Coros y Danzas

Currents in Latin American & Iberian Music

Alejandro L. Madrid, Series Editor
Walter Aaron Clark, Founding Series Editor

Coros y Danzas

Folk Music and Spanish Nationalism in the
Early Franco Regime (1939–1953)

DANIEL DAVID JORDAN

Oxford University Press is a department of the University of Oxford. It furthers
the University's objective of excellence in research, scholarship, and education
by publishing worldwide. Oxford is a registered trade mark of Oxford University
Press in the UK and certain other countries.

Published in the United States of America by Oxford University Press
198 Madison Avenue, New York, NY 10016, United States of America.

Library of Congress Cataloging-in-Publication Data
Names: Jordan, Daniel David, author.
Title: Coros y Danzas : folk music and Spanish nationalism in the early Franco regime (1939–1953) /
Daniel David Jordan.
Description: New York, NY : Oxford University Press, 2023. |
Series: Currents in Latin American and Iberian music |
Includes bibliographical references and index.
Identifiers: LCCN 2022044705 (print) | LCCN 2022044706 (ebook) |
ISBN 9780197586518 (hardback) | ISBN 9780197586532 (epub)
Subjects: LCSH: Folk music—Political aspects—Spain—History—20th century. |
Folk dancing—Political aspects—Spain—History—20th century. |
Coros y Danzas de España—History. | Fascism and music—Spain—History. |
Fascism and women—Spain—History. | Music and diplomacy—Spain—History—20th century. |
Falange Española Tradicionalista y de las J.O.N.S. Sección Femenina.
Classification: LCC ML3917 .S73 J67 2023 (print) | LCC ML3917 .S73 (ebook) |
DDC 781.62/61—dc23/eng/20220928
LC record available at https://lccn.loc.gov/2022044705
LC ebook record available at https://lccn.loc.gov/2022044706

DOI: 10.1093/oso/9780197586518.001.0001

1 3 5 7 9 8 6 4 2

Printed by Integrated Books International, United States of America

Contents

Figures

Acknowledgments

I would like to thank the archivists throughout Spain who have helped make this book possible through their tremendous support and knowledge. Several academics offered crucial advice and guidance when this research began as a PhD thesis, particularly Dr. Matthew Machin-Autenrieth and Professor Marina Frolova-Walker. Finally, I would like to thank my wife, Nataliia Kuksa, who traveled with me throughout Spain and provided unending support.

This book is dedicated to those who have stood up for truth, justice, freedom, and compassion in the face of authoritarian regimes.

Introduction

Exhumations

On a brisk fall day, a light breeze drifted through the tops of cypress trees that surrounded the gray granite arches of a colossal mausoleum. Bronze doors with bas-reliefs of Christ and penitent martyrs opened to the faint sound of Gregorian chant emanating from an obscure interior. Slowly, there appeared from within a dozen pallbearers wearing red and yellow ribbons on their lapels, carrying an oversized casket draped with crimson velvet, a laurel wreath, and a crest with the national motto of Spain, "*Plus ultra.*" With a guttural military shout of "*¡Viva España! ¡Viva Franco!,*" the casket was carefully placed inside a hearse at the bottom of a broad stone stairway, then sprinkled with holy water by a member of the clergy.

The exhumation of the dictator Francisco Franco Bahamonde (1892–1975) on October 24, 2019, from the Valley of the Fallen (Valle de los Caídos) represented a long-sought victory for pro-democratic liberal politicians who wanted to change how his authoritarian regime (1939–1975) is publicly remembered. Today, the monument epitomizes some of the central messages that Franco attempted to bestow upon Spaniards: that the illegitimate, atheist Second Republic (1931–1939)—which he overthrew—had committed grievous sins against the morals and spirituality of Spanish Catholicism. On important dates associated with the dictatorship, several hundred demonstrators gather at this site to give the fascist salute, carrying flags of the yoke and arrows of the Falange Española de la Juntas de Ofensiva Nacional Sindicalista (Spain's fascist party).[1] The chilling ambiance could not be more appropriate for their gatherings; Republican, socialist, and Communist political prisoners of the Spanish Civil War (1936–1939) were forced to build the five-hundred-foot (hundred-fifty-meter) granite cross and mausoleum over twenty grueling years as a form of penance. Underneath this structure lie the bodies of 33,000 Republicans and Nationalists killed in battle, most of whom were buried there without the consent or knowledge of their families.[2] The right to maintain monuments and celebrations related to Nationalist

Coros y Danzas. Daniel David Jordan, Oxford University Press. © Oxford University Press 2023.
DOI: 10.1093/oso/9780197586518.003.0001

Spain is defended by the Francisco Franco National Foundation established by the dictator's family to promote a positive view of his accomplishments.[3]

After Franco's natural death in 1975, Spaniards experienced a transition from authoritarianism to democracy without a transition to justice. The amnesty law of 1977 that freed political prisoners also provided impunity for those who committed atrocities in the name of the regime.[4] Consequently, there were no military trials that punished human rights abuses such as those that took place in Nuremberg between 1945 and 1946 or later in Argentina and Chile in the 1970s and 1980s. Nor were individuals who committed atrocities prohibited from participating as politicians in Spain's new democracy.[5] Instead, politicians settled for the "Pact of Forgetting" (*Pacto del olvido*), an informal agreement of amnesia between the Franco regime and its victims.[6] Only in 2007 did the Spanish parliament pass the Law of Historical Memory intended to remove Francoist symbols from public view (except for those that possess "historical and cultural significance" such as El Valle de los Caídos). In certain conservative regions, this policy took nearly a decade to come into effect. In Madrid, for example, the Law of Historical Memory was only enacted in the capital city in 2015 after being sidelined by the city's conservative mayor.[7] Meanwhile, Spain continues to be dotted with monuments, customs, and bureaucratic structures that derive from or celebrate Franco's dictatorship.

But the Franco regime's influence on Spanish nationalism, society, and religion was immense and varied, and not all its surviving relics are so easy to identify as a five-hundred-foot granite cross or neo-fascist rallies. I encountered a more discrete survivor of the dictatorship's numerous cultural programs while doing research for this book. Today, there is a network of fifty-nine traditional dance troupes with a total of over 5,900 members spread across nearly all the fifty provinces of the nation, known collectively as Coros y Danzas (Choruses and Dances). The ensembles are centrally organized through the Federación de Asociaciones de Coros y Danzas de España (FACYDE), a member of the International Dance Council based at the UNESCO headquarters in Paris.[8] According to the FACYDE's official website, these organizations are "the best guardians and disseminators of traditional Spanish music and dance, as well as important ambassadors of [Spanish] folklore around the world, reaching great national and international prestige for proven seriousness and artistic quality."[9] The FACYDE now runs dance schools throughout Spain, teaching thousands of children and young adults every year. Performances of Coros y Danzas can be seen by Spaniards and tourists alike in public squares during local holidays or cultural festivals at home and around the world. If you, the reader, have ever traveled to Spain and witnessed a group of ten-odd couples in a town square adorned in colorful traditional costumes dancing to an amplified guitar trio, then you have probably witnessed a public performance of one of the many Coros y Danzas ensembles. Audio recordings of these troupes can be streamed on iTunes and Spotify, while video recordings are found on YouTube and group pages on social media.

The FACYDE was founded almost immediately following the end of the Franco regime by Rivera María (Maruja) Josefa Hernández Sampelayo, the national cultural councilor of the Sección Femenina, the official Women's Section of the fascist Falange party. According to their websites, these contemporary groups proudly trace their origins back to the Sección Femenina's Department of Music. Many troupes claim that they continue to perform the settings used during the 1940s and 1950s note-for-note. In fact, the Coros y Danzas de Granada is currently in the process of using song files and video recordings to revive performance practices that had been forgotten after the death of Franco in 1975. Individual troupes of the FACYDE throughout Spain proudly claim that they are continuing the educational institutions and research of the Sección Femenina. Websites for these provincial organizations tally the awards they received in national competitions and list their international tours from the early years of the Franco regime.[10] Consequently, these troupes have become a means of transmitting the Sección Femenina's notions of Spanish culture to future generations. But what makes the Coros y Danzas so fascinating is that they are one of the few cultural legacies of the Franco regime that has not been the center of much political attention; these ensembles are generally considered to be apolitical, and their claims about the ancient origins of their repertoire go mostly unquestioned.[11]

Through my "exhumation" of hundreds of previously untapped archival documents, many of which have only become available after the 2007 Law of Historical Memory, I reveal how the women of the Sección Femenina profoundly influenced Spanish music during the 1940s and 1950s through their collections, interpretations, and performances of rural songs and dances.[12] I focus on the end of the Spanish Civil War (1939) up until the Pact of Madrid (1953) with the United States—a period that saw Spain transform itself from a supporter of Nazi Germany to a faithful ally of the Western Bloc. Through their Department of Music, these women shaped traditional Spanish songs and dances to promote ideas of Catholic morality throughout the nation's culturally diverse regions, helped legitimize colonial involvement in Spain's African territories, and formed political ties with the Allied powers after the Second World War. Moreover, the Coros y Danzas were never simply a one-sided mouthpiece of the dictatorship's nationalist, Catholic underpinnings. Despite the patriarchal nature of the Franco regime, many members were highly independent and negotiated with local cultural elites and foreign political diplomats to further their own careers and personal philosophies. Consequently, the Sección Femenina's definition of Spanish cultural and racial purity was never monolithic, but a malleable concept that was nuanced depending on the geographical and social contexts in which its members were operating.

Hispanidad and Raza Española

Before examining the cultural politics of the Franco regime, it is first necessary to provide some context for the historical roots of Spanish nationalism and the conflicting territorial aspirations within the Iberian Peninsula. Perhaps two of the most important recurring concepts at the center of Spanish nationalist politics over the past hundred and fifty years have been those of "Hispanidad" and the "raza española." Sometimes translated as "Hispanicity" or "Spanishness," the word Hispanidad has taken multiple meanings throughout the nineteenth and twentieth centuries. Contemporary interpretations of the term refer to an international group of peoples who speak the Spanish language, share aspects of Spanish culture, and are (usually) members of the Catholic faith. The idea of a raza española (Spanish race) can be thought of as a subcategory of Hispanidad, and usually refers to an imagined race of people living specifically within the modern boundaries of Spain. Historical, cultural, and linguistic understandings of Hispanidad and raza española became problematic for Spaniards during the nineteenth and twentieth centuries, and the interpretations of these terms were accompanied by different myths and symbols.

The modern regional boundaries within Spain today were mostly created by Christian kingdoms that slowly expanded into Islamic Iberia during the Middle Ages.[13] The peoples of the eastern half of the Iberian Peninsula have been referred to as "Spanish" since antiquity. But this term had little cultural or political significance before the fifteenth and sixteenth centuries because the region of Spain was divided into small, independent kingdoms with separate identities and languages.[14] The union of the kingdoms of Castile and Aragon in 1469, a consequence of the marriage of Queen Isabella I of Castile (1451–1504) and King Ferdinand of Aragon (1452–1516), first paved the way for the formation of a modern Spanish nation-state. Yet, the many languages of these joined territories continued to be spoken, including various dialects of Castilian (otherwise known as Spanish), Aranés, Catalan, Basque, and Galician.

The languages and cultures within the political borders of Spain formed the basis of several regionalist movements in the nineteenth and twentieth centuries. In 1833, the Secretary of State for Development (*Secretario de Estado de Fomento*), Javier de Burgos (1778–1849), proposed a law to the Spanish senate that officially recognized the territorial division of Spain's fifteen historical regions, although the law did not afford any degree of political self-determination. Later, in the 1880s, several constitutions were drafted in a failed attempt to proclaim Catalan, Andalusian, and Basque political autonomy. This coincided with a growth of regional consciousness and a revival of non-Castilian languages, cultures, and music.[15] Francisco Gascue Murga (1848–1920), a Basque regionalist, politician, and musicologist, wrote that Spain was composed of different races, precluding any notion of a "synthetic Spanish culture" or national sentiment.[16] In Andalusia, Blas Infante (1885–1936) claimed that southern Spain possessed unique historical and cultural links to medieval Islamic Iberia, and used his concept of Andalusian nationalism to fuel a movement for political autonomy.[17] In the Northeast, Catalan regionalists Lluís Millet (1847–1941) and Roberto Gerhard (1896–1970) transformed half-forgotten musical traditions into symbols of Catalan nationalism via their ensembles (e.g., Orfeó Català), community programs (e.g., Festes de la Música Catalana), compositions, songbooks, and essays.[18]

The growth of regional identities during the nineteenth and early twentieth centuries coincided with a decline in Spain's political and economic power. The formerly vast Spanish Empire was weakened by the gradual loss of its colonies in the Philippines and Americas (Mexico gained independence in 1821, Chile in 1818, Venezuela in 1811, Argentina in 1816, Bolivia in 1825, Cuba in 1902, the Philippines in 1899, etc.), while European composers, artists, and writers often portrayed the nation as a backwater exotic gateway to the Orient.[19] Fueled by a desire to recover Spanish national pride, another camp of artists, politicians, and intellectuals arose who promoted a concept of a raza española that was devoutly Catholic, politically unified, imperialistic, and culturally and linguistically Castilian.[20] Many of the religious, cultural, and monarchical aspects of Spanish conservatism had roots in the writings of José Zorrilla (1817–1893), the nation's most prominent literary figure of the mid-nineteenth century.[21] Zorrilla's plays are often set during the Middle Ages and typically include derogatory caricatures of invading North African "Moors" being ousted from the Iberian Peninsula by heroic Christian knights.[22] Zorrilla portrayed the historical Muslims and Jews who lived in Iberia before 1492 as invaders whose expulsion from the peninsula was morally justified and predestined by divinity. Yet, this version of the raza española, understood as a centralized (i.e., Castilian) and Catholic Spanish racial identity, mostly influenced Spain's aristocracy and cultural elites of the nineteenth century, with little or no impact upon the nation's lower classes.[23] A cultural gap opened up between the Castilian intelligentsia and the nation's working class who continued to enjoy the popular culture of bullfights and flamenco cabarets—entertainments typical of Spain's southernmost region, Andalusia.[24]

The conservative movement that promoted a Catholic-Castilian brand of Spanish nationalism, summarized in Zorrilla's writings, gained more popularity once the crumbling Spanish Empire surrendered Puerto Rico, Cuba, Guam, and the Philippines to the United States of America after the Spanish-American War of 1898.[25] The possession of colonial territories was the principal means through which the greatness of nations was measured in the nineteenth century. The defeat in 1898 reduced the once vast Spanish Empire almost completely to its European borders, prompting the nation's humiliating subordination to Europe's continental hegemonic powers.[26] This event was labeled the "Disaster of 98" ("El Desastre del 98") by a band of intellectuals who identified themselves as the Generation of '98. Some of the more notable members included the novelist Miguel de Unamuno (1864–1936), the political theorist Ramiro de Maeztu (1875–1936), and the writer Ricardo Burguete y Lana (1871–1937).[27] This group considered the final loss of Spain's territories and colonial power to be the peak of the nation's "moral decay" that had been gradually unfolding since the seventeenth century.[28] To their eyes, Spain's political weakening over the previous three hundred years was the result of Latin decadence, in contrast to the social and economic development that had been occurring in central and northern Europe.[29] Burguete in his manifesto of 1905 Dinamismo espiritualista: Proceso histórico de ética española (Spiritual dynamism: the historical process of Spanish ethics) framed the language and culture of Castile (central Spain) as the nation's "beating heart," providing civilization and political security to the peripheral regions.[30] Ultimately, the Generation of '98 hoped that this brand of Spanish nationalism would culturally reunite an international "Hispanic race" (i.e., Hispanidad), including Spain's former empire in Latin America.[31]

This imperialistic, Catholic, and Castilian model of Hispanidad inspired several ultra-nationalist political movements in Spain throughout the twentieth century. Conservative oligarchs saw military intervention as a solution to restoring religion, economic efficiency, and an old-world social order to the fatherland.[32] Captain-General Miguel Primo de Rivera (1870–1930) seized control of the Spanish government in 1923 after a coup d'état supported by the Spanish king, Alfonso XIII. In the beginning, Primo de Rivera saw his regime as a temporary, ninety-day, military intervention through which he would cleanse the nation's political life of regionalists and leftist politicians whom he viewed as corrupt and incapable of recovering Spain from the disgrace of the Spanish-American War.[33] Primo de Rivera held his dictatorship for seven years, during which time he outlawed regional languages and made Spanish Catholicism an official, national institution.[34] His government was economically and politically mismanaged, however, and the dictator lacked internal support from the military.[35] In 1930, Primo de Rivera peacefully relinquished his power, a move that made possible the establishment of the democratic Second Republic. Despite its weaknesses, Primo de Rivera's dictatorship laid the foundation for future far-right movements in Spain, particularly the concept of an organic authoritarian state based on the ideologies of a hyper-nationalist interpretation of Catholicism.[36]

The democratic values of the Second Republic allowed internal ethnic and regional debates to be temporarily rejuvenated; Catalonia, the Basque Country, and Galicia were granted official statutes of autonomy, and the Catholic Church no longer had an official role in the state.[37] The Church's traditional role in reformatories, the harsh disciplinary regimes that the clergy had enforced in schools for the poor, and the clergy's role in strikebreaking encouraged much of the working class to see Catholicism as an instrument of the Spanish oligarchy's vast architecture of repression.[38] Atheist and egalitarian discourses gained unprecedented popularity, and Spain's Socialist Party became one of the most influential political entities in the nation's coalition government.[39]

Spain's political arena became increasingly polarized between the political right and left, Catholics vs. atheists, and oligarchs vs. working-class socialists.[40] The anticlericalism of leftist political factions persuaded the religious elite to align themselves with nationalist, ultra-conservative, and politically experienced oligarchs who claimed to defend Spain's ecclesiastical martyrs.[41] Cutting across these political divisions were movements for greater regional autonomy, independence, and pro-Spanish nationalists.[42] An economic depression, massive unemployment, and overwhelming poverty of the early 1930s only stoked the fire of political discord.[43]

Movements for women's rights, which had already taken root in Spain during the 1910s, found their first political expression within the 1931 constitution of the Second Republic.[44] Women were promised a socialist "new Spain" that would emancipate them from the guardianship of the Catholic Church.[45] For the first time in the nation's history, women were granted full citizenship and universal suffrage, were mobilized in the workforce, allowed access to education, could own property, and could file for divorce.[46] Women's new civic rights drastically changed Spanish politics due to an electorate that had more than doubled. During the founding of the Second Republic, socialists assumed that women would naturally wish to secure their own political power by incorporating the left's ideals of democracy and anticlericalism.[47] Conservatives, on the other hand, claimed that women's naturally stronger connection to religion would encourage them to use their new civic rights to protect the values of Spanish Catholicism from the "imported contamination" of socialist government intervention.[48]

The conservatives and traditionalist Catholics quickly won the most visible female support, outdoing the socialists or even the more moderate political left.[49] In fact, the political left failed to create a large-scale women's organization until the anarchist Mujeres Libres formed shortly before the outbreak of the Civil War in April 1936. Women's conservative political organizations, the largest of which was the women's section of CEDA (Confederación Española de Derechas Autónomas / Spanish Confederation of Autonomous Right-wing Parties), combined traditional values and conservative female gender roles with women's newly acquired civic duties as voters, social workers, political activists, and propagandists.[50] Using a strategy that was perhaps counterintuitive to their end goal, CEDA encouraged women to leave their families to devote themselves to politics for the greater good of Spanish Catholicism and traditional patriarchal values. Women's participation in CEDA later became a model for the much larger, more powerful, and long-lived women's section of the fascist Falange party.

The Falange Española, later to become the Falange Española de la Juntas de Ofensiva Nacional Sindicalista, was founded in 1933 by José Antonio Primo de Rivera, eldest son of the ousted dictator of the 1920s.[51] The party's twenty-seven-point manifesto denied the socialist leanings of the Second Republic and promoted a centralized state based on Catholic values, a restoration of hierarchical and authoritarian pre-Republican order, and a strong military.[52] José Antonio rebuked dissident regionalists and framed the nation's linguistic and cultural diversity as being bound together by an eternal metaphysical Spanish essence.[53] On the global front, José Antonio wished to re-establish the "golden age" of Spanish imperial power. According to José Antonio, Spain's international influence was not to be accomplished through military force, but by projecting the Falange's understanding of Hispanic culture, history, and religion on its former colonies in Latin America and Africa.[54] In this scenario, Spain would become the spiritual leader of a federation of Spanish-speaking nations.[55]

After a coalition of working-class and centrist parties won the election of February 16, 1936, José Antonio allied the Falange Española de las JONS with a nationalist military aristocracy that attempted to overthrow the government. Hopes for a quick victory for the rebel far right came to an end when impromptu citizen militias and pro-Republican forces managed to halt the uprising in vast areas such as Asturias, Santander, the Basque Country, and parts of Catalonia. What was supposed to be a swift military coup d'état was prolonged into a devastating civil war that lasted nearly three years (1936–1939). An estimated 268,500 Spaniards, foreign volunteers, and civilians died as a direct result of the conflict.[56] Extrajudicial executions were commonplace on both sides, with the Nationalists killing about 151,000 prisoners and the Republicans 49,000.[57] Another 165,000 civilians died from disease and malnutrition and an unknown number were killed in air raids and mass exoduses fleeing the Nationalist military.[58] Even after the Nationalists declared victory on April 1, 1939, the violence was far from over; another 20,000 Republicans prisoners were executed in the following years while untold numbers died in prisons and concentration camps.

José Antonio was among those imprisoned and executed by the Republicans during the first five months of the war. His writings and transcribed speeches, however, became an essential political platform of the emerging dictatorship. General Franco, who led the Nationalist army from the Spanish Protectorate in Morocco, incorporated remnants of the Falange Española de las JONS into a larger political movement of monarchists and other right-wing factions based on traditionalism and clericalism. The Falange's political ideology offered Franco an extraordinary means through which to consolidate his personal power and spread the notion of a culturally, linguistically, religiously, and politically unified Spain.[59]

Until the late 2010s, leading scholarship on the cultural policies of Francoist Spain had focused heavily on the regime's doctrine of National Catholicism—the Catholic Church's almost complete control of public and private life.[60] Michael Richards, Stanley Payne, and Gemma Pérez Zalduondo, for example, investigate how Catholicism was the key legitimating force behind the rebel army's crusade against leftist and atheist "foreign contagions."[61] Franco's concept of the raza española was defined more by religion, cultural tradition, and sentiment rather than by biological connections. According to Richards and others, many of the regime's cultural and educational policies reduced the nearly eight-hundred-year presence of Islamic kingdoms in Iberia to a mere interruption of a "Spanish-Christian continuum" that had its ancestral roots in the pre-Islamic civilization of the Visigoths.[62] Francoism was driven by a "holy crusade" to save religious conservatism, cultural isolationism, and an old-world social hierarchy from the nation's quickly changing economic structure.[63] Supporters of Franco presented the Second Republic as a product of a Jewish-Masonic-Bolshevik conspiracy that threatened the core of Christian civilization through the systematic expansion of urban centers and mass migration from rural villages.[64] Like the Catholic warrior-monks of the Reconquista, Spain's twentieth-century patriotic saviors were tasked with purging Republican "Jewish hordes" and alien ideologies such as "godless" communism, regional separatism, and atheism from the homeland.[65]

Yet this established perspective provides only a limited understanding of Catholicism's role in the Franco regime's propaganda machine. For example, one might be surprised to find that propagandists of the Franco regime occasionally positioned Spain as the direct heir to medieval Islamic Iberia, also known as al-Andalus, especially within the Spanish Protectorate in Morocco. In this context, Spanish history followed a narrative that was separate from National Catholicism. Eric Calderwood, in his postcolonial reading of the cultural and political legacies of Islamic Iberia, examines how the Franco regime highlighted shared traditions and history between Morocco and Spain.[66] The Franco Institute for Hispano-Arab research and Mulay al-Hasan Institute and Center for Moroccan Studies, for example, encouraged academic collaborations between Spanish and North African intellectuals and hosted Arabic language courses for Spanish citizens.[67]

The Franco regime's contradictory relationship with Catholicism was joined to its contradictory relationship with Spain's regional cultures. The

Franco regime attempted to enforce a uniform concept of a *raza española* built upon a plural composition of regional identities.[68] The linguistic and cultural distinctions across Spain's regions, many of which had been Republican centers during the Civil War, were seen as a threat to the nation's stability.[69] The regime's secret police attempted to eradicate all movements for regional autonomy based on distinct ethno-territories outside of Castile. Using phrases such as "*El Imperio hacia Dios*" (The God-made Empire) and "*España, una unidad de destino en lo universal*" (Spain, a unified destiny in universal affairs), Francoist propaganda highlighted Castile as a model for Spanish imperialism and statehood.[70] In a speech delivered via radio in 1941, Franco expressed this national mission as "the struggle of the Patria against the anti-Patria, of unity against secession, of morality against crime, of spirit against materialism, . . . and the triumph of the pure and eternal over bastard, anti-Spanish principles."[71] Censors removed many of the regional customs, songs, street signs, dishes, statues, and dances from public life, the slightest presence of which seemed to destabilize the Francoist conception of a unified nation.[72]

But non-Castilian cultures and languages were not always antithetical to the Franco regime's construction on Spanish nationhood.[73] State-endorsed institutions for folklore research, particularly the Instituto Español de Musicología (IEM) and the Department of Music of the Sección Femenina, collected regional songs, dances, and costumes. Both these institutions were designed to reveal the "peculiarity and uniqueness" of the nation's musical traditions and elevate the status of Spanish culture throughout the world.[74] Researchers within the IEM and the Sección Femenina's Department of Music attempted to find mystical Spanish qualities that would unify the nation's ethno-territories.[75]

The Franco regime's political doctrine was changing and inconsistent. Tumultuous shifts of power occurred regularly between government organizations responsible for the design, implementation, and censorship of national culture, including the Delegation of Press and Propaganda (founded in 1937), the Vice Secretariat for Popular Education (founded in 1939), the Ministry of Education (founded in 1945), the Ministry of Information and Tourism (founded in 1951), and a host of priests and other local authorities who were recruited by the regime to censor culture as they saw fit.[76] Although censorship during the first decades of the regime was inescapable, it was also highly arbitrary; material that was allowed to pass by one censorship body would often be denied by another.[77] Moreover, the autonomy of different media sources varied greatly, and certain institutions, such as the Catholic Church, were exempted from government censorship.[78] Consequently, we cannot speak of an official strategy for censoring music, theater, and art aside from Franco's political strategy of generally suppressing anti-clerical sentiment and sedition.[79] This was useful for those in power; the lack of a clear doctrine on Spanish culture endorsed a fluid, amendable nationalism that enabled Franco to adapt to various political circumstances at home and around the world.

In fact, Franco intentionally created internal conflicts of interest among the ruling elite, a strategy designed to weaken individual branches of government.[80] Through the regime's pluralistic distribution of power, there seemed to be no alternative to Franco's almost unlimited authority while the dictator himself let others take responsibility for the daily administration of the country.[81] Franco's strategy (or perhaps lack of strategy) accommodated the complex coexistence of divergent political aims within the regime's ruling oligarchy such as the Carlists' desire for the restoration of a traditionalist monarchy, the development of Catholic corporatism, and the transition to a Catholic democracy.[82]

For all these reasons, historians would be seriously misled if they merely studied the constitutions, laws, speeches, and writings without investigating how these policies were manifested.[83] Therefore, I have based this book on microhistories of individual people and events that demonstrate how the regime's official policies were translated into social reality.[84] It is only through a close study of the people on the ground—the individual performers, impresarios, music critics, local political leaders, and Spanish consuls—that we can really understand how the Spanish government's nation-building and diplomatic projects were put into effect, received, and changed over time during the 1940s and 1950s.

Gender, Foundational Myths, and Soft Power

On the broadest level, this book seeks to form a better understanding of how states shape and promote ideas of gender and race to legitimate their authority. I conceptualize ethnicity, race, and gender as identities that are created and performed using specific cultural codes.[85] I aim to identify the context in which these codes are negotiated and invoked through the imaginations of individual people working for a state and the publics whom their messages are targeting.

I occasionally refer to the term "nation-state" throughout this book. A nation-state is created by self-proclaimed ethnic groups who have decided that it is in their best interests to govern themselves.[86] A nation-state may be developed by promoting ideas of common ancestry and shared historical narratives.[87] The idea of ancestry, an essential component of race, is associated with the past. Therefore memory—and more often the invention and manipulation of memory—plays a crucial role in building nation-states. Memories that underpin nation-states may be expressed through the practice of rituals that symbolize an ancient national heritage (e.g., religious ceremonies and folk revival movements).[88] When citizens of a nation-state attempt to revive their cultural roots, however, the revived traditions often involve an increased number of symbols and rituals.[89] The process of using ritual, storytelling, and imagination to create memories can be summed up with the term "restorative nostalgia."[90]

The idea of restorative nostalgia is hugely important to the study of music and race. In diasporic communities, for example, the process of momentarily filling in the absence of a homeland can provide a source of cultural creativity and define a community's concept of self.[91] Younger generations may then edit and embellish their parents' missing homeland as they adjust to circumstances in their families' new country. Through art and music, memories of a missing homeland have the potential to give meaning, be creatively productive, and form moral codes that govern a society's identity and sense of belonging.[92]

Culture, particularly music, is an excellent means of projecting a dictatorship's heritage and foundational myths, whether it be the political use of Beethoven's symphonies in Nazi Germany or arrangements of peasant songs in the USSR.[93] But unlike diasporic communities, dictatorships typically take place on land that is associated with the nation-state's ancient ancestral roots. Instead of framing distance or displacement as the principal threat to the nation's sense of self, dictatorships often use narratives related to infiltration of contaminated foreign influences (e.g., Hitler's idea that Jews were corrupting the German people or Franco's idea that American popular music was destroying Spanish culture). The specific process by which dictatorships enforce these invented memories is often accompanied by violence, fear, and political and social oppression. Such violence is often framed as being necessary to protect or revive the endangered virtues of an invented lost golden age.

During the massive migration from rural to urban areas in Spain during the first half of the twentieth century, memories and myths of a rural, culturally isolated peasantry became increasingly important as a tool for building ideas of national culture. One of the great paradoxes of the Franco regime, it seems, was that its economic policies were purposely designed to destroy rural towns and villages while state-run cultural organizations (e.g., the IEM and Sección Femenina) attempted to restore these same communities. Landless peasants and seasonal agrarian workers migrated to city centers not as a lifestyle choice but as a desperate attempt to escape starvation.[94] The Franco regime's failed autarkic economy accelerated the end of Spain's centuries-old rural societies.[95] Between 1950 and 1975, six million rural workers—20 percent of the nation's population—moved to Spain's city centers while another 2.3 million migrated to other nations across Europe.[96] The miserable living conditions of the nation's rural peasantry needed to be reconstructed in the imaginations of Spanish citizens. The migration of peasant workers provided the perfect opportunity for Franco's propagandists to "fill in" the cultural absences left within these devastated communities.

Similar to the Franco regime's nation-building projects at home, Spanish foreign relations during the first decade of the Cold War were built upon invented historical narratives that acted as unifying agents between different nations. Music and dance offered several advantages: performances encouraged interactions with the audience on and off stage; there was no need for language translation; and both music and dance usually provided a clear national stamp. Franco's propagandists used Spanish music and dance as a form of cultural diplomacy.

What do I mean by cultural diplomacy? Cultural diplomacy can be understood as a set of interactions between nations that use "creative expression and exchanges of ideas, information, and people" to further the objectives of foreign policy and increase mutual understanding.[97] In other words, cultural diplomacy happens when a state uses its national culture to get what it wants from other states and the citizens of other states. The term "soft power," the key element of cultural diplomacy, refers to a state's ability to use cultural resources to attract and influence the opinions of foreign publics, rather than coercion or payment.[98]

But cultural diplomacy has its limitations. For example, American politicians during the 1950s and 1960s understood cultural diplomacy as a one-way flow of information into a host nation.[99] Bureaucrats and politicians within the State Department's International Information Administration believed that state-funded concerts in foreign nations allowed American ideas to "pour" into the minds of the civilian public.[100] Things did not always work out as planned. For one thing, American missions of cultural diplomacy relied upon autonomous, non-state actors, such as performers, nongovernmental organizations, and entrepreneurs.[101] These private contractors had independent and sometimes opposing political and economic motivations as they carried out their jobs.[102] When American diplomats hired non-state agents, the policies and objectives of official interests became "blurred and multiplied" and sometimes carried contradictory messages.[103]

Cultural diplomacy has another limitation. People tend to pursue messages that are already in "accordance with their held views," a pattern that can be described as "selective exposure" (think of the modern political echo chambers created by social media).[104] Political propaganda alone rarely has the capacity to change an individual's fundamental beliefs.[105] Instead, it is family, religion, and friends that tend to determine a person's idea of politics. Although propaganda is not very good at changing people's fundamental beliefs, it is very effective at reinforcing preexisting dispositions.[106] In other words, most people's opinions can be altered within certain parameters so long as their basic worldviews are upheld. In the realm of cultural diplomacy, propagandists may be required to temporarily adapt their own national identity and values to the beliefs of the host nation.

Throughout this Introduction, I have emphasized how notions of race, memory, and history are all integral to the formation of a nation-state and its international relationships. Building a distinct, homogeneous, and identifiable community is a creative process in which politicians, propagandists, diplomats, and artists must continuously reinvent historical narratives and traditions to adjust to present conditions. The following chapters of this book explore the Sección Femenina's different musical representations of raza española and Hispanidad in relation to specific geopolitical objectives at home and throughout the world. Chapter 1 begins with an introduction to the Sección Femenina, focusing on the years 1934–1953. The second half of this chapter is dedicated to the Sección Femenina's Department of Music and representations of Francoist gender ideology in musical performance. Chapter 2 explores how instructoras of the Sección Femenina used musical folklore to shape foundational myths of the raza española during the first two decades of the Franco regime. After a summary of the Sección Femenina's activities abroad, Chapter 3 shifts the focus to the organization's tours and educational programs within European-controlled Morocco. During a time of political unrest and movements for Moroccan independence, the Sección Femenina promoted narratives of a Moroccan-Spanish brotherhood based on myths of medieval Islamic Iberia. Chapter 4 explores how the Sección Femenina's missions of cultural diplomacy in the United States, France, and Belgium were designed to fuel anti-Communist sentiments and gain support for the Franco regime during the first years of the Cold War (1947–1953). Chapter 5 reveals how the Sección Femenina used music to promote an Iberian–Latin American sisterhood within Cuba and the Dominican Republic during the 1950s. These diplomatic missions promoted political solidarity and highlighted the common historical, cultural, and linguistic characteristics of Spain and two of its former colonies.

1

Performing Spanish Femininity

On January 10, 1940, several hundred young women in red berets and well-tailored overcoats filled the Teatro Rojas in Toledo. They looked upon a stage set with a long table decorated with ornate textiles and a golden altar crucifix. Curtains depicting biblical scenes from sixteenth-century tapestries served as backdrops. Bordering all of this were banners displaying the name of Carmen Miedes (1902–1936), a female physician of Toledo who had been killed by Republicans in the so-called Modern Persecution.[1] Four top officials of Franco's new government sat at the table (see figure 1.1). In the center were Interior Minister Ramón Serrano Suñer and General Agustín Muñoz Grande. At their sides were two women: the dictator Francisco Franco's wife, María del Carmen Polo (1900–1988), and Pilar Primo de Rivera (1907–1991), the *jefe nacional* (national chief) of the Sección Femenina. After official introductions, Rivera stood and read aloud her plans for a recently developed women's education program:[2]

> For a people to be saved, they must sacrifice themselves because great things can only be achieved through great renunciation. You have seen how thousands and thousands of deaths were required to win the war. . . . And although at this moment we must lead a difficult life, almost completely withdrawn, unbecoming of our youth, in the long run we will have the honor of contributing to the glorification of Spain. . . . All affiliated women will have the most basic knowledge of culture, and they will know about childcare, housekeeping, and hygiene. And through the Sisterhood, they will learn about caring for and selecting domestic animals, artisan work, and local products. And so, we will be able to offer the Leader, by the end of the year, an undertaking carried out . . . by every woman and in every home of the Homeland. . . . *Camaradas: Por Franco, ¡arriba España!*[3]

Rivera's speech sums up the seemingly inconsistent ideas of gender and power within the Sección Femenina. On the one hand, women's function as the defenders of conservative family values implied that they ought to be

Coros y Danzas. Daniel David Jordan, Oxford University Press. © Oxford University Press 2023.
DOI: 10.1093/oso/9780197586518.003.0002

Figure 1.1   Fourth National Congress of the Sección Femenina, January 20, 1940, at the Teatro Rojas in Toledo. (Left) Pilar Primo de Rivera, *jefe nacional* of the Sección Femenina; (center) Serrano Suñer, the interior minister; (right) General Muñoz Grande. ES 28079 ARCM 201.001.45630.2 (IV CONSEJO NACIONAL DE LA SECCION FEMENINA. DEL 10 AL 20-1-40).

removed from the influential realms of politics and business. But, contrary to this stated vision, the Sección Femenina created a number of empowered women who were skilled administrators and leaders within this hyper-patriarchal dictatorship. With more than 30,000 members in 1950, the Sección Femenina was never simply a one-sided mouthpiece of the Franco regime's nationalist, Catholic underpinnings. Despite the fundamentally pa-triarchal nature of the regime, many members negotiated with local cultural elites and foreign political diplomats to further their own ideologies and po-litical objectives. The Sección Femenina's power was constantly challenged by male officials of the Spanish government, foreign agents, and impresarios who maintained very different gender ideologies and conceptions of sexual morality. When we catch glimpses of how the Sección Femenina's programs were being interpreted and experienced, a dramatic power struggle emerges between male and female Spanish officials.

One of the Sección Femenina's primary means of shaping Spanish cul-tural politics was via its vast Department of Music. This organization sent hundreds of young women to remote villages throughout the nation's diverse cultural and linguistic regions to select, transcribe, and compose rural songs and dances. The women documented this material on standardized files to be used in publications, nationalist youth programs, and international tours. Members of the Sección Femenina adapted rural music traditions based on Francoist concepts of female gender roles and cultural purity. However, these concepts were adapted to the geographical and social contexts in which the Sección Femenina was operating. Francoist gender ideologies were fluid and contingent on local conditions and the regime's diplomatic relations with other countries around the world.

Origins of the Sección Femenina

Rivera created the Sección Femenina in 1934 during the Second Republic shortly after her brother, José Antonio Primo de Rivera, founded the Falange Española. Although José Antonio was executed by the Republican army at the start of the Civil War, Rivera survived to direct the Sección Femenina until it was disbanded in 1977. As the national chief of the Sección Femenina, Rivera was one of the most influential political leaders and diplomats of the Franco regime.

The Sección Femenina was initially a reactionary movement against the emancipation that women had acquired during the Second Republic (e.g., women's right to vote, legalized divorce, and their greater inclusion in the workforce).[4] Falangists saw professionally liberated women as susceptible to sexual immorality and cosmopolitan popular culture.[5] The Sección Femenina was created to reintroduce Catholic morality to Spanish women through their traditional roles as mothers and homemakers.[6] But as Spain drew closer to civil war, the Nationalist army relied increasingly on the Sección Femenina as nurses, factory workers, and propagandists.[7] Via the Auxilio Azul (Blue Division), members of the Sección Femenina formed an extensive fifth-column resistance network throughout Spain, smuggling weapons and helping nationalists and clergy to escape Republican territory.[8] Consequently, those women who attached themselves to the Franco regime took on the puzzling function of soldiers, politicians, impresarios, and performers who appeared to be fighting to reduce their own emancipation.

Rivera was a key diplomat for Franco's Spain from the beginning of the Civil War. Besides meeting with the dictators Adolf Hitler, Benito Mussolini, and Antonio Salazar, Rivera was also in touch with Gertrud Scholtz-Klink (1902–1999), the leader of the NS-Frauenschaft (National Socialist Women's League). Scholtz-Klink organized several International Women's Meetings in Berlin between 1941 and 1943 to share feelings of solidarity, strategies, and propaganda with a host of female organizations across Europe. The first of these was held between October 7 and 11, 1941, with pro-fascist participants from Italy, Spain, Romania, Bulgaria, Hungary, Croatia, Finland, Denmark, Norway, and the Netherlands.[9] During this five-day conference, each representative delivered presentations on the values and programs of their women's organization.[10] A Spanish-language circular titled *"La Mujer alemana"* (The German woman) explains how the women of the Nazi party were obliged to fortify the "fertile sap" of the Aryan race.[11] This mission included eliminating all foreign racial and cultural "impurities" from the nation and "raising physically healthy men"[12]—goals that echoed the Sección Femenina's objective to purify Spain from the "corrupting influence" of popular culture and leftist politics. German women were to achieve these goals via their roles as nurses, caretakers, mothers, and the distribution of propaganda through mass media, as expressed in the circular:

> The German woman contributes to the nationalization of the German people by explaining, propagating, and incubating the National Socialist doctrine for future mothers. The NS-Frauenschaft is principally occupied with national education and propaganda service via conferences, press, radio, and film.... After studying the magnificent work of the Frauenschaft and N.S.V., one can appreciate the untainted patriotism and socialism that inspires and motivates the German woman, that encourages her to carry out her admirable work, and that reveals all her ability, intensity, and integrity with which she demonstrates her ideals expressed in the nationalist doctrine.[13]

Researchers on Rivera and Scholtz-Klink describe these women as assertive, independent, and highly organized leaders.[14] Women of the NS-Frauenschaft and Sección Femenina could shape successful careers as politicians and cultural diplomats by harnessing the very misogynistic values that otherwise seemed to be working against them.[15] During a diplomatic trip to Havana in 1954, a Cuban reporter who interviewed Rivera wrote, "For those who hold the erroneous impression that in Spain, women 'only serve in the kitchen'... this magnificent woman has dedicated her entire life to the demands of the Spanish woman."[16] In order to collaborate with male officials on a more equal footing, Rivera encouraged her *camaradas* (female comrades) to be capable of managing their own bureaucratic institutions, as she stated in her 1940 speech in Toledo mentioned previously:

> You will know how to perfectly manage the local headquarters, including its files, its statistics, and its archives; these are all tedious and tiresome things, but they are indispensable, and they will give you a level of knowledge superior to that of the other women of [your] town, so that you can, with decorum, deal with local authorities and bureaucracies, with whom, due to your position, you must be in continuous contact.[17]

Women's unpaid domestic responsibilities for raising children, housework, cooking, and nursing provided them an opening to infiltrate the workforce as paid cultural diplomats, teachers, and nurses. The Sección Femenina greatly increased the number of working women in Spain by providing some of its own members with a regular salary and a voice in politics.[18] In some cases, they may have improved the lives of their female subordinates who were living in what were otherwise hyper-chauvinist, murderous regimes.[19]

The training that Rivera mentions was accomplished, in part, via fifty-six local Escuelas de Hogar (Schools of Home Economics) for girls. The titles of these institutions masked a somewhat diverse program that went far beyond housework. Along with childcare, hygiene, and cooking, girls and young women studying at the Escuelas de Hogar were also trained in physical education, religious morality, Latin, Spanish grammar, agriculture, artisan work, singing, dance, and music theory. Graduates of the Escuelas de Hogar often volunteered for the Sección Femenina's social services branch. Those who came from wealthy families continued their training at one of the three Escuela Superior de Formación (High School of Training), boarding schools for young women located in the historic sites of Castillo de la Mota, Castillo de las Navas, and Aranjuez.[20] Many of the students of the Escuela Superior de Formación were destined for lifelong careers in the Sección Femenina's programs for social and health work, press and propaganda, culture, social services, and primary education.[21]

Rivera supported her vision of women in positions of influence and power by making references to female figures from Spain's glorious past. The Sección Femenina's weekly periodical *Medina* often refers to the work of St. Teresa of Ávila (1515–1582), a Spanish author, intellectual, and religious reformer who was held up as a model of spiritual devotion, celibacy, and scholarly independence.[22] The Sección Femenina linked Teresa's sixteenth-century reformation of the Carmelite Order to the Nationalists' revolution during and after the Civil War. Resembling Teresa's reformation, Rivera encouraged the women of the Sección Femenina to act with a "missionary and national syndicalist spirit, carrying the warmth and brotherhood of [Falangist] doctrine throughout all the lands conquered by Franco's soldiers."[23] Despite the many political rallies that Rivera participated in during the war, she writes in a 1938 circular that the Sección Femenina's accomplishments should be conducted in "a quiet way, without displays and without speeches, because those things are not typical of women—instead [women should pursue their duties] simply, as Teresa did."[24] A similar combination of strength and feminine restraint was bestowed upon Queen Isabella, who was responsible (along with her husband King Ferdinand) for the unification of Spain, the final expulsion of the last Islamic kingdom from Iberia, and funding Christopher Columbus's voyage across the Atlantic in 1492.[25] As the official patron of the Sección Femenina, one of Isabella's old residences, the Castle of La Mota, was used as the organization's headquarters.[26] Along with the administrative work that went on at La Mota, this "mother-house" of the Sección Femenina also operated as its highest-ranking training center. The candidates wishing to advance to the level of music instructors, home economics instructors, or women's physical education instructors trained here in military-like austerity, shielded by the imposing medieval walls and moat that had once protected the Sección Femenina's patron saint.[27]

The Sección Femenina looked to historical figures such as Teresa and Isabella to prove that supposedly masculine virtues of authority and ambition could also apply to women willing to operate within the parameters of Francoist bureaucratic institutions.[28] The Franco regime was never a monolithic system of power wielded by a male autocracy. Instead, its policies were shaped by the consent, collusion, and resistance of women and men from demographics that cut across social classes and regional ethnicities.[29] While women generally suffered great political and economic oppression during the Franco regime, the Sección Femenina allowed some of them to have equal or more power than men within their own social class. This multidimensional power structure created vastly opposing political and social realities in which it was impossible to find a unified expression of femininity.[30]

The Department of Music

The Sección Femenina altered Spain's diverse rural music traditions, which it referred to as *música folklórica* (musical folklore), to transmit its idealized vision of peasant life.[31] The Franco regime designated women as the caretakers of the nation's music. A young woman's musical education was considered to be one of the essential skills for homemaking and motherhood as well as a means of rebuilding Spain after the cultural and political divisions of the Civil War.[32] Even after the Falange party lost effective power in the government in 1945, the Sección Femenina's Department of Music continued to be the Franco regime's primary means of communicating cultural propaganda. Many of the women associated with the Department of Music were able to pursue highly influential careers as performers, folklorists, impresarios, and cultural diplomats.

Cultural institutions such as the Sección Femenina's Department of Music had a heightened importance within Francoist nationalist discourse.[33] The *instructoras de música* (female music instructors) of the Sección Femenina acted as informants who determined the cultural purity of the nation's regional ethnic communities.[34] The Department of Music of the Sección Femenina attempted to save Spanish music from the supposed corruption of republicanism, cosmopolitanism, and what they considered to be trivial forms of popular entertainment.[35] In the more fanatical circles of the regime, jazz represented a savage music of the jungle that had been contaminating Spanish culture for decades.[36] Rivera claimed that the Sección Femenina presented the true face of the nation's musical traditions, free from foreign influences or the exoticized representation of flamenco that had been prominent in the nation's entertainment industry since the nineteenth century.[37] Popular, urban, or risqué musical forms, such as *cuplé* songs that had been used to promote leftist ideologies and regional separatism during the Republic, were condemned as being morally degenerate.[38]

Each of Spain's fifty provinces had about two or three designated *instructoras de música* (whom I will refer to as simply "instructoras" from now on).[39] At least one of them had to be skilled in dancing, another specialized in singing, and a third was able to transcribe melodies to staff notation.[40] This team collected material from around local towns and villages during short field trips that would usually last no more than a week.[41] From the outside, the instructoras' research resembled studies done by men associated with other Francoist institutions. For example, the IEM was founded in 1943 by the priest and musicologist Higini Anglès i Pàmies (1888–1969) and a team of male academics.[42] Through its study of Spanish medieval and current rural music traditions, the IEM sought to locate a "Spanish soul" common to all of the nation's cultural regions.[43] Like the Sección Femenina, Higinio Anglés wished to "resuscitate the nation's authentic folklore" from the perils of twentieth-century modernization and popular culture,[44] as reflected in the IEM's preface to its annual journal *Anuario musical*:

> We aspire to draw back the veil on so many problems contained in our folklore and the scientific study of our musical past; we aspire to awaken in our country vocations for such studies, and to gain worldwide esteem for our heritage, so rich but neglected.[45]

Through the IEM, Higinio Anglés attempted to show the world through his studies and transcriptions of folk songs that Spanish music was worthy of academic research and held all the complexity and profundity of other European traditions. From its foundation, the IEM collaborated with scholars around the world and published articles in multiple languages to promote interest in Spanish musical culture. The IEM also organized what it called folkloric missions between 1944 and 1961 in which groups of researchers collected, transcribed, and published songs from all the regions of Spain.

But the Sección Femenina had a unique role in Francoist propaganda that the IEM could not entirely fulfill. The first volume of the Sección Femenina's publication of songs, *Cancionero español* (c. 1940), includes a prologue by Federico Sopeña (1917–1991) who at the time was a young musicologist working as the Secretary of the Commissary of Music (1940–1943) and as a music critic for *Arriba*, the official Falangist newspaper. In his prologue, Sopeña distinguishes the intentions of the Sección Femenina from academic studies in folklore: "We are not in the presence of a folklorist movement understood as scholarly work. It is something simpler but more vital and important."[46] According to Sopeña, a purely male and scholarly approach to the rediscovery of Spanish folk music would not fulfill the nation's need for a "happy dawn of popular song" that would help repair the culturally and politically divided nation.[47]

The Franco regime augmented a conservative Western gender ideology built to safeguard male authority.[48] Women were portrayed as having a stronger connection to the natural world due to their ability to bear and nurture children, whereas men were portrayed as having more outward signs of power and creativity due to their allegedly superior mental and physical abilities. If the male-dominated IEM was supposedly guided by stereotypes of male intellect, then the Sección Femenina's Department of Music was guided by stereotypes of feminine instinct. According to Sopeña, the Sección Femenina's research on rural music and dance traditions was not less than academia but was supposed to transcend it via women's intuitive connection to the homeland. As a result, some women could perform the academic tasks of researching and collecting Spanish musical songs and dances in the field and local archives while still remaining true to Francoist gender roles. Furthermore, the instructoras' distance from the world of academia may have given them a certain degree of creative license to invent and reinforce various Francoist narratives of Spanish history and culture. Beyond the scrutiny of professional ethnographers and folklorists, their music was adapted to freely invoke and manipulate the nation's foundational myths—from legendary prehistoric Iberian civilizations to fairy tales of the medieval Reconquista. The Sección Femenina's reinventions of Spanish culture and history were designed to legitimize the regime's cultural policies and, as we will see, help the regime cope with relationships at home and overseas.

Coros y Danzas

Besides Rivera, the music activities of the Sección Femenina were directed by Maruja Sampelayo,[49] the Sección Femenina's *regidora nacional de cultura* (national councilor of culture). During the Second Republic, Sampelayo was socially liberated and one of the first female students to earn a degree in philosophy and letters from the Ciudad Universitaria de Madrid.[50] Throughout her studies, Sampelayo was taught by well-known feminist writers such as Maria de Maeztu (1882–1948), Nieves de Madariaga (1917–2003), and Carmen de Zulueta (1916–2012)—all of whom subsequently lived in exile after the Spanish Civil War. Sampelayo's early involvement with women's rights may have inspired those policies and events that lent some women a certain degree of empowerment within the ultra-chauvinist Franco regime, in particular the Sección Femenina's traditional song and dance troupes.

Within the Sección Femenina, Sampelayo organized and managed more than fifty troupes of singers and dancers known as the Coros y Danzas (Choruses and Dances). These ensembles hailed from all the provinces of Spain and were usually restricted to performing songs and dances that were native to their hometown. Within Spain, their performances were typically held in a town plaza, gymnasium, or local casino, with a painted backdrop of an idyllic whitewashed village, olive orchard, or a sunny harbor (see figures 1.2 and 1.3). Performances were held in small towns and major cities alike, usually attended by notables such as mayors and influential businessmen. Before every song and dance, Sampelayo or an instructora gave an introduction through a microphone, recounting the origins of the Sección Femenina and stressing the diversity of Spain's music traditions. Troupes of eight to twelve women in regional costumes performed songs and group dances that were about three and a half minutes each.[51] The songs were either sung in simple two- or three-part harmony and accompanied by a small ensemble of traditional instruments appropriate to the region. An entire program lasted about an hour and a half and finished with the Falangist hymn "*Cara al sol*" with the fascist salute.

The Coros y Danzas rarely showcased solo singers or dancers. A performance that spotlighted individual talent would have been contrary to Rivera's campaign for an altruistic devotion to the national cause. The women's synchronized choreography deprived them of individuality,

Figure 1.2 Coros y Danzas of Granada performing in the tenth annual Concurso Nacional (National Competition), December 1952. The backdrop depicts a view of the Alhambra palace and the Sierra Nevada mountains. ES-AHP Cádiz, Caja no. 13326, no. 3, Tomo I.

Figure 1.3 Coros y Danzas of Cádiz perform in a Concurso Nacional before a backdrop depicting their city's harbor encased in a shell, c. 1960. ES-AHP Cádiz, Caja no. 13326, no. 3, Tomo I.

reflecting José Antonio's writings on the "universal destiny" of Spain's cultural regions and social classes.[52] Songs that were usually associated with an intimate space, such as *canciónes de cuna* (lullabies), were instead performed by choirs. Andalusian troupes almost totally neglected the virtuosic flamenco traditions associated with a trio of guitar, singer, and dancer. Instead, instructoras searched for repertoire, such as couples' dances, that could be easily adapted to suit ensembles of about twelve female performers. For example, an instructora from Cádiz noted that for the dances *el gazpacho*, *el cangrejo*, *el polo*, and *tarantantan*, "A specific number [of dancers] is not necessary, as long as they can be made into pairs."[53]

Until about 1953, all the singers and dancers were single, childless women between eighteen and twenty-eight years of age.[54] According to the "Rules of the National Competition of Coros y Danzas," this upper limit was set because "it is natural that after this age [women's] agility, except in extraordinary cases, is not the same nor is their stamina the same."[55] However, this policy also had symbolic implications. The women of the Coros y Danzas were seen as being of an age in which single women were still eligible for marriage. The performers were presented as fertile virgins on the inside of

Francoist society as opposed to liberated and sexually experienced women "outside" of the system. The women's youthful appearance was intended to represent a rebirth of the nation's supposedly ancient musical traditions.

Sampelayo described the Coros y Danzas as being made up of "university students, peasants, employees, and daughters of families, without distinction between classes, united only in their common desire to serve Spain by showing the world the beauty of their songs and dances."[56] Advertisements and concert programs presented the Coros y Danzas as unprofessional, untrained volunteers who had performed their native songs and dances since childhood—a tactic that was intended to highlight the authentic origins of their repertoire. However, the majority of the women in these troupes, who were almost entirely from urban middle-class families, only became acquainted with these rural music traditions through the Sección Femenina's cultural programs.

Without any monetary incentive, the women joined the Coros y Danzas for recreation, socializing, and to help the Sección Femenina's national mission. The dancers designed and wore the colorful costumes representing their province, made friendships within the troupe, and were occasionally fortunate enough to travel to the regional and national competitions around Spain (The Coros y Danzas de Granada even went on annual skiing trips in the Sierra Nevada mountains from the 1940s onward).[57] Those few troupes who placed in the regional and national competitions toured throughout the world on missions of cultural diplomacy paid for by the government. While abroad, the women were almost always allowed some free time in the mornings to visit local tourist sites, shop for souvenirs, or spend time at the beach in locations such as Cuba and Morocco.[58]

However, the women on these missions were never entirely free of male control—all the performers required the signed permission of their father or a male legal guardian, even when they were well into their twenties.[59] The instructoras maintained discipline by eliminating performers and sending reports on each of their members to the national headquarters of the Sección Femenina in Madrid. Rivera and Sampelayo were often informed of transgressions against Francoist gender roles. After a tour in Argentina in 1948, an instructora wrote the following paragraph about the Coros y Danzas from Bilbao:

> The main defect of the troupe is its great deal of arrogance, perhaps typical of the character of Bilbao, [a people] who believe they are superior

to the rest of Spain. Despite the separatists [among them], they never-theless improved during the trip, incorporating themselves more with the rest of the expedition and all of them demonstrating increasing discipline.[60]

This scenario hints at the parameters of women's power within the bureau-cratic structure of the Sección Femenina. Not only were the Basque dancers chastised for allegedly refusing to conform to the Sección Femenina's con-cept of female discipline, but their "arrogant" and "separatist" tendencies were also framed as being inherent characteristics of the Basque people in general who had largely sided with the Republicans during the Civil War. Female liberty contradicted Rivera's statement that women's behavior must "only revolve around the needs of men . . . and so we shall not make vain public displays, which is not a woman's place, or distasteful arguments."[61] On the one hand, the Coros y Danzas provided its lower-ranking members with certain benefits; the Sección Femenina's Department of Music encouraged women to temporarily leave their families and native towns to train and tour on the international stage, albeit as messengers for the Franco regime's hyper-misogynistic policies. But, as we shall see, women's power to question female or male members of the Spanish government was reserved almost exclusively for the higher-ranking members of the Sección Femenina. Consequently, women's freedom was entirely relative to their status within the Falange. In the Department of Music, one of the most effective ways a woman could raise her rank was to train successful troupes in the Sección Femenina's national song and dance competitions.

The National Competition

Between 1938 and 1941, the Coros y Danzas performed exclusively for polit-ical rallies and propaganda newsreels. In 1942 the Sección Femenina organ-ized the first Concurso Nacional de Coros y Danzas (National Competition of Choruses and Dances) with the added participation of troupes of boys and girls from the Frente de Juventudes (Youth Front).[62] In the first year, 116 troupes competed, with a total of 3,135 performers.[63] Over the next two and a half decades the size of the National Competition increased exponentially, reaching 1,587 troupes and 29,106 performers in 1950; and 2,446 troupes and 48,744 performers by 1967. Through this immense program, the Sección

Femenina used rural musical traditions, dances, and religious songs to construct notions of a *raza española*.

According to the official rules of the National Competition, judges were "chosen from among the nation's most competent musical authorities."[64] Usually, these were high-ranking members of the Sección Femenina itself, such as Sampelayo, alongside male members of the IEM.[65] The National Competition was divided into three stages: the provincial, regional, and national. First, choirs and dance troupes from the same province performed in the style of a local festival. This usually took place in the town square of the provincial capital (e.g., in Córdoba, Almeria, etc.). The provincial winners then competed within their region (e.g., Andalusia, Catalonia, etc.). Only the Sección Femenina's best adult female choirs and dance troupes were chosen from each of Spain's seventeen regions to compete in the National Competition. The final round was performed in a different regional capital every year—a policy intended to celebrate the nation's diverse music traditions as a mystically unified ensemble. Those troupes that were placed in the National Competition often appeared in propagandistic newsreels or feature films (e.g., *Ronda española* [1951]) and toured abroad.

The National Competition held separate prizes for the top troupes of the Sección Femenina and Frente de Juventudes. The troupes of the Sección Femenina were formed entirely by young adult women while the troupes of Frente de Juventudes were a mix of boys and girls between fourteen and eighteen years of age (see figure 1.4). Consequently, the gender balance in the National Competition was roughly three-fourths female and one-fourth male. All the troupes, including the mixed-gendered troupes of the Frente de Juventudes, were directed by female *instructoras* of the Sección Femenina.

Only the instrumentalists remained exclusively male throughout the history of the Sección Femenina's Coros y Danzas. This was consistent with the strong gender divisions in tourist *tablao flamenco* where women's bodies are usually on display while male guitarists play in the shadows as both spectators and performers.[66] Despite upholding these patriarchal gender roles on stage, the male instrumentalists of the Coros y Danzas had no real authority over the ensemble; they were not responsible for organizing tours, nor were they ever permitted to be an instructor of a provincial troupe. There is little evidence in the archives of their formal affiliation with the Sección Femenina, including if they were paid or volunteered. Male instrumentalists did not have a major impact on the artistic course of the Coros y Danzas. Instead,

Figure 1.4 A mixed-gender troupe from the Frente de Juventudes (Youth Front) of Olvera perform for a Concurso Provincial (Provincial Competition) in a local plaza, c. 1960. ES-AHP Cádiz, Caja no. 13326, no. 3, Tomo I.

the men merely followed the female instructoras as the women pursued their own cultural and political goals.

An instructora's first task in the National Competition was to transcribe and catalog rural song and dance traditions from their province upon special files.[67] These documents consist of a single sheet of paper, 46 cm long by 16 cm wide, folded down the middle to create four pages (see figure 1.5). The files contain information such as who collected the music, its origins, the source from which the music was recorded, and a notated transcription of the music. Instructoras were also required to assess the music's "artistic value" and "folkloric value"—terms that I will explore later in this chapter and in Chapter 2. The third and fourth pages were reserved for music transcriptions (see figure 1.6). The files were often accompanied by sketches of the appropriate regional dress with examples of textiles. Except for a few slight modifications, I found that the format remained the same from 1942 until the disbandment of the Sección Femenina in 1977, two years after the death of Franco.[68] Local troupes were only permitted to perform newly collected repertoire once the files had been approved by the *regidora provincial de cultura* (provincial councilwoman of culture) and, afterward, Sampelayo

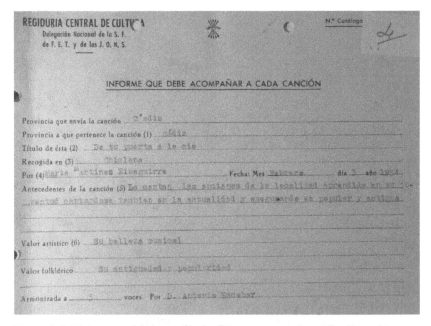

Figure 1.5 First page of the song file for "De tu puerta a la mía" collected in 1954 by Maria Martínez Eizaguirre, an "instructora de música" and provincial cultural councilor of Cádiz. ES-AHP Cádiz, Caja 13324.

in Madrid. Sampelayo received hundreds of song and dance files every year from throughout the nation.[69]

Usually, an instructora would collect songs and dances during a religious holiday or agricultural event in a small town.[70] The instructoras transcribed most of their material from elders and agricultural workers. To underscore the urgency of their work, the instructoras often indicated that a song or dance had never been documented before with the remark "unedited" or "documents do not exist." Music and words were transcribed onsite, and in the rare instances when audio recording technology was used to collect songs, it was only to aid the process of transcription rather than a means of documentation.[71] Once the music was transcribed into standard Western musical notation, any field recordings that were made seem to have been considered redundant—I could find no surviving examples. Information regarding musical qualities that could only be preserved via sound recordings was disregarded, including vocal timbre, microtones,

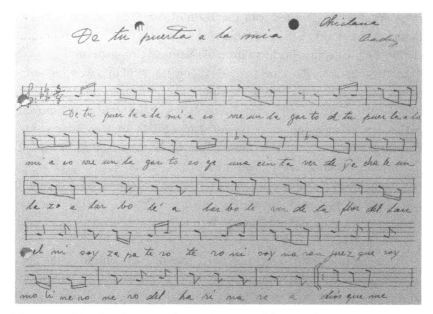

Figure 1.6 Martínez Eizaguirre's transcription of the song "De tu puerta a la mia" on the third page of the same file as in figure 1.5. ES-AHP Cádiz, Caja 13327.

and rhythmic subtleties. Oral and aural traditions collected from community elders were transformed into musical compositions. This procedure contributed to a standardization of the Coros y Danzas' performance practices across Spain and the repertoire of the different cultures they were representing.

Performance practices that tended to be associated with specific rural communities were mostly left out. The troupes of Coros y Danzas across Spain were encouraged to maintain the same pronunciation (when singing in Castilian) and vocal timbre regardless of the musical tradition or cultural group they were representing. The criteria on the guidelines for the National Competition state that the judges were to adjudicate songs based on standardized conceptions of "pitch, diction, and [musical] interpretation."[72] According to judges' comments on written evaluations of performances, they preferred to hear a vocal production that was accurate, open, and "perfectly in tune."[73] For example, when a group from the Andalusian province of Jaén sang a *soleares* with the typical microtones, approximate sense of pitch, and raspy vocal tone associated with that form of flamenco, the jury criticized them for "shouting noisily" and for having a "very lazy and irregular pronunciation" before eliminating them from the National Competition.[74]

In the song files, *villancicos* (religious songs), agricultural working songs, *nanas* (lullabies), and circle dances were usually considered to have the highest "artistic value," a term that intersected with the beauty and simplicity of the ideal Falange woman.[75] The instructora Josefa Romero Baraco writes that the *villancico* "El niño hermoso" from Cádiz has a "joy and simplicity that provide it with an artistic sentiment of great value."[76] An *alegría* (a form of flamenco) from Cádiz is described as the "salt of the earth,"[77] signifying basic, fundamental goodness; and the instructora Pilar Alfonso y Calús from Cádiz writes that the children's song "Terrenilla está bordando" has a "naïve, easy, and gracious melody."[78]

But it became clear when repertoire appeared to contradict the ideal qualities of the Falangist woman. In Andalusian repertoire, the painful and sometimes morbid lyrics found in the more serious flamenco *palos* (forms), especially *cante jondo*, were entirely edited out of the Sección Femenina's representation of Spanish music. However, lighter dances that were at the peripheries of flamenco repertoire, such as the more popular versions of *sevillanas*, *fandangos*, and *alegrías*, were included within the repertoire of Andalusian troupes. Nowhere in the song files is there material that represents bawdy subject-matter or coarse language, as was once the staple of flamenco bars and cabarets throughout the nation earlier in the twentieth century.[79] While the absence of sexual innuendos and scatological humor was certainly related to the instructoras' desire to embody the Francoist portrayal of women's virtue and untouchable beauty, this rather puritanical editing of rural song traditions had also been common among song collectors in Spain since Felip Pedrell (1841–1922) and Antonio Machado y Álvarez (1848–1893).

The song files required the instructoras to provide musical settings for the repertoire that they collected. This usually took the form of simple harmony in two or three voices (see figures 1.7 and 1.8) and settings of instrumental accompaniment. Consequently, members who wanted to work as instructoras of music were provided with two years of harmony, counterpoint, and solfège.[80]

Although the settings were usually written by the provincial instructora, there were some contributions from local professional musicians, such as town organists. In Granada, the guitarists Juan Roman, José Armillas, and

INFORME QUE DEBE ACOMPAÑAR A CADA CANCION

Provincia que envía la canción ___CADIZ___
Provincia a que pertenece la canción (1) ___CADIZ___
Título de ésta (2) ___"El cebollinero".___
Recogida en (3) ___Chiclana___
Por (4) ___Ines Muñoz Perez___   Fecha: Mes ___Mayo___ día ___ año ___1.955___
Antecedentes de la canción (5) ___Recogida de una anciana de 80 años que lo cantaban___
___cuando era niña.___

Valor artístico (6) ___Tiene___

Valor folklórico ___Su popularidad___

Armonizada a ___2___ voces. Por ___Ines Muñoz___

Figure 1.7 First page of the song file for "El cebollinero" collected in 1955 from an eighty-year-old woman in the Andalusian town of Chiclana who sang this as a child. Notice at the bottom the instructora Inéz Muñoz Perez indicates that she harmonized the song for two voices. AHP-Cádiz, Caja 13325, num. 3, libro 1.

Figure 1.8 "El cebollinero" set for two voices by the instructora of Cádiz, Inéz Muñoz Perez. AHP-Cádiz, Caja 13325, num. 3, libro 1.

Ángel Barrios of the popular Trio Albéniz collaborated with the Coros y Danzas, providing virtuoso arrangements of instrumental dances. Regardless of who wrote them, an instructora's ability to provide suitable musical settings was critical to the success of her troupe in the National Competition. The choral harmonization and instrumental settings had to be compelling for an audience to listen to them, yet simple enough to sing and play. On recorded evaluations, judges of the competition frequently criticized instructoras' settings as "having little interest and being very poorly harmonized" despite the supposedly "great folkloric value" of the original material.[81] If the judges from the annual National Competition felt that the repertoire of a certain group was suitable for high-profile performances or propagandistic newsreels, composers in Madrid such as Rafael Benedito (1885–1963) and Benito García de la Parra (1884–1953) might rework the musical setting and choreography.

The Sección Femenina tailored the nation's rural music traditions to suit their completely female ensembles. Instructoras frequently noted on the files that certain dances could be performed "by men and women, or by women only," implying that they would choose the latter.[82] For example, the light flamenco *palo*, *peteneras clásicas*, catalogued by Bella Moreno in 1954, was noted as being "easily adapted as a girls' dance due to its naïve and simple choreography."[83] For repertoire in which men were considered to be essential, women performed in men's costume (see figures 1.9 and 1.10).[84]

In the same way that the Sección Femenina allowed some women to participate in the male-dominated sphere of politics, the Coros y Danzas could temporarily impersonate men, taking on their costumes and choreography. On the one hand, the cross-dressed women emphasized the gender imbalances and differences between the types of activities men and women were "supposed" to be engaged in. But at the same time, the absence of male influence gave these female ensembles considerable autonomy to shape the way in which rural Spanish music traditions were presented via their music programs at home and on international tours. The instructoras' attempt to portray themselves as sexually chaste yet empowered female representatives of Franco's Spain, however, was not always realized. As we will see in the following pages, the Sección Femenina's autonomy and representations of Catholic virtue were contested by male Spanish politicians who saw the public performances of the Coros y Danzas as a signal of their sexual availability.

Figure 1.9 Costume design depicting a woman dressed in the male garments of the *majo gaditano* (dandy from Cádiz). Cádiz ES-AHP, Caja 13327.

Power Dynamics and Abuse on International Tours

During the Coros y Danzas' international tours, social gatherings after performances were a means of building relations with foreign civilians and diplomats. At these events, the young female performers were encouraged to charm foreign male officials and sell Spanish culture. However, the women often found themselves in degrading and dangerous situations with unruly men, alcohol, and drugs. Occasionally the women would be in danger of rape when a group of intoxicated men followed them home after an event or continuously demanded more performances.[85] Abuse from male politicians and bureaucrats threatened the women's safety and caused the moral principles

Figure 1.10 Women dressed as male *bandoleros* (highwaymen) while dancing with other women dressed as *Gitanas* (Roma/Gypsies) in Cádiz, 1960. Notice the male instrumentalists seated in the background. Cádiz ES-AHP, Caja 13327.

of the Sección Femenina to conflict with the organization's important role in Spanish cultural diplomacy.

In London on June 28, 1947, the final day of the Coros y Danzas' first international tour, the Spanish diplomat Juan Puchals invited troupes from Segovia, Córdoba, and Ferrol del Caudillo[86] to perform at the Instituto de España[87] (Spanish Institute) in London. Although the Coros y Danzas were departing for Madrid the following morning, Sampelayo agreed to this last-minute request. After the women had gone to Mass that evening, Puchals arrived with several cars to collect the troupes up from their dormitories in the convent of the Sisters of the Immaculate Heart of Mary. The women were brought to an empty room of the Spanish Institute where they waited alone for several hours.[88] In her travelogue, Sampelayo writes that "From that moment, we all took notice of this unnatural treatment."[89] Eventually, the women were called to dance for a cocktail party downstairs. According to Sampelayo—and much to her dismay—the Spanish diplomat did not introduce the young women as the Coros y Danzas of the Sección Femenina, but as professional entertainers. After their performance, the troupes were served alcoholic beverages and were mostly ignored by the other guests. Once Sampelayo realized that the event was so "cold and unwelcoming" to the women, she told Puchals that her troupes needed to return to the convent where they were residing. In her travelogue, Sampelayo implies that the diplomat made sexual advances and prevented the performers from leaving. Finally, an intense argument quickly arose between these two Spanish officials about who should pay for the transportation of the women to their accommodations:

> I told him that it was he who had to think about how we were going to get back because we did not attend the party particularly for our own pleasure, rather we attended the party as representatives of Spain and that, especially as ladies, male courtesy forced him to take us home at those hours of the night. . . . Quite quickly, he brought us the taxis and told the *camaradas* to pay for them. Our embarrassment in the face of this was so great that I could not even be bothered and all I could tell them was that they were ignorant of who we were. When we arrived at the convent, I sent the taxis [back] to the Institute to receive their pay.[90]

According to Sampelayo, Puchals denied her rank as an authoritative figure within the Spanish government. Moreover, Puchals seemed to hide women's influence on Spanish cultural politics in general by omitting an introduction to the Sección Femenina and the Coros y Danzas. Political, sexual, and monetary power dynamics were constantly being negotiated between the Coros y Danzas and the Spanish male officials with whom they collaborated. Diplomats were frequently enthusiastic about using the Coros y Danzas' services but refused to acknowledge the official authority of the *instructoras* that allowed them to overcome traditionally proscribed gender roles.

In 1951, Rivera and Fernando Fuentes of the Franco regime's Servicio Exterior (Foreign Service) arranged several performances of the Coros y Danzas in Morocco.[91] This tour was part of an annual international festival known as the Semana de Tánger—a week-long celebration that allowed Western colonists operating in the Tangier International Zone to share their culture with the Muslim and Jewish Moroccans through sports activities, theater, food stalls, and live musical performances.[92] The *jefe de expedición* (leader of the expedition), María de Miranda y Quartin, was placed in charge of thirty-five female dancers and twelve male instrumentalists representing Madrid, Málaga, and Cádiz. Miranda y Quartin writes in her travelogue that the three troupes gathered in Algeciras, an Andalusian port town, before traveling to Tangier by boat. When the troupes disembarked from their ship at nine in the morning, they were greeted by several Spanish officials and a large crowd of Moroccans and Spaniards.[93] Fuentes was already inebriated, behaving in ways that Miranda y Quartin describes as "very reckless."[94] Miranda y Quartin asked Fuentes to take the troupes directly to their accommodations at the Hotel Continental because seven of the women were ill after the sea voyage across the Strait of Gibraltar. But Fuentes insisted that all the women must parade through the city on foot behind a marching band and thousands of Spanish flags. Unknown to Miranda y Quartin, Fuentes was leading the women straight from the port to a stage in the city center where they would be expected to perform for an enormous crowd of Spanish and Moroccan men. An argument followed in which the male diplomat tested Miranda y Quartin's authority over the dance troupes and how the cultural programs of the Sección Femenina were to be presented abroad:

> First, they told me (as we were walking) that they were taking the girls to the fair just to be seen and greet the public from a stage. But once we were there, they wanted them to dance. I defended [the girls] as much as I could because the process of taking them directly from the port to dance [in the square] seemed inhumane to me (and some girls were still seasick). But when I was almost ready to give in because of [the men's] persistence, some professional flamenco dancers came on stage—I then flatly refused to let our girls dance, explaining to those gentlemen that we, as a rule, never perform with other organizations or professionals. Then they finally gave up.[95]

After Miranda y Quartin's initial victory, Fuentes arranged performances in venues that did not support the Sección Femenina's concept of feminine virtue. Later that evening, the three troupes performed for Spanish and Moroccan diplomats at the Parque Brook, a club that Miranda y Quartin describes as "a very chic place, with pool, dance floor, tables, nice lighting etc. etc."[96] The women performed in traditional dress on a small dance floor crowded with tables while the instrumentalists played on a stage designed for jazz orchestras. Because of the club's intimate and cosmopolitan atmosphere, Miranda y Quartin reports that "It was very pleasant to have dinner and spend time there, but it was not appropriate for a show of the Coros y Danzas."[97] Miranda y Quartin mentions in her list of "Mistakes to Correct" that Fuentes should never again be responsible for organizing tours of the Coros y Danzas. She then suggests that it would be preferable to have someone who understands the Sección Femenina's values—preferably someone from the Sección Femenina itself—to scout out performance venues and arrange international tours.[98]

The Coros y Danzas' tours abroad were an arena in which Francoist gender ideology was constantly debated; the women of the Sección Femenina fought for dignity and greater autonomy as they attempted to articulate their own definition of feminine virtue. These inconsistencies between the Sección Femenina's gender ideology and the male diplomats' demand for disempowered, sexualized entertainers were part of a larger paradox: Francoist notions of religious virtue and the nation's enormous, legalized prostitution industry. Despite National Catholicism's disdain for sex outside of marriage, prostitution and sexually transmitted diseases skyrocketed after the Civil War. In 1941 about 65,000 cases of syphilis were reported within Spain, rising to 268,000 in 1947.[99] Since the number of legally registered prostitutes remained below 10,000 until the 1950s, the rise of venereal diseases was likely due to a clandestine sex trade practiced by women who were trying to supplement the starvation wages of their official work.[100]

It has been argued that Western capitalist societies tend to polarize the roles of adult females between those who are "outsiders" (e.g., public women, courtesans, lesbians) and "insiders" (e.g., those considered to be suitable marriage partners).[101] Sexually mature women who are "insiders" have more access to socioeconomic systems and therefore can pose the greatest threat to male authority. Consequently, "insider" women tend to have their roles, including music-making, restricted to the domestic sphere.[102] Outsider women, however, have these restrictions lifted because their insecure access to wealth and power often does not place them in significant competition with men of the establishment. The Coros y Danzas did not entirely correspond to Koskoff's "insider" or "outsider" conceptions of female gender roles; these single women were very much on the "inside" of Francoist society and strove to embody the regime's ideals of female sexual virtue, yet they had certain restrictions lifted on their public performances and travel. Male officials repeatedly attempted to break the women's status as "insiders" by sexualizing the dancers, challenging the authority of the *jefe de expedición*, and ignoring the existence of the Sección Femenina altogether. In return, the instructoras of the Coros y Danzas made themselves into independent, yet chaste, mother figures who challenged the male-dominated world of foreign diplomacy.

An "Excessive Feminine Element"?

During international tours, the Sección Femenina adapted its portrayal of gender and Spanish rural music traditions to the expectations of their foreign audiences. Several folk festivals were founded in the years immediately following the end of the war as a means of restoring world peace, in particular the annual Llangollen Festival of Wales (1947) and the British-based International Folk Music Festival (1949). These events provided Rivera excellent avenues through which to organize regular missions of cultural diplomacy on behalf of the Franco regime.[103] During international collaborations, however, the Sección Femenina was encouraged to adapt its portrayal of femininity and Spanish culture to the expectations of foreign publics.

In early 1949, Rivera applied for the Coros y Danzas to participate in the first annual International Folk Music Festival held in Venice from September 7 to 11, 1949. Funded by a grant from the Arts Council of Great Britain, the festival ran until 1967 and was held in a different country every year. The festival was publicized as a "scientific" event that hosted performances of rural dance and music traditions alongside readings of academic papers by prominent musicologists, cultural anthropologists, and folklorists. Cambridge University Press published the proceedings in the annual *Journal of the International Folk Music Council* (1948–1968). Three prominent British folklorists and composers managed both the festival and journal, including Ralph Vaughan Williams as president from 1947 to 1958, William Stanley Gwynn Williams as treasurer, and Maud Karpeles as secretary.

The London-based team searched for international participants by sending pamphlets with enclosed application forms to embassies located throughout the British capital. According to the pamphlet, the internationality of the participants was intended to promote an "understanding and friendship among nations" and help undo the socio-political division that remained after the Second World War.[104] Such a utopian view of music's ability to bridge national divides was sometimes questioned by those who were present. Tola Korian (1911–1983), a Polish actress based in London who attended the 1949 Venice festival, wrote the following in the journal's proceedings:

The Inauguration took place in the Sala dello Scrutinio and we heard several warm speeches of welcome on behalf of the Italian authorities. . . . Just at the point when things seemed to be getting too serious, because we were told that the peace and future of the world depended largely upon us, we had a very simple, human speech from the Honorary Secretary, Miss Maud Karpeles, with a touch of British humor that put everybody at ease.[105]

Regardless of such questions about the festival's ability to help heal the wounds of the war, academics and performers from eighteen nations participated in the event, representing almost the entirety of the Western Bloc.[106] The absence of any representation from the Eastern Bloc begs this question: Did the festival work more to strengthen the West's solidarity rather than deal with the quickly escalating international crisis of the Cold War?

With its gigantic, elevated stage in St. Mark's Square illuminated by floodlights and amplified through loudspeakers and microphones, the festival featured seven hundred singers, dancers, and instrumentalists from fifty international troupes.[107] A surviving pamphlet shows that the festival directors made stark distinctions between popular and rural music traditions in a way that intersected with the philosophies of the Sección Femenina's Department of Music:

The festival is designed to illustrate both the survival and revival of folk music. The performers may therefore be either members of accredited folk dance and folk song societies or peasants and others who have acquired their art by the traditional methods. Preference should be given to the latter category. The dances and songs presented must be genuine examples of "folk" as distinct from "popular art."[108]

While the festival organizers state that they place higher value on performances of "peasants," they also suggest that organized troupes of dancers and musicians may apply as an alternative (I interpret their use of "peasants" as poor people living in rural, somewhat isolated agricultural or fishing communities). This dichotomy was linked to how the festival directors understood their objectives for the "survival" and "revival" of "peasant" music and dance. Here, "survival" refers to fostering performances by the "original" practitioners of the repertoire, specifically "peasants"; "revival" refers to the recreation of "peasant" traditions by trained troupes or societies, often situated in urban centers.[109] While the society preferred the "authentic" peasants over trained troupes, the latter were seen as a necessary evil to help prevent the loss of rural customs that were fading due to mass migrations to city centers. Of course, this view can be seen as problematic if we consider that any intervention on the part of an academic organization dedicated to preserving the customs of rural societies is bound to influence and change those very customs—whether they be performed by the original members of the rural community or by urban outsiders.

In principle, the state-organized Coros y Danzas of the Sección Femenina would have fit nicely into the festival directors' definition of "folk revival." Yet, it seems that the Sección Femenina's portrayal of gender in Spanish music was a step too far. After Rivera made an initial inquiry about entering the Coros y Danzas into the festival, Karpeles informed her that the troupes would not be allowed to participate due to their complete lack of male dancers. "Dances which are intended for men, or men and women together," Karpeles writes to Rivera, "should not be performed by a group consisting solely of ladies."[110] Consequently, the festival organizers did not consider the Spanish troupes to be "strictly traditional." Karpeles explains that she had brought this issue up when she adjudicated troupes of Coros y Danzas two years earlier at the first Llangollen International Musical Eisteddfod Festival in Wales.[111] Karpeles highlights her androcentric vision of Spanish music and dance when she writes that the festival directors would be "particularly glad if there were an opportunity of having some of the very spectacular ritual dances for men in which Spain is so rich."[112] We do not have Rivera's letters to Karpeles, but considering the apologetic tone in Karpeles's following letter on August 16, it seems that Rivera was offended by this critique of the Coros y Danzas' authenticity. Karpeles replied with the following:

> As regards the nature of the groups that you had proposed to send, please do not misunderstand me or think that I am lacking in appreciation. I have seen and adjudicated several of the women's groups at the Llangollen Eisteddfod and I have expressed my great admiration of their dancing. Although there may be a certain number of dances which are traditionally performed by women I think you will agree that the most typically Spanish dances are those which are performed either by men alone or by men and women together and as there has, unfortunately, to be a narrow selection of groups, it is natural that we prefer to have either groups of men only or mixed groups. The Venice Festival is not a competition in which any group

can take part but a Festival at which only selected groups are invited to perform. It is, at the same time, a scientific congress so that we should like dances that are performed, as far as possible, in the authentic traditional way.[113]

Karpeles remarks favorably on the skill of the Coros y Danzas but claims that the lack of men in their dance ensembles is an inauthentic representation of Spanish dance, which is inherently masculine. Gendered readings of rural music traditions during the postwar era were not exclusive to Francoist Spain. Although the dancers and singers of the Coros y Danzas during the late 1940s and early 1950s were exclusively female, Karpeles proposes a similarly subjective perception of Spanish dance by saying that it was not traditional for Spanish women to perform independently from men—and that most of that nation's repertoire ought to be performed by "men alone." These exchanges reveal that the world-renowned directors of the festival also had a skewed view of gender in Spanish music, ignoring the fundamental contribution of women to the development of Spanish popular and rural music traditions in both commercial and private settings during the twentieth century.[114] Instead of Rivera's Coros y Danzas, Karpeles invited a dance troupe directed by the Spanish musicologist and composer Manuel Chausa.[115] In a report of the festival, however, this troupe is not to be found, and in its place are four Coros y Danzas representing Salamanca, Saragossa, Cabezon de la Sal, and Santander.[116] We are left to speculate on the internal maneuverings that took place in Madrid to produce this result.

Foreign critics often commented on the gender distribution of the Coros y Danzas. Three years after the Venice festival, between February and March 1952, the Spanish ambassador to the United Kingdom hosted a series of performances by several troupes of Coros y Danzas under the title "The National Spanish Company of Dancers, Singers and Instrumentalists" at London's Stoll Theatre. A London-based reporter for *The Scotsman* complained of an "excessive feminine element" and a lack of "mixed couples" in the dance troupes.[117] An anonymous critic for *The Times* wrote that the strong "female bias" was the result of an amateurish "conscious desire to revise and preserve traditions" also found in unprofessional English song and dance societies.[118] A critic for *Theatre* using the initials G.S. (possibly the Scottish poet and critic George Sutherland Fraser [1915–1980]), wrote of the same show:

The serious lack—and it became obvious after the fourth or fifth item—was of male dancers; for reasons undisclosed . . . the group consists of about six women to every man, and the majority of the men are instrumentalists, not dancers.[119]

G.S. expresses that all displays of "masculine elegance . . . vitality, virility and virtuosity," which he believes to be an inherent component of Spanish dance, were missing from the Coros y Danzas due to the performers' gender.[120] According to G.S., the only moments when the troupes displayed these traits was during those dances in which "women were obviously substituting for men."[121]

It seems that G.S.'s conception of "masculine virtuosity" may have clashed with the "artistic value" and performance practices of the Sección Femenina's Department of Music mentioned earlier in this chapter. The English critics expected to witness the "swift footwork" and "expertise" found in the tourist flamenco venues in Andalusia and Madrid and performed by touring international artists. While the English critics wished for more virtuosic skill and flair, the members of the Sección Femenina were concerned with portraying the women's beauty, appeal, and ability to dance and sing within large ensembles. In the conclusion of his review, G.S. alludes to what he thinks are the politics behind the Sección Femenina's representation of Spanish music: "Unless Spanish dancing is suffering a newly-imposed cultural twist under the existing regime, and for reasons far from obvious, this program is not strictly representative."[122] Not only does G.S. consider the performance to be inauthentic due to a lack of male dancers, but he suspects that the Franco regime is deliberately altering the gender roles of Spanish music for political reasons. In the last paragraph of his article, G.S. contrasts the Coros y Danzas with a cultural movement born out of a bourgeois group of artists in Granada during the first three decades of the twentieth century:

Any attempt to square this show with both the avowed objects of its presenting organization and with the present-day condition of Spain, must take into account both the notable paucity of male dancers provided and one's awareness of the importance of the male element in popular Spanish dancing, music-making and poetry reciting. Are only women interested in spreading contemporary Spanish culture abroad? Are men no longer interested in dancing in Spain? Or are there too few good male dancers available for this kind of government service? And, on second thoughts, one recalls that none of the items dwelt significantly upon those masculine qualities of pride, integrity and tenacity which are celebrated in, for instance, much Spanish popular literature of previous ages and specifically in the poetry of Garica [sic] Lorca in our own day.[123]

The murder of the internationally renowned poet Federico García Lorca in 1936 by the Nationalists was well known outside of Spain and added to the atrocities that politically stigmatized the Franco regime after the Second World War. Lorca and his circle of artists, writers, and composers known as the Centro Artístico believed that flamenco represented Andalusia's (and by extension Spain's) most ancient and "profound" qualities.[124] Our London critic, G.S., was aware of this Andalusian artistic movement. G.S. implies that the regime replaced the "masculine qualities of pride" associated with Lorca's vision of flamenco with artificial, docile, and feminine music and dance manufactured by the state. G.S. concludes that the performance of the Coros y Danzas, although fascinating and well executed, had been "twisted" by the cultural policies of the Franco regime.[125]

Not surprisingly, accounts of performances from the mid-1950s onward show that the Sección Femenina added considerably more men to the Coros y Danzas while touring abroad, an adjustment that contradicted the organization's associations between femininity and folklore and the title of the Sección Femenina itself. The male performers were selected from the members of the Frente de Juventudes mentioned earlier. Given the timing, it seems likely that this was linked to the reception of British critics (already during the North American tour of 1953, the gender balance had been significantly altered to forty-nine women and thirty-five men [see Chapter 4]).[126] Thus, the Sección Femenina's tours of Europe during the late 1940s and early 1950s show how successful cultural diplomacy requires a complex set of interactions between the representatives of the visiting and host nations.[127] Cultural diplomacy is a two-way street. As the representatives of the Franco regime shaped foreign ideas of Spanish culture, they were also obliged to negotiate their notions of gender roles and ideas of Catholic morality.

The instructoras strove to express the Franco regime's understanding of women as subservient and maternally preoccupied through their collective acts of cultural preservation. But some members of the Sección Femenina who transmitted this misogynistic ideology via the Department of Music gained a certain kind of empowerment. This process had several logistical stages. First, instructoras promoted the notion that Spanish folk music was

under threat of contamination from foreign popular culture and leftist politics.[128] They then proposed that women's maternal instincts made them the
ideal candidates to safeguard, repair, and salvage the nation's supposedly ancient musical heritage. Instructoras next used the National Competition and
the song and dance files to invent, authenticate, and codify Spanish female
identity according to their own moral, religious, and political values. Finally,
the higher-ranking instructoras built careers as teachers and impresarios for
their troupes.

The instructoras' interactions with Spanish male diplomats reveal, however, that the ruling oligarchy of the Franco regime was not ideologically
consolidated and would not universally support their mission. Moreover,
the Franco regime's continuously evolving portrayal of the female gender
roles in Spain was not completely manufactured by propagandists such as
the Sección Femenina, but also through the feedback and expectations of
critics abroad. As discussed in this book's Introduction, the various political players in Franco's bureaucratic authoritarian regime were directed by
diverse and conflicting interests, obeying written and unwritten rules that
were open to interpretation.[129] The instructoras of the Sección Femenina
operated within a network of political circles at home and abroad that reinforced different ideas of Spanish culture and femininity. As we shall see in
the following chapters, this ambiguity was generally useful for those in the
highest circles of the Franco regime: over time, the lack of a clear ideological doctrine endorsed a fluid conception of gender and race that enabled the
Spanish government to adapt to various political circumstances throughout
the world.

2

Songs and Dances of the Raza Española

In her speech given at the third annual council of the Sección Femenina in
the Castilian city of Zamora in 1939, Rivera conveys the comeradas' duty
to be knowledgeable of all the regional cultures within the political borders
of Spain:

> We joined the Falange because we were unhappy with Spain. And the
> Falange changed our whole being. Frivolous and insubstantial as we were
> before, it made us realize that we could be of use for something, that in
> Spain there was music that we did not know, that there were mountains,
> that there were rivers, that there were seas that united us with the world,
> that there were men capable of dying for Spain. That being Spanish is one
> of the few serious things that one can be in life. . . . When all Spaniards have
> within them the slogans of the Falange Española Tradicionalista y de las
> J.O.N.S., when the Catalans know how to sing the songs of Castile; when
> the *sardanas* are also known in Castile and the "*chistu*"[1] is played; when
> Andalusian *cante* is understood in all its depth and philosophy instead of
> knowing it through the *tabladillos zarzueleros*; when the songs of Galicia
> are sung in the Levante;[2] when fifty or sixty thousand voices come together
> to sing the same song, then yes we will have achieved unity among men and
> among the lands of Spain.[3]

Rivera's dream of a culturally diverse but mystically unified raza española
would soon be realized through her Department of Music. Troupes of
Coros y Danzas representing Catalonia, the Basque Country, and Galicia
performed local songs and dances in their regional languages at political
rallies, national competitions, and on international tours. After a devastating
civil war that was fueled largely by cultural and socioeconomic boundaries,
this was perhaps one of the regime's most incongruent acts regarding its cultural policy; as the above speech was being delivered, Franco was enforcing
centralist policies that attempted to eliminate any trace of regional culture

Coros y Danzas. Daniel David Jordan, Oxford University Press. © Oxford University Press 2023.
DOI: 10.1093/oso/9780197586518.003.0003

from public life. Many of the same Catalan, Basque, and Galician dances, songs, and languages that Rivera refers to above were banned with penalties of imprisonment and death. While the Franco regime attempted to erase non-Castilian languages, dances, and songs from the repertory of private performers, the Sección Femenina's mission was to discover common cultural and historical threads that would be shared and recognized by the entire nation.

As I have shown through my account of the 1949 festival in Venice, one of the principal factors that distinguished the Sección Femenina from mid-twentieth-century British folklorists was their complete focus on the "revival" rather than the "survival" of rural music and dance traditions. The Coros y Danzas never presented actual "peasants" to the public, as the directors of the Venice Festival understood the word. All the performances immortalized in the Sección Femenina's newsreels and sound archives are of urban, professional, or semi-professional musicians dressed as rural agricultural workers, shepherds, and fishermen. This chapter explores how instructoras of the Sección Femenina attempted to revive and rewrite rural music traditions throughout the cultural regions of Spain as a means of constructing an ancient and shared history of the raza española.

Informants and Sources

The instructoras considered material collected from their community's elders to be of the highest "folkloric value," a nuanced term frequently used by the Sección Femenina's Department of Music that I will continue to examine throughout this chapter. A quarter of the files that I have studied mention the age of the local people who provided material as being between seventy-five and ninety-eight years of age. In other instances, they simply mention that a song or dance was transcribed "from an old lady of the village."[4] The instructoras often state that a song or dance was popular during the elder's youth but has since been forgotten by the younger generations. For example, an instructora of Los Barrios (a small town in the province of Cádiz) provides the source of a fandango that she collected from her community in November 1955:

> It is a dance that is intended for the countryside since that is where it is customarily performed. Today only the elders remember this dance because

the youth have never learned the steps. . . . It was not collected from a song-book, but from the elders of the area.[5]

Again, Inés Muñoz writes that the *fandango callejero* that she documented in the small village of Algodonales on October 20, 1959, could only be obtained from elders of the area: "It is [transcribed] from the local elders—there are no existing documents on this dance other than [what] . . . the elders remember from their youth."[6] The instructoras presented these songs and dances as endangered traditions that were on the brink of oblivion due to modern neglect of Spanish heritage and values. The repertoire, still preserved in the memories of elders living in rural towns, was seen as a window into an authentic Spanish past that could guide the nation into a more moral and authentically Spanish future.

The instructoras often claimed to save songs and dances that had not been performed for a half-century or more. According to the instructora María Carmen del Castillo, the dance *la bata* was performed in the small village of Grazalema in southern Spain only until the late nineteenth century.[7] Another instructora, Carmen Carrascosa, reports that she transcribed a *malagueña* in 1955 from an eighty-year-old man named Toribio Campos Muñoz who lived in Siles, a town outside of Jaén.[8] This informant claimed that the people of his town often danced to this song during "his time," but he was the only one still living who remembered it.[9]

Songs, dances, and designs for traditional clothing were revived from sources that had been compiled decades or centuries before the beginning of the Franco regime, including songbooks, oil paintings, and surviving garments. For example, in Cádiz, instructoras often looked to costumes and instruments in local museums. The instructora María Torres submitted a costume design in 1955 based on clothing that she found on a nineteenth-century puppet in the Fábrica Museo de Muñecos Marín [Marín Doll Museum Factory] founded in 1928.[10] At the bottom of the dress file under the heading "Does there exist an authentic example?," María Torres remarks, "No authentic dresses of this type currently exist, except within the Marín museum."[11] The dresses that Coros y Danzas from Jeréz de la Frontera wore while performing the dances *tanguillo, caracoles*, and *fandango* were copied from eighteenth-century oil paintings, etchings, and drawings of idealized *majas* and *majos* by Francisco José de Goya (1746–1828).[12] Once again, a version of the song "El Gazpacho" was transcribed from a songbook titled *Danzas populares de algunos pueblos de la Sierra* (Popular dances from towns in the Sierra Mountains) compiled by an anonymous author in the year 1797.[13]

Sometimes instructoras reconstructed songs, dances, and traditional costumes using incomplete sources. In Granada, a local musician named Don Miguel del Castillo submitted several dance files copied from a songbook compiled by Rafael Salguero Rodríguez (1875–1925),[14] who had once been an organist of the city's cathedral.[15] Castillo states that the music he transcribed "clearly had Gypsy origins."[16] Consequently, he choreographed the dance himself, borrowing gestures from the *alboreá* (a flamenco *palo* performed during Gitano[17] marriage rites) that he observed in the neighborhood of Sacromonte.[18] This dance, titled *la reja*, and its accompanying songs, "Niña asómate a la reja" and "Quiero vivir en Graná," were then cataloged and submitted by the instructora Angustias Franco in 1942 with a simple form of notated dance choreography.

The examples above reveal that many of the customs documented on the instructoras' files were partially invented or no longer representative of local traditions during the century in which they were recorded. As discussed in the following pages, rural traditions that had been either forgotten or only partially preserved provided the instructoras with an opportunity to create a new cultural heritage using their own imaginations. The instructoras used these invented musical traditions to shape the regime's present conceptions of a national and religious identity that every Spaniard could call his or her own. By experiencing this music, even those Spaniards who were born and raised in the nation's larger cities could seem to relive the traditions of their imagined rustic ancestors.

"Folkloric Value" and the Origins of the Raza Española

The information under the sections of the song and dance files marked "folkloric value" and "history" generally concerns the repertoire's age and the character of the community where it is performed. Such descriptions were always read aloud by a narrator during the national competition and missions of cultural diplomacy abroad. Sampelayo, who helped design the song and dance files as the director of the Sección Femenina's Department of Music, was concerned with the history of the repertoire that the instructoras collected just as much as its "artistic" qualities; footnote number 6 printed on the song files cautioned instructoras that a "song can have great musical beauty while not being folkloric."[19] These accompanying narratives encouraged the audience and performers to "relive" an invented origin story of the raza española.

The instructoras placed the origins of most songs and dances within an ambiguously remote past. Under the heading "Age of song or dance," the most common answer is "Date not known, danced since ancient times," or "It is not possible to be precise—it is very ancient, and is currently danced in all its purity."[20] The instructora Dolores Torres from Seville writes that a certain *villancico* she collected in Jaén in 1940 was "very popular and ancient, known and sung by all the social classes since the time of our grandparents and ancestors."[21] Later, in 1944, María Uribe Zores wrote the following statement about the song "Pícaros gitanos" that she transcribed in Seville: "we have sung it to our children, to ourselves, our parents, [and] our grandparents. There is no doubt of its antiquity and authenticity, and we cannot explain why it does not exist in any songbooks."[22] As we shall see, the instructoras' assessments of "folkloric value" framed the nation's musical traditions as being ancient, unchanging cultural artifacts.

The instructoras occasionally attributed contemporary rural music traditions to ancient Bronze Age Iberian civilizations. Such origin stories were probably not wholly the instructoras' invention; there were many similarities with earlier and contemporaneous writings by the musicologist Higinio Anglés (the director of the Instituto español de Musicología previously mentioned) and various intellectuals who were active during the decades preceding the Franco regime. According to Anglés, contemporary rural Spanish music had roots in Mozarabic chant, medieval *romanceros*, ancient Greek culture.[23] Such references to antiquity and the Late Middle Ages fit with Anglés's desire to portray Spanish culture as having roots in exclusively pre- and post-Muslim Iberia (711–1492). As Moreda Rodríguez points out, Spanish musical folklore "had to be fitted within Hispanidad, and this made it necessary to minimize or erase any connections to religions other than Catholicism."[24]

However, it was the pro-Republican and Andalusian regionalist Blas Infante (1885–1936) who probably first linked contemporary Spanish rural culture to ancient, quasi-mythological people in southern Spain. In Infante's essays "Ideal andaluz" (1915) and "La verdad sobre el complot de Tablada y el estado libre de Andalucía" (1931), the author attempts to justify his movement for Andalusian regional autonomy by examining the region's distinct culture.[25] Inspired by contemporaneous publications and excavations in southern Spain by the German historian and archaeologist Adolf Schulten

(1870–1960),[26] Infante claims that contemporary Andalusian character was first formed in Tartessos, an ancient harbor city close to modern-day Cádiz. According to Infante, Tartessos represented a fundamental milestone in the development of an ahistorical "Andalusian being" that continued to shape the region's culture and music in the twentieth century. Such writings inspired Andalusia's artistic and intellectual elite, including García Lorca. In his essay "Arquitectura del cante jondo" (1931), García Lorca writes that the basis of contemporary flamenco song was formed by ancient polytheistic Tartessans, and later given special expressive color by the Abrahamic religions that inhabited the Iberian Peninsula in the Middle Ages.[27] Although both Infante and García Lorca were executed in 1936 by the Nationalists for being Republican sympathizers, the instructoras of the Sección Femenina reframed their perspectives on Spanish and Andalusian cultural history to support their own political agenda, sometimes even quoting García Lorca's works.[28]

Like the writings of Infante and García Lorca from previous decades, the song and dance files of the Sección Femenina are filled with unverifiable lineages for the Spanish race going back to antiquity. But, unlike Infante's "Ideal andaluz," the Sección Femenina's references to ancient peoples were rarely connected to egalitarian ideals or a distinct regional character. Referring to scenes from the Hebrew Bible, an anonymous instructora operating in Granada suggests the dance *fandango cortijero* from La Herradura was first performed for King David by ancient slave women from Tartessos brought to the Eastern Mediterranean. The instructora's method of research is rather untrustworthy and reveals her desire to project Francoist ideas of race onto her imagined history of Spain:

> Were the dances [of Tartessos] the origin of the *fandango cortijero*? There is no written data that can confirm this—but as the *fandango* has only been transmitted orally through the generations, the comparative study of Spanish Folklore leads us to the conclusion that this hypothesis is well founded.[29]

The song and dance files of the Sección Femenina are filled with invented traditions and imaginings of fictional or unverifiable lineages for the Spanish race. For instance, Angustias Franco tells us that the *fandango de Almuñecar* was danced in the Bronze Age and brought to Andalusia from modern-day Israel by Phoenicians.[30] In an English-language program note from 1955, the traditional dance *el pericote* from Asturias is said to have been of the Neolithic Period: "This dance was performed before the region's prehistoric site of Peña Tú,[31] an idol made of stone by the Celts in Asturias ten centuries before Christ, although [the dance] now has modern influences."[32] In the same program, the *sardana*, a Catalan dance, is attributed to an ancient race of people who had immigrated to Iberia from Sardinia. Apparently, this dance was performed to worship the sun, "thereby explaining its circular formation."[33] This history includes the following explanation: "The theory that the *sardana* is a dance devoted to the sun is strengthened by the 24 measures which correspond to the 24 hours of the day."[34] In reality, the *sardana* was invented in the nineteenth century as a composite of several traditional dances, a result of the cultural movement known as the *Renaixença* (Renaissance) that accompanied an awakening of Catalan nationalism.[35] During the twentieth century, this dance was appropriated as a symbol of Catalan independence, and was vehemently prohibited by both the Primo de Rivera dictatorship and the Franco regime in all contexts of life except for the Department of Music of the Sección Femenina. Instead of eliminating the dance from their repertory, the instructoras incorporated the *sardana* into Francoist propaganda, cleansing its regional ethnic symbolism with a politically neutral historical narrative.

Along with references to prehistory and Bronze Age Iberian civilizations, the instructoras were also fond of connecting contemporary rural music traditions to the medieval re-Christianization of Spain. If a song and dance did not contain some reference to the Reconquista in its lyrics, an instructora would often find some means of connecting the repertoire to a relevant historical figure. For instance, the origin of the *seguidillas*, danced in the town Puebla de Don Fadrique to the northeast of Andalusia, is attributed to the town's patron, a renowned knight who was granted the surrounding land by the Catholic Monarchs after his exploits during the final conquest of Granada (1492). The local cultural councilor of the Sección Femenina claimed that the choreography is similar to dances from Aragon brought to the area by the caballero himself and presumably his cohort. Another reference to the Reconquista can be found in the words to the *fandango de Almuñecar*: "Long live Pérez de Guzmán/ long live his sacred land/ and long live Granada as well."[36] Guzman was a thirteenth-century Christian knight made famous by the playwright Antonio Gil y Zárate (1793–1861) in a scene where Guzman provides a dagger to the Moorish abductors of his son to demonstrate his unwillingness to succumb to the siege of Tarifa.[37] The instructoras framed these heroes of the Reconquista as personifications of the values of National Catholicism.

The instructoras juxtaposed local secular folk songs with religious music such as Gregorian chant, songs of pilgrimage, and religious carols, highlighting the role of the Catholic church within Franco's idea of the raza española. The Sección Femenina performed church music for holidays and marched in religious processions during Semana Santa and Corpus Christi.[38] During the national competition, troupes were required to perform one *villanacico* (Christmas carol) and one example of Gregorian chant, and separate prizes were given to those troupes that excelled specifically in those categories.

The Sección Femenina frequently participated in the Fiestas de Moros y Cristianos (Festival of Moors and Christians) celebrated throughout Spain, a holiday commemorating Christian victories of the Reconquista. Fiestas de Moros y Cristianos are local holidays in which towns parade and re-enact medieval battles between Christians and Muslims, inevitably resulting in a victory for the former. For example, the first public performance of the Coros y Danzas de Granada was in 1943 during a commemoration and solemn civic procession for the 451st anniversary of Queen Isabella and King Ferdinand's conquest of that city.[39] In addition to performances of local music and dance, instructoras were expected to stage plays about the expulsion of Muslims from Spain with young students from the School of Home Economics. The instructoras frequently used texts from the Spanish Golden Age that celebrate Catholic imperialism. A text used by the Sección Femenina in Granada written by an instructora ended with the defeated Sultan kneeling before a statue of the Virgin Mary, repenting for his transgressions against her and the "true faith." The play concludes with the following monologue:

> Sultan: (Kneels before the Virgin) You have the most atrocious man, the boldest, at your feet, surrendered. . . . What delight, what glory, what happiness! Today, I will prove to be a fine slave by receiving baptism this afternoon. And although you have captured a thousand soldiers by force of arms for that most excellent obligation, your slaves rightly acclaim you, all ask for your grace and also feel their baptism is delayed.[40]

The Sección Femenina used this music, dance, and theater to nourish and shape the symbolic world of Francoist Spain.[41] These cultural projects were linked to an official policy of racial preservation that attempted to justify the violence committed by male members of the Spanish government. The theologian and Nationalist sympathizer Manuel García Morente (1886–1942) wrote of a Spain defined by the "Christian faith and Iberian blood," while those of leftist ideologies were conflated with the so-called Anti-Spain of the "morally degenerate" "Moors" and Jews.[42] According to Francoist ideology, the Nationalist army was obliged to defend Spanish cultural heritage using whatever means necessary, including war, mass executions, and concentration camps. The Sección Femenina's cultural programs helped enforce a dichotomy between the "virtuous Spanish race" and the "corrupted" Republicans and Communists in exile. Through its Department of Music, the instructoras of the Sección Femenina edited and performed traditions that the soldiers of Nationalist Spain were encouraged to protect with violence. Yet, the metaphor that linked the failed Republican army to the corrupting "Moorish invaders" was only useful to the Franco regime within the Iberian Peninsula. As we shall see in Chapter 3, when the Sección Femenina sent women to perform for Spain's colonized peoples in Morocco, the "Moor," paradoxically, became an image of inclusiveness and cultural unity.

Regional Identities and Social Class

As discussed in the Introduction, Franco considered Spain's diverse languages and cultures to be a potential threat to the unification of the nation, especially those that had once been associated with movements for regional autonomy under the Second Republic.[43] The regime's repression of regional cultures has often been described as cultural genocide; non-Castilian languages and regional customs were prohibited from the public domain, including administration, education, media, and publishing houses.[44] Meanwhile, the names of people, cities, natural landmarks, and companies were "Hispanicized," meaning that they were exchanged for Castilian equivalents.[45] But the unique cultural traditions and languages of Catalonia, the Basque Country, Galicia, and Aragon were not entirely eliminated. In fact, many of them were co-opted by Francoist propaganda.

In an effort to overcome, and in essence depoliticize, Spain's non-Castilian languages and traditions, the Sección Femenina promoted a "*sano regionalismo*" (healthy regionalism) in which the nation's diverse cultures were presented as mere variations of a Castilian center.[46] In a quote used in the Sección Femenina's propaganda campaigns throughout the 1940s and

1950s, José Antonio Primo de Rivera stated that "Spain is diverse and plural, but her diverse peoples, with their languages, customs and characteristics, are irrevocably bound in a unity of destiny on a universal plane."[47] This unity between the lands and people of Spain would be partly achieved by a "beautiful mix of regional music" that characterized the Sección Femenina's cultural programs (see figure 2.1).[48]

From the founding of the Sección Femenina's national competitions in 1942, instructoras collected, published, and performed songs and dances from all the regions of Spain, even those in languages that were otherwise strictly prohibited in public life. The Sección Femenina's first publication of music was a 643-page hardbound color illustrated compendium of songs from all the nation's regions, simply *Cancionero* (Songbook). Non-Castilian languages are represented throughout the work in separate chapters. Such displays of the nation's different regional cultures became a staple feature of the Sección Femenina's vision of the raza española, as reflected in Sampelayo's speech before a performance of the Coros y Danzas in 1955:

> The first thing that attracts one's attention when observing this show is the diversity of Spanish folklore. Each province has its totally unique costumes, dances, [and] music. This show reflects, better than any scholar's study, the soul of each [region] and that of Spain.[49]

The nation's different regions received equal representation in the programs of the Coros y Danzas, and the first prizes for the national competitions between 1942 and 1948 were distributed fairly evenly between the different regions. For example, a troupe from the city of Gerona won first place in the first competition in 1942 even though Catalan culture and language were otherwise prohibited from being performed or spoken by ordinary civilians.

Winning Province and Region: 'Dance'	Barcelona, Catalonia	Lérida, Catalonia	Zaragoza, Aragón	Zaragoza, Aragón	Burgos, Catalonia	Seville, Andalusia	Encinasola, Andalusia

Figure 2.1 First place for "song" and "dance" categories in the National Competition for the Coros y Danzas of the Sección Femenina between 1942 and 1948.

The Sección Femenina portrayed regional songs, dances, and costumes as being inherent and timeless national traditions. The possibility that Spanish musical folklore was influenced by innovative individuals within a community or cultural exchanges between different regions was antithetical to the regime's representation of an eternal Spanish race. Instead, the instructoras ascribed Spain's diverse regional cultures to natural causes resulting from the nation's diverse landscapes. This geographical explanation for Spain's regional diversity disassociated regional music traditions from their previous separatist political connotations. For example, in the program notes for a performance of the Coros y Danzas in 1953, the people of the Basque Country are portrayed as being "tenacious and self-reliant" due to the wild, mountainous region they inhabit.[50] Apparently, this produced a local musical tradition that is "clear and strong," lacking the "lively and exuberant exclamations" performed elsewhere in Spain.[51] The same program describes the region of Galicia as "washed by the Atlantic and persistent rains, an enchanted land with infinite shades of green always overshadowed by a vague melancholy."[52] Over the ages, these characteristics of Galicia's geography supposedly produced a people who were "serious, thoughtful and serene, with eyes that reflect their character and their intuition."[53] The program links the inherently "thoughtful and serene" qualities of the Galician people to characteristics of the region's music (as quoted here in the original English): "The typical musical instrument of Galicia is the 'gaita' (bagpipe) whose wild and untamed notes are . . . always dominated by one monotonous long drawn out note which gives the air of a melancholy tone."[54]

The instructoras used Spain's different regional music traditions as a metaphor for the nation's diverse economy. At national rallies, portrayals of Spain's various landscapes and products reinforced a vision of the nation as strong, unified, and self-sufficient. One such demonstration celebrated Nationalist victory after the Civil War in Castile on May 30, 1939.[55] During the rally, young women clad in regional dress along with beasts of burden approached a podium to place their regions' produce at Franco's feet.[56] After this homage to Franco, the women sang and performed regional dances including "the Galician *muñeira*, the Basque arch dance, the Aragonese *jota*, the Catalan *sardana*, the Andalusian *vito*," while men accompanied them on traditional instruments such as bagpipes, Basque *txistu* flutes, guitars, and castanets (see figure 2.2).[57]

The Sección Femenina's depictions of a culturally diverse but united Spain paralleled the Franco regime's desire for an autarkic economy in which every

Figure 2.2 Coros y Danzas of Galicia performing a circle dance, c. 1940. Fundación Joaquín Díaz, Joaquín del Palacio, jp0097, Nº de negativo 97.

region would serve a critical function for the nation's survival. Workers in rural communities, especially in Andalusia, were seen as having a "biological mission" to be submissive to the superior "racial and spiritual essences" of the people of Castile and the governing metropolis of Madrid.[58] Through their choice of repertoire, costumes, and spoken narrations, the instructoras reinforced this socioeconomic and racial hierarchy. For example, program notes from a performance of the Coros y Danzas in 1953 distinguished "the authentically rustic dances" of Andalusia from the "nobility, elegance, and courtliness" of Castilian musical folklore.[59]

Although other branches of Francoist media portrayed Andalusians as a "lazy and degenerate caste" from a "*país del jornaleros*" (land of unskilled day laborers),[60] the Sección Femenina presented a more positive view of the region's southern agricultural workers. In fact, Andalusians' poverty and alleged "simplicity" were seen as contributing to the region's cultural purity. Instructoras prioritized the songs and dances of smaller, isolated, agricultural communities. On a dance file from the province of Granada submitted in 1944, Angustias Franco describes how people labeled as "poor farmers" around the town of Otivar in the Sierra Nevada mountains performed *el robao*. According to the instructora, the farmers' supposed isolation from the corruption of external influences had added to the authenticity and "folkloric value" of their traditional music and dance:

> Its grace lies in the simplicity, coarseness, and energy that the entire population breathes. It is a tumult of rhythmic jumps and turns inherent to these strong young men and women, sun-tanned, who know nothing of affected, modern choreography. . . . It is extremely ancient and danced today in all its purity.[61]

To celebrate the productivity of such "strong young men and women" living in the Andalusian countryside, the instructoras collected an enormous number of songs associated with local staple products. For example, songs, dances, and traditional costumes from coastal provinces such as Cádiz and Málaga invoked the fishing industry. The 623-page songbook mentioned earlier in this chapter depicts a barefoot woman from Málaga carrying baskets of sardines from the ocean. The practical, working garment worn by a Cádiz *coquinera* (shellfish merchant) of Cádiz symbolized the town's productivity:

> The *coquinera* dress was worn by the poor class and was essentially a daily, working outfit. Derived from the gypsy suit, it has been modified for simplicity and comfort. [It is] shorter, so as not to hinder movements. It has simple and sober decorations.[62]

These idealized displays of rural life contrasted greatly with the hardships experienced by the nation's working class and landless agricultural workers, many of whom would have been present in the audience at the first local stages of the national competitions. As mentioned in the Introduction, the Franco regime relied on a policy of economic self-reliance that was "characterized by serious food shortages which caused widespread famine among the poor" up until the Pact of Madrid with the United States in 1953.[63] Like other fascist states such as Nazi Germany and Italy, the Franco regime of the early 1940s attempted to sever ties with the world economy, a policy that ultimately led to an economic and humanitarian disaster.[64] Minimum wages were lowered and the working class relied on food stamps to survive. Food was often unattainable on the rationing system and could only be accessed on the black market for double or triple the official price.[65] In 1949, 400,000 Spaniards were unemployed in the agrarian and construction industries, and even those adults who managed to find a job were undernourished and their children often died of starvation.[66] During the bleakest period, from 1939 to 1945, about 200,000 Spaniards starved to death.[67] Diseases linked to poverty and poor housing conditions such as typhus, pellagra, and tuberculosis ravaged the rural working class.[68] To make matters worse, the victorious pro-Franco aristocrats and landowners imposed a 66 percent drop in wages, policies that were designed to destroy any remnant of the militant peasantry that had spontaneously risen in 1936 to defend the Second Republic.[69] As a punishment to these communities for having supported Republican Spain, Franco allowed the famine to continue unabated for nearly fifteen years.[70] In fact, we could say that the Department of Music of the Sección Femenina served as a means of filling the cultural and physical voids left in these devastated rural societies.

Rivera attempted to gloss over the regime's quasi-feudal economic structure and the severe hardship experienced by the nation's laborers. In a text published in 1939, she expressed the Franco regime's policy titled "*no hay castas*" (there are no social classes). Adopting rhetoric similar to that used in German National Socialism, Rivera wrote that the Sección Femenina would unify "the men, regions, and social classes of Spain . . . to ensure that no talent is lost due to a lack of economic means."[71] Of course, this "unity" only applied to those with the following qualifications:

> those who work will deserve all our consideration . . . [while] the vagrants will never be granted any privileges. . . . The nation does not pay the slightest regard to those who do not perform any function and only aspire to live as guests at the expense of other's efforts.[72]

The regime's policy of "*no hay castas*" was used as a pretext to alienate individuals who were thought to be a burden on society. Only those citizens who were seen as contributing to the greater good of Spain were valued by the government. Likewise, regional cultures were only celebrated in so far as they seemed to unify the rest of the nation socially and economically.

The instructoras used their imaginations to reinterpret, canonize, and categorize Spain's complex and multilayered history. Promoting a unified idea of a raza española, however, was a difficult task; the Sección Femenina had to contend with the nation's many languages and existing cultures and the enormously complex religious history of the Iberian Peninsula. The instructoras' process of reinventing cultural and historical memory had several stages. First, Rivera and her instructoras promoted the notion that foreign contamination was threatening Spanish traditions and values through popular culture, cosmopolitanism, and leftist politics.[73] Then, the instructoras proposed to safeguard, repair, and salvage the nation's supposedly ancient heritage via their music programs. Finally, the instructoras transformed these folkloric practices to support the Sección Femenina's values and strategies for national unification. But the Sección Femenina's constructions of the raza española were subject to change; in the following chapter, I examine how the instructoras sometimes altered their ideas of race and religion when on missions of cultural diplomacy abroad.

3

Mementos of al-Andalus
in Colonial Morocco

In the holy city [of Chefchaouen], next to the beautifully illuminated
Alcazaba accompanied by the sound of the water from its fountains,
the great Hispano-Moroccan family sings a hymn of peace, joy, and
fraternity during their jubilant celebrations. In front of the city, the
high points of the Kasbah . . . are nests of calm, industriousness, and
coexistence. . . . The performance of the Coros y Danzas of Spain
could not help but evoke the past like a golden bridge through time.[1]

The above is an excerpt from a newspaper article titled "Paz y alegría en
Chauen" (Peace and happiness in Chefchaouen) published in 1955 in the
Spanish-language Tangier periodical *Telegrama del Rif*. The article refers to
a performance of the Coros y Danzas during a tour throughout the North
African territories then known as the Spanish Protectorate. According to the
author, the juxtaposition of Iberian traditional music and medieval Islamic
architecture highlighted the common history and lineage of all Moroccans
and Spaniards. The event reflects the Franco regime's wider political agenda
between 1939 and 1958 as propagandists attempted to create a Hispano-Arab
community within Spain's North African territories. Drawing on the notion
of a historical connection between Spain and Morocco, Francoist institutions
sought to legitimize colonial rule via cultural exchanges. Here, music served
the regime's purposes very well. The Sección Femenina promoted alleged
musical affinities between certain Spanish genres and the native musical
traditions of the Islamic world in general. A degree of mutual understanding
between Muslims and Christians was central to the Sección Femenina's activities in Morocco, to the extent that Franco even presented himself as the
friend of Muslims. Yet, as I have sketched out previously, such a narrative ran

Coros y Danzas. Daniel David Jordan, Oxford University Press. © Oxford University Press 2023.
DOI: 10.1093/oso/9780197586518.003.0004

against the grain of Franco's raza española rooted in the Catholic Reconquest of Spain.

Over the next three chapters, I examine the intricacies of the Sección Femenina's numerous interpretations of Hispanidad on the colonial and international stage as the Franco regime attempted to improve Spain's relations throughout the world. I choose to focus on the geographical regions of Morocco, the Western Bloc in Europe and North America, and Cuba and the Dominican Republic in Latin America. These locations represent some of the Franco regime's most important diplomatic relationships during the Cold War era as the Spanish government attempted to retain its colonial territories and extract itself from political exile. These case studies also provide vastly different contexts in which the regime had to modify its notion of an international Hispanidad to best match local conditions. Throughout the second half of this book, I propose that the troupes of Coros y Danzas were a powerful means of promoting a somewhat flexible image of Spain, an image that was adapted according to different geopolitical circumstances.

The scale of the Sección Femenina's tours outside of Spain was enormous; from 1947 until the organization's dissolution in 1977, groups of forty to eighty performers toured internationally several times a year for a week to three months at a time. The tours covered most of the nations of Western Europe, North America, Latin America, the Middle East, North Africa, and parts of Asia (see Appendix II). The Sección Femenina's tactics of nation-building within Spain, colonization in European-occupied Morocco, and cultural diplomacy with foreign powers in Europe, North America, and Latin America were all very much interrelated—in all these political contexts, the Sección Femenina established cross-cultural relationships by inventing notions of shared history and racial "blood" with citizens of other nations. However, the nature of these imagined communities varied greatly, often contradicting the narratives of Spanish history and race that were expressed by the same performers within Spain itself. To complicate matters even further, newspapers published in Spain exposed Spaniards to all these versions of Hispanidad, some of which seemed to directly contradict the Franco regime's idea of National Catholicism. As a result, the events described in the following chapters confounded and mixed Francoist ideas of raza española and Hispanidad on both the home front and within an international context.

Spain was involved in intermittent wars in Morocco during the decades leading up to the rise of the Franco regime. In 1860, Morocco lost a bloody three-month war with Spain over a dispute about territory around the coastal area of Ceuta. The resulting Treaty of Wad-Ras required a great monetary debt be owed to Spain that depleted Morocco's financial reserves.[2] This political and economic defeat made Morocco economically dependent upon the West, opening up the nation for European colonists from France, Germany, Spain, and the United Kingdom.[3] Morocco thus became a "subaltern state feeding European expansion" as it was forced to offer up natural resources and cheap labor within an unprotected market.[4] This uneven power dynamic greatly diminished the authority of Sultan Mohammed IV and eventually culminated in the establishment of the French and Spanish Protectorates in 1912 under the Treaty of Fès.

Following the loss of Spain's last colonies to the United States as a result of the Spanish-American War in 1898, further expansionism in Morocco enabled the Spanish monarchy to reclaim its status as a global power.[5] However, from the outset, Spain had to compete with the French Protectorate in southern Morocco and British and American influences in the Tangier International Zone.[6] Also, Spanish authority was always at risk of a Moroccan nationalist revolt, such as took place during the Rif War (1920–1927) fought between Berber tribes and the colonial powers of Spain and France.[7] The neighboring French Protectorate struggled against decades of resistance, particularly from an underground separatist party known as the Istiqlal Party founded in 1937. Opposition to European rule continued into the 1950s when Sultan Muhammad V appealed to the United Nations for Moroccan independence.[8] This contact, combined with the Sultan's refusal to dismantle the Istiqlal Party, inspired the French government to exile the Sultan to Corsica in 1953 "amid howls of protest" from Moroccan nationalists.[9]

Unlike the French Protectorate and previous Spanish administrations, the Franco regime experienced relative peace in its own territory, discounting a few comparatively small Berber uprisings in the East.[10] This may have been due, in part, to the regime's efforts to foster trust and comradeship between Spaniards and the Muslim inhabitants of North Africa by sheltering Moroccan nationalists fleeing the French Protectorate.[11] Moreover, the Spanish Nationalists owed many of their victories during the Civil War to the 80,000 Muslims who fought in in the Moroccan units, including the dreaded shock troops, Regulares Indígenas.[12] From its very beginning, the Franco regime used cultural diplomacy to promote the idea of a common history and culture between Spain and the Arabic-speaking world—a narrative with roots that went back to the nineteenth century.[13] These strategies aimed to legitimize Spanish colonial rule in North Africa while undermining French authority, which Spain portrayed as merely an invading colonial power.[14]

The Franco regime had some sensitivity to the cultural filters of Moroccan Muslims and was even willing to temporarily alter Francoist narratives of a hyper-nationalistic, Catholic race to achieve its political ends and maintain the protectorate. As mentioned in the Introduction, one of the primary aims of cultural diplomacy is to create feelings of mutuality, common interest, and values between the visiting and host nations.[15] But how could the Franco regime, after spending so much effort and so many resources on its brand of National Catholicism, foster feelings of mutuality between Spaniards and Muslim Moroccans? Although the regime tended to enforce Spain's Catholic identity at home, and the regime tended to enforce Spain's North African historical connections in Morocco, the firewall that divided these two narrations was highly permeable. As I have already explained, the regime's censorship was all-pervading and well-funded but often highly arbitrary—notions of Hispanidad and raza española were in constant flux as governmental departments responsible for propaganda were created and dissolved.[16] Spaniards reading the official newspaper of the Spanish government, *Arriba*, at home in Spain during the 1940s and 1950s would have been bombarded with writings on Catholic values and a notion of raza española free of Jewish or Arab blood. But on the next page, the same citizen would read a review of a performance in Tangier celebrating a Hispano-Moroccan brotherhood. As a result, it was possible for politically aware Spaniards to learn that Franco's centralist, fervently Catholic visions of Hispanidad and raza española were being altered abroad for political gain.

The idea of a Hispanic-Moroccan brotherhood was not an invention of the Franco regime; in fact, Franco's propagandists drew upon writings by cultural theorists from across the political spectrum dating back to the beginning of the century. The Arabist Julián Ribera (1858–1934) was an early proponent of the cultural legacy of al-Andalus in contemporary Spain. Using a highly subjective methodology, Ribera found loose connections between medieval Arabic music and the *Cantigas de Santa María*, a collection of thirteenth-century poetry in the Galician-Portuguese language with musical notation.[17] According to Ribera in his study *La música de las Cantigas. Estudio sobre su origen y naturaleza* (1922), the influence of al-Andalus continued to be present in musical traditions throughout contemporary Spain (e.g., the contemporary Aragonese *jota*).[18] Ribera's theories were later dismissed by Spanish musicologists, particularly the director of the IEM, Higinio Anglés, who objected to a history of Spanish culture that included any non-Catholic elements.[19]

Similar views to those of Ribera were upheld by a group of intellectuals in the early twentieth century living in Andalusia, including the composer Manuel de Falla (1876–1946), García Lorca, and Blas Infante. Linked by a cultural organization known as the Centro Artístico, these artists believed that remnants of ancient musical traditions from medieval al-Andalus could be found in contemporary Andalusian culture, especially the music of flamenco.[20] Infante portrayed Andalusians as a "polyethnicity" made up of descendants of medieval Iberian Muslims, Jews, and Christians. Infante fueled a movement for Andalusian self-government that he justified by his perception of the region's distinct history and culture. Infante's goal was to create an autonomous, bilingual Andalusia with speakers of both Spanish and Arabic.[21] In Ronda in 1918, Infante presided over an assembly that drafted a charter for Andalusian autonomy.

Although Infante's regionalist views led to his assassination by Nationalists in 1936, and Julián Ribera's theories were rejected by the regime's IEM, the idea of a shared Moroccan-Spanish cultural identity and history proved to be a useful tool for Francoist propaganda in the Protectorates. The writer, historian, and political philosopher Rodolfo Gil Benumeya (1901–1975) adapted Infante and Ribera's interpretations of Andalusian and North African culture to the Francoist political agenda. While defending Spain's "natural rights" to its protectorate in Morocco, Benumeya used the history of Muslim-ruled Iberia to distinguish contemporary Spanish culture from the "corrupting" influences of modern Europe.[22] The Muslims and Jews who were expelled to North Africa after 1492 merely continued to reproduce the culture of medieval al-Andalus, according to Benumeya's essays *Andalucismo africano* (1953) and *Claroscuro andaluz* (1966).[23] By retaining the Spanish Protectorate, Benumeya claimed that the Franco regime was reuniting Spaniards with Moroccan-Andalus diaspora.[24] The idea of a shared Hispanic-Moroccan identity was compatible with the Francoist desire to unite Spain's diverse cultural regions, as expressed in the motto "*España . . . ¡Una, grande y libre!*" (Spain . . . United, great, and free!).[25] Benumeya framed the Muslim inhabitants of the Spanish protectorate as members of yet another peripheral Spanish region, thus legitimizing the Franco regime's continued presence in Morocco.

During the Spanish Civil War, Franco promoted the idea of a shared Hispano-Moroccan identity by establishing several cultural organizations within the Spanish Protectorate and sponsoring a pilgrimage to Mecca protected by the Spanish navy and air force.[26] Benumeya helped Nationalists located in Northern Morocco found the Franco Institute for Hispano-Arab Research, and later the Mulay al-Hasan Institute and Centre for Moroccan Studies. As mentioned previously, these organizations highlighted the "historical and cultural connections between al-Andalus, Morocco, and Francoist Spain," encouraged academic collaborations between Spanish and North African intellectuals, and hosted Arabic language lessons for Spanish-speaking residents.[27]

Benumeya was an avid supporter of the Coros y Danzas as these women of the Falange attempted to create cultural bridges between North Africa, the Middle East, and Spain. The following paragraph is from an article published by Benumeya on January 12, 1950, in the *Telegrama del Rif*, a state-run paper published and distributed in the Spanish Protectorate dedicated to defending the interests of Spain in Morocco:[28]

> The reviews published in Arabic and Spanish have judged that the tour of the Coros y Danzas . . . are relevant to the entire world of Arabic culture across the Mediterranean Sea. . . . Melodies that seem to be the most Spanish are those that share a common musical background with Turkish and genuine Arab music—the basic elements of these compositions originated in the south of the Iberian Peninsula, that is in Andalusia, when this region was the center of the [Islamic] Spanish-medieval civilization. Consequently, the music of the Coros y Danzas de España is not foreign to the patriotism nor emotional aesthetic of the Turkish, Syrian, Lebanese, and Palestinian people. . . . It is hoped that the girls of the Coros y Danzas de España will one day bring their embassy of art and feeling (which they have already shared with Morocco) to Egypt, Syria, Jordan . . . and to all the Mediterranean Levant where Hispanic culture is seen as something attractive and familiar.[29]

In this excerpt, Benumeya suggests that the musical traditions of Spain, North Africa, and the Middle East are linked by a shared history and innate sense of beauty. It was this mutual sense of music and art, or an "emotional aesthetic" to use his own words, that Benumeya wished to exploit during the Coros y Danzas' missions in Morocco.

Many of the Sección Femenina's instructoras followed Benumeya's example. In the second class of the Sección Femenina's bachelorette course for students between the ages of fifteen and sixteen, students were taught that Castile had historically "assimilated other cultures as nutrition for [the nation's] future."[30] According to the instructoras, the conquered peoples throughout the Spanish Empire provided a rejuvenating force for Christian Spain as Catholics consumed, absorbed, and reinterpreted the cultures of their defeated subjects. Students in the Sección Femenina were taught that traces of ancient interactions between Christians and Muslims could be found in the Spanish-speaking world even in the twentieth century, transforming the nation into a "transmitter of the orient to the Christian world."[31]

A similar reading of Spanish history was reflected in the Sección Femenina's music education course, but with an emphasis on the Jewish, rather than Islamic, ancient al-Andalus. In the Sección Femenina's textbook for music history written by Rafael Benedito, *Historia de la Música: La música a través de los tiempos* (1946), the author claims that Gregorian chant derives from ancient Jewish religious chant, citing the Jewish ethnologist and musicologist Abraham Zevi Idelsohn (1882–1938).[32] This was a wildly accepted origin history of Gregorian chant during the twentieth century that has since been disproven.[33] The importance of Benedito's lesson on the connections between Gregorian chant and ancient Jewish chant was not merely historical; it directly applied to the religious music that the students and instructoras were performing every day. Further in his chapter, Benedito speculates that Jewish chant may have also influenced the development of Andalusian *cante jondo*, a category of flamenco song characterized by long, improvisatory melismas and a highly emotional delivery:[34]

> I will contribute something from a modern author who finds similarities in the spirit, expressive intensity, and melodic form . . . between certain songs that are still preserved and practiced in synagogues today and certain forms of "*cante jondo*," such as the *saeta*, the *seguidilla* and the *fandanguillo*, even reaching to suppose that the term "*cante jondo*" is an alteration of "*jon do*," derived from the influence and wear of the vulgar pronunciation of the [Hebrew word] "*jom tob*," whose translation is "holy day," or, even more literally, "good day." Lacking evidence, and having not delved into the investigation, we limit ourselves to providing this information as a matter of curiosity.[35]

The "modern author" that Benedito refers to here is the German-Jewish historian, novelist, and Spanish citizen Máximo José Kahn (1897–1953). In his article "Cante jondo y cantares sinagogas" published in *Revista de Occidente* in 1930, Kahn proposes that the term *"cante jondo"* derives from the Hebrew *"jom-tob,"* or *"yamin tovim,"* meaning "holy day."[36] Benedito's reason for omitting Kahn's name was certainly because the latter was a supporter of the Second Republic who had managed to escape certain death by fleeing to Mexico as an exile.[37] Nevertheless, Benedito thought that Kahn's theories on the origins of flamenco were useful for the Sección Femenina's nation-building project. When Benedito mentions the *saeta* in the quote above—an improvised song of lament addressed directly to sculptures of Jesus or Mary from balconies in Gitano neighborhoods during the religious processions of Corpus Christi and Semana Santa (Holy Week) in Andalusia—he proposes another historical connection between the religious music of Judaism and Catholicism. In Benedito's *Historia de la música*, the religious music of Judaism and Catholicism are intimately connected and consequently so are the origins of the Spanish and Jewish races. Given how the Franco regime frequently portrayed Jews as Bolshevik conspirators bent on undermining the Spanish state and the cultural purity of the raza española, Benedito's music history textbook exemplifies the complexities of Francoist cultural politics.

Drawing upon the writings of pro-Republicans such as Infante, García Lorca, and Kahn, the performances and programs of the Coros y Danzas often presented Spain as having a multilayered identity with cultural roots in Europe, North Africa, and the Middle East. For example, the composer and virtuoso guitarist Ángel Barrios (1882–1964), who often performed with the Coros y Danzas of Granada, writes in a program from the 1940s: "Spanish folklore is the richest in Europe, incomparably more varied and emotional than that of any other nation. . . . Our fiery Oriental spirit is mixed with a Celtic sweetness—a melting hue of two contrary lights."[38] Andalusia was particularly important for maintaining this narrative because of the region's proximity to the Islamic world and the fact that the city of Granada was the capital of Iberia's last medieval Islamic kingdom. In her script for the Coros y Danzas' tour of the United States in 1953, Sampelayo claims that Andalusian music was a mixture of European and Arab traditions of North Africa:

> The Andalusian dance, which is different from anything else in Europe, is the product of a very old civilization which developed in the south of Spain during the Moorish occupation: Anybody who knows the East cannot but

bring to mind Arab music when listening to the "*soleares*" or any other kind of "*cante jondo*."[39]

These alleged cultural links between Spain and North Africa were frequently mentioned during the Coros y Danzas' tours throughout Morocco as the instructoras and Spanish diplomats tried to use music to improve Spain's relationship with Muslims and Jews in North Africa.

From 1950 until the loss of the protectorate in 1956, Rivera, with the help of Spanish diplomats, organized performances in the Spanish and French protectorates and the Tangier International Zone. Andalusian troupes were usually selected to tour Morocco, likely because of this region's historical connections to medieval Islamic Iberia. The instructoras from Andalusia chose a repertoire that underlined the cultural relationship between southern Spain and North Africa, often referring to specific historical figures found in *Historia de la conquista de España* (1926) by Julián Ribera, *Los musulmanes de España* (1920) by Reinhart Dozy, and even translations of ancient texts by the medieval Muslim alchemist and philosopher, Jabir ibn Hayyan (721–813). On a dance file completed in 1948, the instructora María Martínez writes that the choreography used to perform the dance *ocho y zangano* from Cádiz was introduced to Andalusia in the ninth century by the Muslin king Umar ibn Hafsun.[40] On another file, Adela Rojas, the provincial cultural councillor of Cádiz, writes that the twelfth-century Andalusian writer Al Saqund introduced a percussion instrument known as the *pandereta* to the Iberian Peninsula.[41] There seems to be some evidence to support an Arab introduction of the *panderereta* to Andalusia, Asturias, and Portugal, although I have found no verification connected to the story of Al Saqund in the works of Ribera or Dozy.[42] It seems that the Sección Femenina simply invented these details to give their narrations a sense of legitimacy and interest.

The dance files from Andalusia illuminate the complex ways in which the Sección Femenina emphasized an alleged musical and cultural kinship between Spain and Morocco. According to a dance file from Cádiz, flamenco styles such as the *zambra* and *caña* were considered to be musical artifacts that had been adapted "to the popular customs of the [Christian] victors" by converted Muslims who remained in Iberia after the Reconquista.[43] On the file for the *chacarrá* (a dance with a triple meter related to the fandango), Angustias Franco writes that "the most assiduous and learned Arabian philosopher," Yahya ibn Yahya, taught the *chacarrá* to "beautiful, young, Christian girls" living in Tarifa (a city close to Gibraltar) during the eighth century.[44] The *chacarrá* was performed by the Coros y Danzas of Cádiz in a dress known as the *cobijada* (see figures 3.1 and 3.2). The *cobijada* vaguely resembles contemporary garments worn by some Muslim women that partially cover the face.

The *instructora* Angustias Franco provides the origins of the *cobijada* by citing the "most authorized legend" of a Muslim nobleman of the ninth century named Abdelcader Ben Mohamed el Uayzani. Apparently, Uayzani was

Figure 3.1 Dress design of the *cobijada* worn by dancers of the Coros y Danzas from the province of Cádiz. ES-AHP Cádiz, Caja 13324.

Figure 3.2 Photo from 1958 portraying a member of the Coros y Danzas from Cádiz wearing the *cobijada*. ES-AHP Cádiz, Caja 13325.

captured by a Christian army and fell in love with the daughter of one of his jailers. While in prison, Uayzani supposedly came to "abhor Muhamad," asked to be baptized, and taught the Christian youth to dance wearing the *cobijada*.[45] According to Angustias Franco, the *cobijada* blurred the boundaries between what was considered to be Hispanic and Arab, and male and female, while eliciting a romantic nostalgia for Muslim-ruled Iberia:

> When a girl from Cádiz comes out to dance the *chacarrá* wrapped in a cloak that covers her face, one inevitably recalls the women of Old Islam. And

when they dance to the rhythm of castanets and the strings of the guitar, one's mind is carried very far back in time, way back to the times of the Caliphs of Cordova. Who does not forget their worries while watching the intricate and timeless steps of these dancers? The Islamic origin of these dances, now Hispanic due to their acclimatization [to Iberia] during the most fascinating Hispano-Arab civilization, is clearly visible in the dancers' movements and their technique as well as the *cobijada*, which they wear while dancing. It is a Moorish garment of a purely folkloric flavor that almost entirely covers the woman's form and hides almost all her face, revealing only the eyes.[46]

Such connections between the *cobijada* and Muslims of al-Andalus, however, are an invention of the romantic imaginations of nineteenth-century travel writers, beginning with Richard Ford (1796–1858) in his *A Hand-book for Travellers in Spain* (1845).[47] Contemporary researchers suggest that the *cobijada* does not have Islamic, but rather Christian origins.[48] Variations of this garment had been worn in Andalusia and Castile during the religious ceremonies of Semana Santa since only about the late seventeenth century, almost two hundred years after openly practicing Muslims were expelled from Iberia or forced to convert to Christianity.[49] Nevertheless, this dress was useful for the *instructoras* as they tried to create historical and cultural connections between the Spanish and Islamic world.

Throughout the Coros y Danzas' tours of the Protectorates, Spanish newspapers noted how their performances exemplified the cordial relationship between the two nations, in particular the "peace, joy, and fraternity of a greater Hispano-Moroccan family."[50] The *Telegrama del Rif* reported that the women's performance in Chefchaouen, mentioned earlier, functioned like "a golden bridge" connecting Muslims and Christians to their common past.[51] Wherever the Coros y Danzas toured in Morocco, they collaborated with local musicians. The Coros y Danzas performed at a festival in Tétouan, the Spanish Protectorate's capital, alongside a group of Muslim women to whom the Spaniards extended their "most sincere expressions of affection and friendship."[52] The Sección Femenina also formed local Muslim and Christian troupes of Coros y Danzas throughout the Spanish Protectorate, including at Tétouan, Ceuta, and Melilla. According to the results of the Sección Femenina's thirteenth National Competition, held in Tétouan in the year 1955, these Moroccan-based troupes performed programs of Arabic songs and Gregorian chant, participated in the Sección Femenina's national competitions, and toured throughout North Africa.[53]

The Coros y Danzas' most publicized performances in Morocco were in the Tangier International Zone, a shared territory governed by a group of Western nations including Belgium, France, Great Britain, Italy, the Netherlands, Portugal, Spain, and Sweden.[54] From 1950 until the independence of Morocco in 1956, diplomats of these occupying nations organized the Semana de Tánger (Week of Tangier) mentioned previously in Chapter 1, a summer event that included games, food, theater, and music. Western diplomats designed this festival to strengthen their relationship with Morocco and to foster international alliances throughout the Western Bloc. A journalist for the Spanish paper *Arriba* described the event as a "splendid conglomerate of races and nationalities that constitute our city . . . bringing [to Africa] the gentle wind of the West."[55] According to this article, Tangier was engulfed in nine thousand flags representing the various European nations. Each consulate hosted an event associated with Western cultures, such as sporting events organized by the English, classical ballets staged by the Portuguese, and beauty pageants hosted by the French.[56]

Rather than simply imposing another Western tradition on Tangier, the Franco regime approached the city as an extension of Spain's political and cultural territory. José Truijo, Spain's director of cultural relations in Tangier, wrote to Rivera that the Semana de Tánger was a "magnificent act of propaganda" that could strengthen Spain's ties with the city's Moroccan population and assert Spain's "natural" right to North Africa.[57] According to a journalist from Madrid covering the Semana de Tánger, the city is "by geography—and history, Spanish. And Spanish is the most widely spoken language, and [our] currency is the most widely circulated."[58] Judging from newspapers and private correspondences, the Spanish attractions at the festival seem to have been the largest and most funded. Spanish-themed festivities included bullfighting in Tangier's Plaza de Toros (Bullring), a concert of Falla's "El sombrero de tres picos" (The three-cornered hat) by the Sinfónica de Madrid, and performances of Coros y Danzas from Andalusia and Tétouan. A traditional Feria Andaluza (Andalusian Fair) was constructed outside the Spanish Legion where sixty booths sold trinkets such as painted fans and castanets. According to *Arriba*, these events seemed to "convert Tangier into a province of Andalusia."[59]

At the Semana de Tánger, Rivera's concept of an international Hispanic community was expanded to include Morocco's Muslim and Jewish citizens.

Francoist journalists rejoiced as members of the three Abrahamic religions participated in Spanish traditions at the fair, writing that "there was hardly a resident of Tangier, . . . Christian, Muslim, or Jew, who did not pass through the Feria Andaluza at least once."[60] In his 2003 study "*Taurolatras periférica*," Gonzáles Alcantud observes that even in Tangier's Plaza de Toros, a "curious Spanishness defined by cultural plurality continued to exist."[61] Fights often starred three *matadors* (professional bullfighters) or *novillos* (apprentices) represented by a Catholic, Muslim, and a Jew. Well-known matadors from Spain and Latin America, such as Miguel Báez Espuny "El Litri" (1930–2022), presented the corpses of the slain bulls as gifts to prominent members of Tangier's Jewish and Muslim communities.[62] According to an article published in *Arriba* by the journalist Vicente Cebrián Carabias (1914–2010), the Coros y Danzas performed immediately after one of these fights in a double billing while the sand of the ring "still bore the recent traces of the Spanish game of death" (see figures 3.3 and 3.4).[63]

Cebrián Carabias reports that the audience in the bullring consisted of "more than six thousand people of different religions, nationalities, and races . . . heterogeneous in their composition, unanimous in their reactions."[64] Unsurprisingly, the group from Cádiz danced the *chacarrá* while wearing the niqab-like *cobijada* mentioned earlier in this chapter.[65] According to Spanish papers, the Muslims in the audience reconnected with their lost Hispano-Moroccan cultural roots while watching the double bill:

> Muslim men with white, perfumed beards and their women in *djellabas*[66] inlaid with rich cloth, and also workers from Malaga and Algeciras, the Indians of Zoco Chico [a neighborhood in Tangier], the Moors of the old Medina—all of these were crowded into the stands of the arena to learn about our songs and dances. . . . And all the people of Tangier learned once again about those things that are Spanish.[67]

Such glowing descriptions of Francoist cultural diplomacy in surviving news articles are likely biased in favor of a pro-colonialist point of view. While it is impossible to know how individual Moroccan spectators reacted to Spanish propaganda, the attempts of Spanish diplomats and touring artists to win over Moroccan hearts through a supposedly shared cultural heritage could only have been marginally successful at best. Although some Moroccan nationalists, such as the Istiqlal Party, welcomed Franco's victory in 1939, they realized that strong diplomatic

Figure 3.3 Performance of the Coros y Danzas of Málaga, Cádiz, and Madrid in the bullring of the Tangier International Zone, 1951. The caption reads: "IBERIAN BULLRING. —In the bullring, a classic scene of triumph for the Spanish people, the Coros y Danzas obtained the loudest and most resounding successes. More than six thousand people of different religions, nationalities, and races applauded all at once, praising those who brought the name of Spain to Tangier." "Bailes y canciones españolas en Tánger," *Arriba*, July 1951. Ministerio de Cultura y Deporte. Archivo General de la Administración, Fondo de la Delegación Nacional de Sección Femenina, IDD (03)051.023, Caja 12/00644.

ties to Spain would no longer provide a clear economic advantage after the Axis powers fell.[68] Attempts by Western powers to create propaganda that was appealing to Muslim and Jewish Moroccans were thwarted by severe economic depression, poor housing conditions, and famine in the late 1940s and early 1950s.[69] Already in 1947, Sultan Muhammed V began to deviate from French and Spanish policy, aiming for a unified Morocco under Arabo-Islamic leadership.[70] His exile to Corsica, imposed

LAS HURIES, EN PRIMERA FILA.—Enbutidas en ricas chilabas, velado el ros

Figure 3.4 Muslim women watching a performance of the Coros y Danzas in the bullring of the Tangier International Zone, 1951. The caption reads: "HOURIS IN THE FIRST ROW. —Clothed in rich robes, their faces veiled with a handkerchief, these two Muslim women attend the show." "Bailes y canciones españolas en Tánger," *Arriba*, July 1951. MCD. AGA, Fondo de la Delegación Nacional de Sección Femenina, IDD (03)051.023, Caja 12/00644.

by the French government in 1953, only fueled calls for Moroccan sovereignty.[71] The Franco regime may have been able to achieve more stability in its protectorate than its French neighbors by presenting Spain as historically and culturally related to Muslim and Jewish North Africa. Nevertheless, Franco's colonial ambitions in Morocco, rationalized by the myth of a Hispano-Arab brotherhood, failed when the Sultan successfully negotiated Moroccan independence in 1956.

As mentioned in the Introduction, one of the "strategic imperatives" of cultural diplomats is to foster a sense of shared values.[72] The Franco regime reframed its official narration of Spanish history and culture in an attempt to increase its popularity among Moroccan Muslims and Jews. In Tangier and the Spanish Protectorate, the performances of the Coros y Danzas celebrated the myth of al-Andalus in which Christian, Islamic, and Jewish cultures were portrayed as integral aspects of Spanish civilization. Spain's cultural diversity, which often appeared to threaten the formation of a cohesive national identity, was used to the regime's colonial and diplomatic advantage; the instructoras chose and adapted various historical narratives from the Iberian Peninsula to strengthen the nation's diverse geopolitical relationships around the world.

4

Divide and Conquer

The Sección Femenina in the United States, France, and Belgium (1950–1953)

> Even with my black eye I did not quit—I kept right on going, because
> I know you and your organization—and the people of Spain deserve
> it—and His Excellency, Generalissemo [sic] Franco. . . . I am proud
> to fight for a man like him and for you and your organization.[1]

These are the words of Hollywood agent and merchant Henry ("Harry")
Sokol written to Rivera on August 29, 1953. Sokol is referring to the injury
he received during one of many violent outbreaks that occurred between so-
called "commie" Spanish Republican refugees and troupes of Coros y Danzas
during a five-month tour of the United States. Despite the protests during
some eighty performances, the troupes and their American representative
persevered, combining pro-Franco propaganda with Spanish traditional
song and dance in some of the most prestigious venues in the United States.
At a time when Spain was politically isolated and in economic crisis after
the fall of the Axis powers, these tours were intended to connect Spain with
the West via professed common values while capitalizing on the communist
witch hunt of the McCarthy era.

Previous authors have claimed that the instructoras of the Coros y Danzas
presented the group as politically neutral to avoid a public uproar while performing in the United States and Europe.[2] Such fights mentioned above,
however, were not uncommon. In fact, at times these tours seem to have
been designed to fan the flames of political discord. This chapter evaluates
the strategies, successes, and failures of the Coros y Danzas as they attempted
to create a bond between Spain and the West via their common campaign
against the USSR.[3]

Coros y Danzas. Daniel David Jordan, Oxford University Press. © Oxford University Press 2023.
DOI: 10.1093/oso/9780197586518.003.0005

At the start of the Second World War, Franco openly expressed his sympathy for the German cause, identifying the Allied powers with the ousted Spanish Republican army.[4] Spain maintained an "active neutrality" while offering supplies and unofficial "volunteer" troops to assist the German and Italian armies fighting the Soviets in Eastern Europe.[5] Despite his early connections with European dictatorships, the only real principle guiding Franco's foreign policy throughout the 1940s and 1950s was the survival of his regime. This objective necessitated many diplomatic concessions and sudden incongruous changes of policy from day to day.[6] Sometime after October 1, 1943, as the Allied powers slowly got the upper hand, Franco began to disassociate his regime from Germany and Italy, and permitted the United States to use military ports and air bases in Spain.[7] Franco tried to conceal the potentially damaging contradictions in Spain's foreign affairs with a tactic he described as "*dejar hacer*," or "let them do as they will," making his subordinates liable for any compromising liaisons.[8] After 1945, Spanish propagandists presented Franco's brother-in-law, Ramón Serrano Suñer, as the sole politician responsible for the regime's former relationship with Nazi Germany.[9] Franco denied that Spain had ever supported the Axis—even after the United Nations published captured German documents that proved his regime provided asylum to thousands of escaped Italian fascists and Nazis.[10]

Nevertheless, the Franco regime's internal politics and diplomatic relations were in a precarious situation at the end of the Second World War. Relentless police persecution made the establishment of consistent policies and steady governance almost unfeasible.[11] Meanwhile, tens of thousands of exiled supporters of the defeated Republic remained throughout Europe and the Americas, some of whom re-established the Republican government in Paris.[12] Within Spain, Republican supporters who had been cut off from a means of escape formed an underground guerrilla army known as the National Alliance of Democratic Forces (ANFD) that continued to resist the dictatorship.[13]

Public opinion on Francoist Spain within Western Europe and the United States remained volatile after the Second World War. Two conflicting views of the dictatorship took root. In one camp, Franco's Nationalists were cast as the defenders of Christianity, conservative family values, and patriotism from foreign communist infiltrations.[14] In another camp were those who believed that the Spanish Republicans had defended freedom, democracy, and peace from fascism. The anti-fascists viewed the Franco regime as an anachronism, the survivor of a disappeared ideology that was irrevocably crushed after the end of the Second World War.[15] News of the Franco regime's humanitarian crimes during the 1940s and 1950s spread throughout the United States and Europe, such as the imprisonment of two million Republican supporters, the execution of over a hundred thousand Spaniards, mass starvation, and homelessness.[16] Within the United States, the nearly three thousand international volunteers who had fought for the Republicans during the Spanish Civil War organized themselves under the Friends of the Abraham Lincoln Brigade (FALB) and Veterans of the Abraham Lincoln Brigade (VALB). Together with the exiled Spanish Republicans, these organizations protested meetings between local governments and Spanish ambassadors, formed picket lines outside of Spanish consulates throughout the United States and Europe, and held fundraising banquets to support the pro-Republican guerrillas still within Spain.[17]

During the Potsdam Conference of 1945, the Soviet delegation presented a memorandum that portrayed the Franco regime as a serious threat to the freedom of European and American nations.[18] Stalin encouraged the victorious Allied Powers to break all relations with Franco and assist the exiled Republican government situated in France to form a new military.[19] But the Soviet proposal was unacceptable to the British and American delegations. Prime Minister Winston Churchill and President Harry Truman feared that restarting the Spanish Civil War could result in pro-Russian Communist guerrillas transforming Spain into a Soviet satellite state.[20] The British and American governments, which were still largely dominated by an aristocratic elite, saw the relatively liberal Second Republic in exile as a threat to existing Western socioeconomic hierarchies.[21] Instead of a military confrontation, the Western Bloc condemned Spain in a tripartite statement between France, Britain, and the United States, excluded Spain from the United Nations, withdrew all diplomats from Madrid, and placed punitive trade sanctions on the Franco regime in an effort to peacefully cause its downfall.[22] By 1947, the only ambassadors who remained in Madrid represented Argentina, Portugal, the Dominican Republic, and the Holy See.[23]

But a fortuitous turn of events favored Franco's dictatorship. The bipolar hegemony between the USSR and the United States created an inevitable confrontation between the world's capitalist and communist powers.[24] Almost immediately after the end of the Second World War, the Allied nations, led by the United States and the USSR, began a new struggle for political and economic dominance.[25] Soviet intervention in Eastern Europe, the communist takeover in Czechoslovakia (1948), the blockade in Berlin (1948), and the successful explosion of the Soviet atom bomb (1949) generated a second "Red Scare" within the United States and Europe.[26] The House Committee on Un-American Activities (HCUA), the American congressional organization responsible for investigating involved in what it called "subversive activities," intensified its investigations and public trials of private citizens and organizations accused of being associated with communism.[27] Congress defined "subversive activities" as "the extent, character, and objects of un-American propaganda activities in the United States," particularly referring to threats to the American form of government as defined in its constitution.[28]

The Franco regime's history of anti-communist rhetoric and the Iberian Peninsula's strategic geographical location for American military bases made Spain a useful ally for the Western Bloc.[29] American and British governments attempted to improve the Franco regime's image abroad while presenting the supporters of Spain's Second Republic as part of an international "communist enterprise."[30] The FBI began investigations on and blacklisted members of the VALB while Congress halted their public demonstrations and refused to acknowledge them as veterans.[31] Anti-communist executive orders allowed private companies to persecute and discriminate against members of the FALB, VALB, and the Joint Anti-Fascist Refugee Committee.[32] In May 1953, the VALB was labeled as a communist front and forced to register as a subversive group. Those members who were blacklisted faced social exclusion, devastating unemployment, and intense government surveillance.

The United States and Spain approved the Marshall Plan in 1948, granting more than a billion dollars in military and economic aid to the devastated countries in Western Europe after the Second World War.[33] In the case of Spain, however, the Marshall Plan was largely for show at first. Spain had to wait until September 23, 1953, for any tangible support when President Eisenhower enacted the Pact of Madrid that permitted the American military to use strategic locations on the Iberian Peninsula during the ongoing Cold War in exchange for large loans to the Spanish government, re-establishment of diplomatic relations, and "drawing a veil over Franco's past alliances" with Nazi Germany.[34] As these international agreements were being made, politicians in both Spain and the West were busy using soft power to recast the Franco regime in a new, friendlier light.

Foreign Friends and Impresarios

Local private agents can provide cultural diplomats with invaluable input that can "make or break" performances and exhibitions, including knowledge of customs in the host country, the appropriateness of venues, advertising, and connections with local politicians.[35] Consequently, every international mission of the Coros y Danzas relied on hundreds of individuals, all of whom contributed to the success of the tours and the ways in which Spanish culture was represented abroad. These participants included the performers of the Coros y Danzas and their supervising *jefe de expedición* (leader of the expedition), male Spanish diplomats, local impresarios, music critics, and foreign musicologists.

The shift in American-Spanish relations during the late 1940s and early 1950s was clearly felt by diplomats, politicians, entrepreneurs, and private citizens in the United States and elsewhere throughout the Western Bloc. While planning a tour of the United States in 1953, Pérez del Arco, the Spanish diplomat stationed in Los Angeles, wrote to Rivera:

> Spain's sympathizers and circle of friends has increased exponentially in recent years . . . it will not be difficult for us to establish a large committee—of forty or fifty people, mostly influential North Americans—who will contribute to publicity, contacts, and support.[36]

Spanish diplomats often arranged meetings with local politicians and private citizens to create friendly relationships and spread a positive image of the living conditions in Franco's Spain; informal social gatherings as well as newspaper and radio interviews helped the members of the Coros y Danzas shape foreign perceptions of the Franco regime just as much as their performances. During the 1947 trip to the "First International Festival of Folk Music" in Llangollen, Wales, Sampelayo, the expedition's leader, reports in her confidential travelogue that a local man named Morrison Jones invited her to his home for tea with his family. During her visit, Sampelayo "explained what the S.F. [Sección Femenina] is and what is currently happening in Spain."[37] According to Sampelayo, Morrison Jones appears to have believed Sampelayo's portrayal of living standards in Francoist Spain:

> [Mr. Jones told me that] everything the English newspapers were saying about us was political counterpropaganda. With the philosophy of a simple,

kind man, he told me that a people with such healthy enthusiasm and such sincere cordiality [such as us Spaniards] could not be bad. . . . He also told me that he had talked about this with many people there [in Llangollen] who thought like him.[38]

The youthful performers of the Coros y Danzas often socialized backstage with government officials and high-profile businessmen such as American governors, British MPs, and representatives of the Rockefeller Foundation. On March 22, 1952, a reporter from the *Brighton and Hove Herald* interviewed a group of Coros y Danzas members about the political environment and living conditions in Spain:

> I asked them what liberty they had in Spain.
> Reply: We have plenty liberty; it is you here who have not any. We wanted to have some music at night and we were told we must not to make a noise. In Spain we dance and sing all night. You can't drink when you want. We have many things you have not here.
> What food do you have while in England?
> Reply: Here in England you have everything out of the tin. Why no meat? Why no real food?[39]

Naturally, in both encounters, the visiting Spaniards did not mention the legal and financial difficulties that most people in their country were experiencing at the time. As mentioned previously, the autarkic economy of the first thirteen years of the Franco regime led to severe food shortages that resulted in widespread famine.[40] From the end of the Second World War until the middle of the 1950s, the civilian population was afflicted by starvation, disease, and a lack of adequate shelter.[41] Social encounters with the touring Spaniards provided citizens of the Western Bloc with an opposing vision of Franco's Spain, refuting reports of famine and political prosecution that regularly appeared in European and American papers.

During foreign tours, hired foreign agents often declared their support for Franco, even if they were primarily motivated by their own financial interests. For these entrepreneurs, Spain's shifting international relationships provided a new territory ready to be commercially exploited. As the director of the Sección Femenina, Rivera always selected foreign representatives who were sympathetic to Nationalist Spain (or who could be encouraged to appear so) and kept files on the personality and political affiliations of those with whom she collaborated. One report concerns Colonel Wassily de Basil (1888–1951). De Basil was a Russian impresario who managed the Office Artistique Continental based in Paris and the Original Ballets Russes (the latter was a fragment of Sergei Diaghilev's Ballets Russes that split in two after his death in 1929).[42] A file on de Basil held by the Sección Femenina points out that he was a "White Russian" originally named Vasily Grigorievich Voskresensky, who had been in exile for thirty years after fighting against the Bolsheviks during the Russian Revolution of 1917.[43] As an enemy of communism, de Basil is described as "a great defender of [Franco's] Spain for which he has great admiration."[44] Rivera wrote de Basil's obituary in 1951 for *Arriba*, making the most of her connection with this international figure.[45] Rivera presents de Basil's first encounter with the Coros y Danzas as a kind of religious epiphany for the impresario. According to the obituary, de Basil discovered the Coros y Danzas on a trip to Madrid in 1948 and was more impressed by their performance than those of the European companies he managed. Apparently, this first meeting in Madrid was a "revelation" for de Basil's soul, leading him to despise the work of professional "creators, composers, and choreographers."[46] In reality, however, de Basil took great pride in his past involvement with the Ballets Russes and Original Ballets Russes.[47] In fact, Vicente García-Márquez in his book *The Ballets Russes* (1990) writes that de Basil was forced to represent the Coros y Danzas because of his "desperate financial situation."[48] Despite what may have been de Basil's lack of genuine enthusiasm for the Spanish troupes, Rivera used the passing of this well-known impresario as an advertisement for the cultural achievements of the Sección Femenina. As we shall see, Rivera hired foreign impresarios such as de Basil primarily as a means of attaching a local, familiar voice to the propagandistic performances of the Coros y Danzas.

The Coros y Danzas' tours of the United States attracted many agents to Spain's embassies in the United States, eager to take advantage of new prospects in Spanish tourism, culture, and goods. On March 12, 1952, Henry Sokol (born c. 1896),[49] who ran an import-export business in Hollywood, paid an unexpected visit to the Spanish consulate in Los Angeles. Like de Basil, Sokol claimed to be another "White Russian" in exile who had fought for the tsar during the 1917 revolution.[50] Now trying his career as a talent agent, Sokol persuaded the Spanish consul general in Los Angeles, José Pérez del Arco, to arrange a meeting between him and Rivera in Madrid the following week. Pérez del Arco allowed the meeting to take place, but advised Rivera to take "extreme caution" should she make any legal contracts with the agent due to Sokol's tendency "to stumble upon financial difficulties."[51] Pérez del Arco warned Rivera that Sokol was a "speculator and a gambler," desperate for a chance to use the Coros y Danzas as a means of making money quickly.[52] Pérez del Arco concluded with the following advice in his correspondence to Rivera:

> I repeat, therefore: Be careful! . . . be vigilant and have your back covered, so that if the company is not as economically prosperous as Sokol projects, the only evil would be that he personally suffers, which would be a very unfortunate thing considering his loyalty to us, but would not harm the interests of the Sección Femenina.[53]

But Rivera was not looking for a huge monetary gain from the tour provided that Sokol was ready to finance and represent Franco's Spain abroad. Rivera needed a local agent to lend the visiting Spaniards a sense of legitimacy, while the monetary outcome was of secondary importance to the political mission of the Sección Femenina. After their meeting, the aspiring American impresario agreed to arrange and fund all transportation, food, lodging, advertising, and the rental of performance venues for an ensemble of eighty-four performers for a four-month tour (later extended to five), through thirty-three states and several ventures into Canada.

Sokol claimed that the tour would cost him $100,000.[54] According to his letters, he obtained the money by taking loans and courting sympathetic organizations such as the Rockefeller Foundation. In return for his financial investment and time, Sokol was to receive 5 percent of the profits, and "the company would be fundamentally his."[55] Additionally, Sokol was allowed to keep merchandise that he robbed from manufacturers in Madrid, paying them with a check linked to a bank account with no funds. These items, consisting primarily of handbags of Spanish leather, traditional head shawls known as mantillas, and seven tables of porcelain dolls dressed as toreadors, were used in an exhibition of Spanish goods in conjunction with the performances of the visiting troupes (see figure 4.1).[56] Sokol believed that the success of the tour would allow him to make an income and create a long-term relationship with the Sección Femenina in which he would continue to represent the Coros y Danzas in the United States every two or three years.[57]

Sokol's contract contrasted greatly with that of his more successful European counterpart. The agreement with de Basil's company, Office Artistique Continental, gave the European agents 10 percent of the profits,

Figure 4.1 A photograph taken in a Los Angeles venue of Harry L. Sokol's exhibition of Spanish merchandise imported from Madrid, 1953. MCD. AGA, Fondo de la Delegación Nacional de Sección Femenina, IDD (03)051.023, Caja 12/00666, exp. 1.

while the Sección Femenina was responsible for all expenses.[58] The contract with Office Artistique Continental was the only scenario in which a foreign impresario could make a significant income when representing the Coros y Danzas. The international tours of the Spanish troupe were not designed to make an overall profit, and it is likely that the bottom line was usually in the red. The fact that Sokol was willing to find funding for the Sección Femenina himself (or at least that he claimed to do so) may have been the initial reason that Rivera chose to hire him as an agent, considering his reputation for being a "very poor businessman."[59] Rivera's goal for these expeditions was to spread Francoist propaganda and find a representative who would openly support Francoist Spain. Economic gain was of secondary importance, and Rivera was unconcerned if the tour happened to financially ruin Sokol.

As Pérez del Arco had anticipated, Sokol was mostly inadequate as an agent beyond serving as a figurehead, and it was the Spanish diplomats who arranged most of the advertisements and rented the performance venues. Pérez del Arco sent the following summary of Sokol's contributions to the tour in a letter to Rivera:

> He does not seem to possess great competence as an entrepreneur, and this is due to his failures and financial evasions; he has chosen a terrible time of year to bring our artists to America. The summer is unbearably hot, and the public withdraws from attending shows in the local market. Also, there is a lack of advertising and, above all, of appropriate advertising, without which it is impossible to be successful in this country.[60]

To make matters worse, Sokol did not plan the tour far enough in advance, leading to periods of up to ten days between performances, and the Spanish consulate was obliged to print flyers and posters throughout the tour.[61] Yet, Sokol frequently exaggerated his personal physical and financial sacrifices when writing to Rivera:

> the group complain to me that I should rest—but I work all day and night— and am enjoying all this hardship for which I would not exchange it for a million dollars. . . . I did not undertake this mission for the almighty dollar—the reason is that I feel the people of Spain deserve recognition in the United States and Canada.[62]

However, Sokol's primary interest was always money, and he exploited the tour as much as he could for his own financial gain. As the group was traveling up the Pacific Coast, Pérez del Arco informed Rivera that there were "some disturbing reports" about Sokol provided by a bank in California.[63] Sokol gave a check backed by no funds to pay the airfare for the Coros y Danzas to the United States, forcing representatives from Trans World Airlines to seize ticket sales directly from box offices in California, Oregon, and Washington. Meanwhile, the University of British Columbia informed Pérez del Arco that Sokol neglected to pay for using a performance venue.[64]

Sokol was likely dishonest with the Spanish government as well. He borrowed money from the Spanish consulate on several occasions, claiming that he lost $200,000 due to multiple interferences from "communist" protesters. However, considering his dishonesty in other financial transactions, Sokol may have hidden some of the earnings of the tour from Sampelayo, the group representative responsible for dividing the proceeds. Moreover, Sampelayo reported to Rivera that Sokol was abusing the members of the Coros y Danzas, overcrowding them in cheap hotel rooms and underfeeding them. Considering their almost militaristic discipline and the harsh conditions that the members of the Sección Femenina had previously endured during their tours of Morocco, Sampelayo's frequent complaints to Rivera were likely justified. However, Sokol dismissed these grievances, saying the group was "a little bit spoiled."[65] Meanwhile, Sokol asked the Spanish embassy in Los Angeles for a loan of $50,000 to finish the tour and was unable or refused to pay for the return flight of the troupe, thereby breaking the original contract.[66] Sokol's involvement in the American tour of 1953 only ended when he was arrested in San Antonio on October 27 and charged for passing $2,129.19 worth of non-funded checks for services throughout the United States and Canada.[67] Sokol's nephew, Dave Jacobson of Winnipeg, promised to pay the missing funds from the bounced checks when he learned his uncle was in jail.[68]

Rivera had many opportunities to hand over the group to a more competent impresario. A team of agents from Los Angeles followed the Spaniards throughout California, bribing the bus drivers to stop working for Sokol. On one occasion a mysterious "young lady" told Sampelayo that she knew an agency that "could take the group and do a better job."[69] However, Rivera chose to continue working with Sokol and even permitted him to extend the tour by another five weeks to "make some good American money."[70] All the above raises the question: why did Rivera allow this fraudulent and incompetent agent to continue representing the Coros y Danzas?

Sokol's enthusiasm for Franco was enormously successful at dividing the American and Canadian public and isolating individuals who expressed anti-Franco views. The Sección Femenina needed this swindler as a figurehead—an American representative who would publicly support Nationalist Spain under any circumstance. Whether by original intent or through evolution, Sokol's duty as a theater agent was a pretense. Once Rivera had attained Sokol's loyalty, she was not concerned about making a significant economic return from the tour—in fact, she was even willing to endure major financial losses. The leaders of the Franco regime had larger ambitions: gaining access to the economies of the wealthiest nations in the West.

Stehrenberger has suggested that the administrators of the Coros y Danzas disassociated the group from fascism by changing their title from the "Coros y Danzas de la Sección Femenina de la Falange" to the "Coros y Danzas de España." According to Stehrenberger, the group presented itself in the United States and Europe as a neutral "civic organization promoting and perpetuating interest in the country's folklore."[71] Although the politics behind the tours may have been somewhat dampened at certain strategic moments, the troupes were usually advertised as a cultural branch of Franco's government and even the Falange party. As the reader will soon discover, the majority of private citizens and politicians on both sides of the Atlantic were well aware of the Coros y Danzas' political connection to the dictatorship in Spain.

Sokol's financial interests, whether he was successful in them or not, encouraged him to cater to the political agendas of the Spanish diplomats and publicly declare his affinity to Francoist Spain. His letters to Rivera and other representatives of the Spanish government are saturated with rambling praise of Franco and his own loyalty to the Falangist cause:

> You know there is no man living, whether Spanish or American, who would do what I have done for you and your organization and His Excellency, Genrallissimo [sic] Franco and his Government and the people of Spain. I did it with all my heart, because I have seen what you are doing for your country and for your people, and you deserved it and anything anybody could do for you.[72]

Along with his groveling letters to Spanish officials, Sokol was keen to advertise the Coros y Danzas as a product of Nationalist Spain to the American public, praising Franco during the introduction to every performance. In a newspaper interview after the troupe's return to Spain, Sampelayo reported that "Sokol, that great friend of Spain, often spoke about our country and about our Head of State."[73] Sokol's portrayal of the Coros y Danzas as a cultural organization of either the Falange party or the Spanish government was consistent with how the troupes were promoted throughout the United States and the Western world.

One Dallas newspaper advertised the troupe as "cheerful Spaniards, dancers and singers from the country's National Youth Chorus, and Generalissimo Franco."[74] In the 1953 tour of the United States, the American and Spanish flags served as a backdrop to the dancers, and the women sang the fascist anthem "Cara al sol" (the lyrics of which were written by José Antonio) after the American national anthem as preludes to every performance. In an interview afterward in Madrid, Sampelayo commented that "One thing that excited the American public was that we always inaugurated our program with two national anthems—the Spanish and the American—both sung in English. You cannot imagine the effect this had."[75] At the 1947 International Folk Music Festival in Llangollen, Wales, Sampelayo reported in her travelogue that Spain's Nationalist anthem was well received, and the locals said it was "very nice and dashing."[76] When Sampelayo was asked in Llangollen what the words of the song meant, she responded, "It is the anthem that the Spanish youth brought to the war. The Spanish revolution had been fought with it, and, above all, this anthem continues to give us courage and joy."[77] On this same tour of the United Kingdom, the girls flew the Falangist flag of the yoke and arrows when departing after a performance in the Spanish Institute in London.[78] Mainstream American and British journalists rarely reflect upon how the Coros y Danzas sang the Falangist anthem beyond mentioning that they did so. But the reception of "Cara al sol" in the West could not have been as easygoing as the above accounts suggest, considering the political protests that are recorded in the American press, Sokol's letters, and internal correspondences between Spanish diplomats and politicians. After all, journalists writing for Spanish papers would only want the Spanish public to be aware of the success of the Franco regime in its diplomatic missions. I hesitate, however, to completely write off the accounts of the positive reception of Falangist propaganda that are recorded in the travelogues written by the instructoras because these documents often go into great detail about the difficulties and failures that the troupes of Coros y Danzas faced on their missions abroad. I doubt that most of the public in the United States and Europe would have been aware of the origin of "Cara al sol," who wrote it, what it represented in Spain, and that it would normally be performed while giving the fascist salute.

But once rumors of the Francoist dance troupe had reached exiled Spanish Republicans and foreign veterans of the Spanish Civil War, the Coros y Danzas were hounded by anti-fascist demonstrators on both sides of the Atlantic. In the United States, a few of the anti-fascist protests were successful, on one occasion putting a halt to four nights of performances at Carnegie Hall from October 1 to 4, 1953. The Musicians' Union and the American Guild of Musical Artists (AGMA), in an act of solidarity with the VALB, adopted one of the most effective methods of resistance against these performances of Francoist propaganda. These organizations did not accept the Coros y Danzas as a not-for-profit organization and demanded that Sokol hire musicians, managers, and press agents from among their AGMA union members. Sokol refused their demands, and after the protests outside of

Carnegie Hall, the venue's managers refused to admit the audience for a total loss of about $30,000 (the equivalent of $290,017 in 2020) for the troupe.[79]

Despite a few cancellations and major financial losses like the one mentioned above, these confrontations ultimately helped Spanish officials ostracize those organizations and individuals who opposed Nationalist Spain. In his letters throughout the 1953 tour of the United States, Sokol repeatedly accuses the protesters of being communists who were subverting the cultural and political values of the West:

> the Communists walk[ed] around with signs and [told] the people not to patronize the group, but it didn't do them any good, because I did everything possible to overcome that, and told the people to pay no attention to those Commies because Spain was the first country who fought Communists, and His Excellency, Generallissimo [sic] Franco, should be congratulated for what he did and for how hard he fought the Communists and how wonderfully he succeeded in winning the liberation of his country.[80]

Sokol paints a scene in which he is contending with a crowd of angry anti-fascist demonstrators for the attention of confused onlookers. The protesters accused Sokol and his troupe of spreading fascist propaganda, while Sokol, and later the American press, labeled the protesters as "commies"—an accusation that proved to be far more damning in Cold War America.

Rivera and the Spanish diplomats encouraged Sokol to agitate and at times attack the protesters. For instance, Sokol wrote to Rivera that a "Spaniard who did not like Spain" hit him at the University of British Columbia in Vancouver, Canada:

> Four Spanish Communists were there, got a little smart, and I didn't want them around—so one of them hit me over the head with a bottle so I had a black eye for the first time in my life. I could have had them locked up there but it would have been bad publicity so I let them go. But I shall return there some day [sic] by myself and will take care of them the way they ought to be taken care of.[81]

But in fact, a report from the Spanish embassy tells us that it was Sokol who initially attacked the protesters, not the other way around. Sokol had a tendency toward physical aggression that delighted the Spanish diplomat in Vancouver who wrote to Rivera, "His admiration for Spain seems to be sincere; in Vancouver, he attacked a red Spaniard who dared to insult the regime with such violence that the Spaniard repelled Sokol with punches."[82] After receiving similar reports of Sokol's heroism from Sampelayo, Rivera wrote these encouraging words to the American agent:

> [These protests] indicate that the propaganda of Spain's enemies continues to this day, and it is this progressive poisoning that makes them so insolent. I want to thank you very much for your assertiveness and I feel the discomfort that you have had to go through to defend our position.[83]

Sokol's pugnacious style appears to have become more valuable for generating anti-communist propaganda than his ability to make money. In fact, his violent tendencies may have contributed to Rivera's original decision to hire him. In an official report on Spanish artists and touring groups throughout the United States, the Spanish consul in Los Angeles, Pérez del Arco, described Sokol as "a rough, rude man, who fluctuates between spontaneous acts of violence and sincere regrets for his conduct."[84] Sokol himself often boasted of his own violent nature in his correspondence to Rivera and the Spanish diplomats, claiming: "My loyalty to Spain is such that I would fight anyone who ever said anything against your wonderful country."[85]

Literature on cultural diplomacy usually focuses on the reinforcement of peace and camaraderie between nations.[86] Mahiet writes that musical diplomacy can be a "mediating activity" that "lubricates international relations . . . and forges shared understandings, coexistence and cooperation."[87] But can the opposite motivations also be present at times? Would a government ever use music to create discord between certain segments of a foreign population? Was Sokol's black eye merely an outcome of Rivera's failure to gauge the political sentiments of the American public? Or was this violence part of some ulterior plan for the advancement of Spanish-American political relations?

Contrary to the above writings on cultural diplomacy, Rivera and the Spanish diplomats with whom she collaborated predicted and even encouraged the anti-fascist protests within the United States and Europe— a strategy intended to provoke the already growing political divides within the West at the beginning of the Cold War. Schneider writes that successful cultural diplomats aim to "offer a vision of hope, foster a sense of common interest and values, and isolate and marginalize violent extremists."[88] On one hand, the Sección Femenina's tours of the United States and Europe were designed to create a sense of common values with that segment of the public who were predisposed to be open to friendly relationships with Francoist Spain. At the same time, these international tours helped ostracize exiled Republicans and other anti-fascists who were immune to the propaganda of the Coros y Danzas. In the context of the 1953 tour, Sokol's acts of aggression served Rivera's goals in the United States and Canada; physical confrontations further divided the supporters from the critics of Francoist Spain and steered the public's attention away from the issues that the protesters were attempting to confront. Once the picketers were labeled as communists, regardless of what their actual political views may have been, Spanish diplomats and pro-Franco Americans had little difficulty in vilifying them.

While Sokol's troupe was touring in California, a columnist for the *San Francisco Chronicle* called members of a picket line around the city's opera house an "indignant group" of fourteen youths who spent the "afternoon looking for someone to accept their protests."[89] The author's statement about the protesters' age is clearly misleading and is an example of how conservative America at the time—and indeed conservatives throughout the West—had a habit of equating the political left with youthful ignorance and hotheadedness. In reality, at least half of the protesters were members of the VALB, making them at least old enough to have fought in Spain during the late 1930s. Confusingly, the author points this out himself when he mentions that those protesters who were affiliated with VALB were recently marked as being part of a subversive organization by the Department of Justice.[90]

After a performance in Dallas, Texas, "Tex" Sanderson, a co-director of the annual Texas State Fair, sent his compliments to the Spanish troupe, expressing his desire for closer diplomatic ties between the two nations: "Your families, teachers, the mayor of your town, General Franco, everybody in Spain, can be proud of your artistry here in the U.S.A. You have been the greatest diplomatic mission ever dispatched by anybody to any place."[91] In his letter, "Tex" denounces the "commies" and "5th column rats" of the VALB who disrupted the performance at the state fair, calling them an "unwarranted parade of hideous rodents," who only wanted to "subvert" the hymns of the "Coros y Danzas de España."[92] The festival director consoled the troupe of visiting Spaniards, reminding them that "the kindly, Christian America that I know so well, but which is not always represented in official circles in Washington, loves you—madre España."[93]

Meanwhile, in Europe, crowds protesting against the Coros y Danzas were denounced by politicians and underwent intense encounters with police.

After a performance in 1952 at London's Stoll Theatre, a critic from the paper *Theatre* writes, "A different kind of importance was attached to the occasion for political reasons."[94] The troupe's conspicuous association with the Spanish government encouraged a demonstration in the gallery from which protesters threw leaflets and shouted, "Down with Fascism" and "Franco the assassin."[95] During a performance in Marseille on that same European tour, a hundred Spaniards affiliated with the exiled National Workers Confederation (CNT) and the Iberian Federation of Anarchists (FAI) disrupted a performance of the Coros y Danzas for a half an hour, shouting and throwing anti-fascist pamphlets. A Spanish consul described the scene as a contest between the "awful screaming" of the Spanish exiles and the applause of the loyal French public. Of the hundred or so arrests made by the police, sixteen to eighteen of those protesters who were Spanish were kept for background checks with the possibility of being deported from France.[96]

In the United States and Western Europe, there was a strong contrast in how papers with opposing political leanings reported on similar events. During the European tour of 1951, a series of violent confrontations occurred in Paris and Brussels between anti-Francoist demonstrators and police. The protests were led by the World Federation of Democratic Youth (WFDY). With its headquarters in Budapest, Hungary, this organization was endorsed by the United Nations in 1945 to unite the world's youth against fascism, war, and nuclear armament.[97] At its conception, the WFDY included more than thirty million students from sixty-three nations.[98] However, with the increasingly strained relations between the USSR and the West in the early 1950s, WFDY members were blacklisted by the US government for their left-leaning politics. Only those members who identified themselves as strictly communist or socialist remained affiliated.[99] Throughout the postwar era, the WFDY opposed financial relationships between Western democracies and dictatorships around the globe, especially the Marshall Plan that provided funds to help strengthen the economy of Franco's Spain.

In April 1951, members of the WFDY learned that the Spanish diplomats would arrive in Paris and Brussels to meet with European politicians for the first time since the Spanish Civil War. The diplomats were to be accompanied by a troupe of 150 Coros y Danzas members scheduled to perform in the Palais de Chaillot and the ABC Theatre. In Paris, hundreds of WFDY members and other anti-fascist protesters gathered around the Spanish embassy, later attempting to block the entrance to the theater.[100] A columnist in the socialist paper *Libération* compared the members of the Sección

Femenina to the Nazi Hitler-Youth.[101] The next week, in Brussels, the WFDY published the following statement in the official paper of the Communist Party of Belgium, *Le drapeau rouge*:

> We denounce the policy of friendship proposed by the [Belgian] government with these Francoist bandits who were the allies of the Nazis—the oppressors of our nation. . . . The opening of diplomatic relations with Franco and the authorization for demonstrations of Francoist propaganda to be held in Brussels represent an insult to democracy, an insult to all those who are struggling and fighting against the war on fascism, of which Franco is one of the most revolting symbols.[102]

According to this article, a crowd of forty protesters composed of local students and Spanish refugees postponed the show in Brussels' ABC Theatre for about an hour as they threw stink bombs and leaflets around the hall, chanting "Down with Franco" and "Long live Republican Spain."[103] The messages on these leaflets attacked the Belgian government for its initiatives toward the restoration of diplomatic relations with Spain, recalling the horrors of the Spanish Civil War and the Miranda de Ebro concentration camp (see figure 4.2).[104]

Outside the theater in Square Sainctelette, cobblestones were torn from the street and thrown at policemen guarding the entrance.[105] The audience, including the ambassador of Spain and many members of the Spanish embassy in Brussels, countered these protests by vigorously applauding the troupes as they continued to dance and sing "with complete composure."[106] Sampelayo, however, who was commenting on the origins of the repertoire over a loudspeaker, was forced to leave the stage for her own safety.[107] After the performance, the few members of the audience who had managed to stay till the end of the show were jeered and heckled by an angry crowd of 350 demonstrators as they left.[108] *Le drapeau rouge*, with its Marxist viewpoint, provides this melodramatic account of the performance in Brussels, presenting the protesters as heroic martyrs resisting the barbarity of the visiting fascists and corrupt local government:

> We know that a few days ago the representatives of Franco, the executioner of the Spanish people, came to the capital. It was not by chance that this troupe of Falangist dancers passed through Brussels this Friday. It was not by chance, nor merely for the pleasure of dancing, that the friends of

Figure 4.2 Images of starving children and military officers in Barcelona
with the headline "Images of Barcelona: Documents against Franco," from the
Marxist paper *Le drapeau rouge*. "Vive le 14 Avril: Journée de solidarité avec le
peuple espagnol," *Le drapeau rouge*, April 13, 1951. MCD. AGA, Fondo de la
Delegación Nacional de Sección Femenina, IDD (03)051.023, Caja 12/00644.

Franco and Degrelle[109] developed this program. These people intended to
spread propaganda for Franco's bloody and sinister regime: . . . At about
eight o'clock the A.B.C. [Theatre] was empty, desperately empty. A few
people began to arrive only at about eight-thirty. Oh! So few! . . . Shortly
after nine o'clock [an hour behind schedule], the curtain was finally raised.

As a Falangist appeared on stage to announce the show, her speech was interrupted by a spectator shouting "Barcelona!" and shrill whistles. This surprised Franco's envoy who stopped for a moment before returning behind the velvet curtain. The Falangist dancers had hardly appeared on stage when a multitude of voices screamed: "Franco the assassin! Franco the executioner!" The dancer who was responsible for announcing each dance was ill at ease. She could not say anything and was hardly even seen. Her brief appearances were greeted by boos and whistles and even a joyful trumpeter. . . . The [police] agents advance with batons in hand. We witnessed scenes of savagery. An officer pursued a woman who was running away and clubbed her from behind. The woman took three steps and fainted after a blow from the baton across her face. . . . Then the police evacuated entire rows. We shouted, we clung to the benches. The protesters were separated while shouting "Franco the assassin" "Long live the Spanish Republic." A hundred or so Democrats have been arrested.[110]

Even the more moderate papers associated with the political left portrayed the visiting Spaniards negatively. A Belgian critic in *Germinal* commented sardonically on this premiere performance of the Coros y Danzas in Brussels: "I imagine that the Spanish ambassador spent the rest of the night writing a pitiful report to the Caudillo . . . [that] our country is not yet ready for the revival of fascism."[111] A columnist for the liberal paper *Le soir* wrote that the performers' depiction of the "tourist beauties" and idyllic life of the Spanish countryside was merely the propaganda of "warmongering fascists" attempting to stifle the outrage of Belgium's working class.[112]

As in America, Belgian and French journalists and editors adapted their narrations of the protests according to their own political views. While the above reports from left-leaning and Marxist papers took the side of the protesters, several news sources on the political right ostracized the protesters as "Russian" communist provocateurs—regardless of their actual political affiliation or country of origin. French papers such as *Le méridional de Marseille* reported that the crowd consisted entirely of criminal Spanish "anarchists" who were "sent packing" by the city's police force.[113] In Brussels, an article headlined "A Stupid Protest" in the center-right Christian socialist paper *La libre belgique* concluded that the Belgian government should "immediately reinstate the undesirable protesters to the border," including those who were Belgian citizens.[114] According to the reporter, the communist protesters attempted to sabotage a healthy, politically neutral cultural event:

The idiotic scene provoked by the "Moscow-teers"[115] of Brussels deeply pained the spectators who were drawn to the theater to witness a timeless performance of Spanish culture. These Spanish dance troupes represent neither the Spain of Franco, nor that of the "Frente Popular." It was the Spain of Goya, Velasquez, Granados; it was the Spanish people themselves—and the most that can be said about the "protesters" in Brussels is that they displayed only their own vulgarity and stupidity.[116]

Meanwhile, *La nation belge* stated that there was nothing politically provocative about the performances in Brussels, April 1951, besides the "intolerant nature" of the "Muscovites."[117] Both *La nation belge* and *La libre belgique* are silent about any physical confrontations between police and protesters, such as those scenes from *Le drapeau rouge* mentioned above. It can be argued that the presence of the Coros y Danzas enforced a polarized view of the political left and right that helped to isolate and ostracize those opposed to the Franco regime in Europe and the United States. The greater the fear of communism in the West, the easier it was for Francoist propaganda to be successful and for foreigners loyal to Franco to associate Spanish refugees and anti-fascist protesters with the threat of the USSR.[118]

As Johnson-Cartee writes in her analysis of political campaigns, propaganda is more effective at strengthening people's views rather than changing them.[119] While cultural diplomacy can promote a sense of mutual understanding, it can also help enlarge strategic political divisions within the host nation. Rivera appears to have acted very shrewdly as a propagandist. She knew it would be impossible to gain the support of foreign citizens who were already anti-Franco and convert them to become friendly to Nationalist Spain. In fact, she and the Spanish diplomats saw these demonstrations as unavoidable. Rivera and Spanish diplomats relied on the fact that they would inevitably win the support of Western politicians and businessmen during the late 1940s and early 1950s; the Iberian Peninsula was too important as a strategic location for military airfields and bases, and Franco's dictatorship seemed to pose no threat beyond its own borders. The best chance for Rivera to increase public support for the Franco regime in the Western world was first to divide the political middle ground in the United States and Europe, and then create a bond between those Spaniards, Americans, and Europeans who were already pro-Franco and held strong anti-communist sentiments. Therefore, the members of the Coros y Danzas served both to charm foreign politicians and citizens with their interpretation of Spanish culture while also presenting the Franco regime as an ally against communism at the beginning of the Cold War. Once Republican exiles and the VALB were labeled as subversive organizations in the United States and Europe, Spain's negative association with fascism was dwarfed by the new fear of communism from the East. In this way, Spain capitalized on American and European anticommunist fear and rhetoric to create new diplomatic ties to the West and extract itself from political isolation.

5

Sorority in the Americas

During the 1940s and 1950s, the Coros y Danzas made numerous visits to Spanish-speaking communities and nations throughout the Americas, connecting Spain via narrations of shared history, culture, and race. Such interactions are comparable with the Sección Femenina's attempts to build a shared cultural history with Muslims and Jews in Morocco. In the Americas, however, the instructoras of the Sección Femenina promoted a shared language, religion, and narrations of white European heritage. These exchanges served both the Franco regime and the officials of the country they were visiting. Instructoras from the Sección Femenina's Department of Music became deeply involved in local cultural politics in a way that helped maintain their hosts' officially sanctioned perceptions of race.[1]

Writings by Spanish historians such as Miguel de Unamuno (1864–1936) and Menéndez Pidal (1869–1968) formed the basis of the Sección Femenina's concept of an international Hispanic hermandad (brotherhood). These intellectuals conceptualized an intercontinental and egalitarian Hispanic race shaped by the historical legacy of the medieval Catholic Monarchs and the Spanish Empire's sixteenth-century conquest of the Americas.[2] The connections the Franco regime made between religion and race, explored in the Introduction and Chapter 2, represented not only a means of nation-building at home but also a tool of cultural diplomacy between the Franco regime and other hyper-conservative states located in Latin America.[3] Gómez-Escalonilla, in his book *Imperio de papel* (1998), explores how the Franco regime relied increasingly upon its diplomatic relations in Latin America for economic and political support after 1945. During the years immediately following the end of the Second World War, the Franco regime sought to form constitutions with nations in Latin America, proposing a Hispanic joint intervention program against foreign aggression; mediation in inter-Hispanic conflicts; the protection and promotion of a common cultural Hispanic heritage; the strengthening of economic ties via a customs union and an inter-Hispanic bank; and a pan-Hispanic citizenship.[4] In collaboration with almost all of

Coros y Danzas. Daniel David Jordan, Oxford University Press. © Oxford University Press 2023.
DOI: 10.1093/oso/9780197586518.003.0006

the Hispanic-American republics, the Franco regime helped form an international confederation of academic and research programs dedicated to building relations between Spanish-speaking people, including the Asociación Cultural Hispano Americana (Hispanic-American Cultural Association) and the Instituto de Cultura Hispánica (Institute of Hispanic Culture).[5]

The Sección Femenina played a critical role in positioning Spain as the cultural and spiritual leader of the Hispanic Americas. To recruit foreign Catholic, Hispanic, and conservative female elites to Falangism, Rivera founded feminine cultural circles abroad and disseminated the Sección Femenina's propaganda in thousands of brochures, books, magazines, and photographs.[6] The first Female Congress of Hispanic America (Congreso Femenino Hispanoamericano) was held in 1951, notably not in the Americas but in Madrid, and included 479 female representatives from North, Central, and South American nations and the Caribbean, including Argentina, Bolivia, Colombia, Cuba, Chile, Ecuador, Mexico, Panama, Puerto Rico, El Salvador, Uruguay, Paraguay, Peru, and Venezuela.[7] The year was highly significant because it marked the five hundredth birthday of the explorer Christopher Columbus, a figure idolized in conservative Spain as a national hero who brought Catholicism to the Americas with the support of Isabella I of Castile almost immediately after the sack of the last Islamic kingdom of Iberia in 1492. According to Rivera, music was to be a primary way for Spain and its former colonies across the Atlantic to become culturally and politically reunited:

Because music unites those who are most distant, and because music reminds us, sometimes with sorrow and at other times with joy, of the best moments of our lives . . . that is why the Falange, which [means] above all unity, has preferred music, better than any other means, to unite our spirits, and from music we have chosen the part most accessible to all: the song. The song that Americans and Spaniards sing in the same language. The song that remains in the ear, that is repeated, that is not forgotten; the one that has no author but was born in the village. . . . For this reason, Americans and Spaniards must know our songs and sing them together; because when fifty or sixty thousand voices of Spaniards and Americans come together to sing the same song, then our spirits will also unite and we will understand each other better and we will love each other more. Then the sea that separates us will be only an accident of Geography, which will serve to bring and carry from here to there—and from there to here—the culture of your Republics and that of our Homeland.[8]

To facilitate this transatlantic "reunion" of Hispanic peoples, Rivera created programs that trained female music instructors throughout Latin America and provided scholarships for female foreign representatives to study voice, dance, and musical pedagogy in Madrid within the Palacio de Bellas Artes and the Sección Femenina's private gymnasium on Calle de Zurbano.[9] Women from Latin America studied music at the Sección Femenina's headquarters in Castillo de la Mota (in addition to nursing, home economics, and all other aspects of the Sección Femenina's responsibilities).[10] Between 1947 and 1952, the Sección Femenina awarded eighty-nine scholarships to foreign female students for study in Spain, while seventeen scholarships were awarded to students of the Sección Femenina by foreign nations to study abroad, including six scholarships from the United States.[11]

"Old Spanish Days" in California

The Coros y Danzas used music to connect Spanish-speaking communities throughout the Americas to an international "Hispanic brotherhood." In a 1948 circular, Rivera told the performers that they had the "responsibility and honor to make known to the Hispanic-American world the immense wealth of our folklore so that these people will feel more united to Spain."[12] Spanish papers reporting on the tours of the Coros y Danzas throughout Latin America claimed that capitals such as Cuzco, Buenos Aires, and Havana were linked to Spanish history "just as much as Seville or Toledo."[13]

Such narratives were also used when the Coros y Danzas toured Hispanic communities within the United States, particularly those in Southern California and throughout the Southwest. The group leader for the first-ever tour of the United States in 1950, Sampelayo, explained her choice of itinerary during an interview for a Málaga newspaper:

> The comrades of the Sección Femenina are going to carry out a cultural and artistic campaign through the lands of America—specifically through the lands that were once Spanish in California. There, in the cities that still preserve the traditional Spanish holy names, the air will vibrate again with the songs and dances of our young comrades, full of pure beauty. . . .

—And where will you go?

All of California, and especially areas that still have a lot of Spanish people such as San Diego, Los Angeles, Santa Barbara, San Francisco and others of particular importance. . . . The Spaniards of California, children of Spaniards, will revive in their spirit the clear example of Spanish purity, whose art, full of religious mysticism, has no example in the world.[14]

The Coros y Danzas and Spanish press made the most of Spain's historical and cultural connection to the territory within the modern state of California, referring specifically to a period of fifty-two years from 1769 to 1821 when its lands and people were colonized by the Spanish Empire. Before a tour of California in 1950, the Málaga newspaper, *Sur*, portrayed the American state as a former Spanish colony with profound cultural and linguistic ties to the "old country." According to this anonymous columnist, it was the responsibility of the Coros y Danzas to enlighten Californian citizens about their ancient Hispanic heritage through performances of traditional Spanish music and dance:

There, amid skyscrapers and imposing modern machines, the churches founded by our colonizers are still preserved and the language of Cervantes is [still] spoken. . . . That is where they will resurrect the love and affection for the chivalrous and wonderful Spain that is preserved in the legends and traditions of California. . . . And [the women of] our Sección Femenina will be the ambassadors for this racial mission.[15]

California is depicted here as a cultural time capsule from the Spanish Empire's "Golden Age," a land where the archaic language in Miguel de Cervantes's (1547–1616) famous novel, *Don Quixote de la Mancha* (1605), is still spoken by modern descendants of sixteenth-century conquistadors and missionaries. Of course, this is historically impossible because, among other reasons, the area that now makes up the modern state of California was not colonized by Spain until the late eighteenth century, more than 150 years after the death of Cervantes. However, Franco's propagandists were not solely responsible for inventing this false history; as we shall see, they were responding to aspects of American popular culture and Southwestern ideas of race that had already become well established in the United States by the end of the nineteenth century.

The first performance of the Coros y Danzas in the United States was held at the Hollywood Bowl in August 1950, followed by a series of performances at the annual "Old Spanish Days Fiesta" in Santa Barbara. Continuing to this day, the festival celebrates the city's Spanish historical and ancestral roots around one of California's best-preserved eighteenth-century Franciscan missions. The fair is meant to recreate the culture of the Spanish colony of "Old California," celebrating the music, clothing, and food associated with the region when it was first colonized by the Spanish Empire. A Californian reporter writing for the *San Marino Tribune*, on August 17, 1950, described the event as a ". . . fiesta in which thousands of residents and visitors join in to relive again a romantic era from the city's rich and ancient Spanish heritage."[16] An article printed in the New York newspaper, the *Olean Times Herald*, on September 21, 1950, provides this picturesque description of the fair and its significance to the local community:

> Descendants of old Spanish families here recently dusted off sombreros and carefully unfolded their antique mantillas and stirred palatable Latin American dishes for the Old Spanish Days of the nation's most spectacular and colorful festivals. . . . Nearly two centuries ago the Spanish grandees, senoritas and padres transplanted a bit of Spain in California. More than any place, this flavor is retained in the architecture and customs of Santa Barbara. . . . For four days, Santa Barbara is transformed into a Spanish village.[17]

The ancestral background of California's original Spanish-speaking colonists is quite different from what the articles above seem to suggest. From the beginning of Spain's colonization of California in 1769 until its annexation from Mexico by the United States in 1848, most of the Spanish-speaking settlers in the area were of Native American and African descent.[18] The few citizens with pure Iberian blood tended to be the higher-ranking clergy, the majority of whom returned to Europe in the early nineteenth century. Granted, there was a strong racial hierarchy in place in California during the late eighteenth and early nineteenth centuries, with Hispanic landowners referring to themselves *Californios* or *gente de razón* (people of reason) to distinguish themselves from unconverted and non-Spanish-speaking Native American peoples. However, following the annexation of California by the United States in 1848, *Californios* became second-class citizens themselves among the new protestant Anglophone settlers.[19] According to the historians Castro-Salazar and Bagley, after the Mexican-American War, "Mexicans were robbed of their lands, cheated in commercial transactions, professionally diminished, utilized as commodities and considered inferior in regard to language, customs, and religiosity."[20]

Throughout the twentieth century, Americans with Mexican ancestry and Mexican immigrants continued to be subjected to political and economic oppression. During the economic crisis of the 1930s, five hundred thousand people categorized by the federal census as "Mexican" were deported from the United States regardless of their citizenship, including many families that had lived in the American Southwest long before the territory was annexed from Mexico.[21] A decade later, labor shortages caused by the Second World War prompted the United States to persuade unemployed citizens in Mexico to legally cross the border as temporary workers, particularly farmhands. By the mid-1950s, Mexican citizens accounted for a quarter of agricultural laborers in the United States but were subjected to work for long hours on starvation wages, living in poor conditions, while suffering from the effects of exposure to pesticides.[22]

The misrepresentation of a landowning Hispanic elite of pure white Iberian ancestry living in the frontier of Alta California, first invented by the *Californios* during the eighteenth and early nineteenth centuries, established a permanent racialized mythology of the American Southwest. Stories about white landowners of Spanish and Mexican California became staples of Anglo-American popular culture, including Helen Hunt Jackson's 1884 romantic novel, *Ramona*, and Johnston McCulley in his popular 1919 novel about a mysterious swashbuckling hero, *The Curse of Capistrano*, later adapted into the 1920 Hollywood film *The Mark of Zorro*.

The same racial myth was at the heart of the annual Old Spanish Days festival when it was founded in 1924. According to Paul Sweetser, the former vice consul of Mexico in Santa Barbara and former president of the Santa Barbara Historical Society, the festival "reminds our Spanish Californians that they are from Andalusia, where the music was soft, and coquettish, and the colors were gay," words that seem to be taken from a list of Latin American stereotypes.[23] Frances Price, the festival's founder and director, modeled the event after the annual Feria de Sevilla (Seville Fair) that takes place just outside that Andalusian city in May and involves hundreds of colorful traditional private tents (*casetas*) that line the dirt paths.[24] In a 1950 publicity article in the *Santa Barbara News Press*, Prince provides photographic comparisons between Andalusian costumes, foods, and dances and those traditions of Southern California. Prince's choice to imitate the Feria de Sevilla is curious given that this Andalusian tradition did not begin until 1846—twenty-five years after Mexican independence from Spain! Nevertheless, Prince's fictitious cultural connections between Southern California and Andalusia fed into the Franco regime's narration of racial purity and Spain's glorious imperial past.

The Old Spanish Days festival of 1950 featured sixty of Spain's "most talented folk-dancers," according to the *Santa Barbara News Press*.[25] This diplomatic mission was propagandized just as widely in Spain as it was in the United States (see figure 5.1). Surviving Spanish news columns indicate that the Coros y Danzas were well received by the Californian public,

El grupo de Vigo, de los Coros y Danzas, baila en un tablado al aire libre en Santa Bárbara, California

Figure 5.1   An image from a press clipping of the Vigo group of the Coros y Danzas dancing on an outdoor stage in front of the Santa Barbara Mission in Santa Barbara, California, October 1950. "Activo programa para el Grupo Folclórico Ibero." *La prensa*, May 28, 1953. ES-AGA, (03)15.23, 12/643. MCD. AGA, Fondo de la Delegación Nacional de Sección Femenina, IDD (03)051.023, Caja 12/00643.

with several events explicitly linking the visiting dance troupes to Franco's government. In an interview for a Spanish paper, Sampelayo says that Catholic priests and local citizens greeted the troupe with shouts of "¡Viva el Caudillo!" (Long live the Leader!) as the troupe arrived in a caravan of cars decorated with Spanish and American flags.[26] The Spanish-language programs for the Coros y Danzas include a brief narrative of Santa Barbara's founding by the seventeenth-century Spanish explorer Sebastian Vizcíno, as well as the coat of arms of Franco's Spain. Religion played a major role in connecting the values of the Coros y Danzas with the conservative American public; according to the Spanish newspaper La prensa, the troupes entered the eighteenth-century Spanish mission of Santa Barbara to "thank God" for their successful performance as the words of the Catholic Mass "floated over a sea of [Spanish] flags while cries of acclamation were heard for Spain and Franco."[27] Later in the festival, the women of the Coros y Danzas attended a party titled Hijas de España (Daughters of Spain) dedicated to the female descendants of the city's remaining colonist families.[28]

During the Coros y Danzas' second tour of the United States three years later, publicity for the show frequently targeted Spanish-speaking Americans, while advertisements and posters were printed in both Spanish and English. Sokol, the Russian-American impresario discussed in the previous chapter, sought out locations with a high demographic of Hispanic Americans, writing to Rivera that "if we play at San Antonio, which is a big city and has 60% population of Spanish and Mexicans . . . I am sure it will be a great success."[29] An interview in the Diario Madrid after the tour indicates that Sokol's speculation may have been correct. The group leader, Sampelayo, reported that "for many Spanish residents who have been there [in America] for some time, the performances were like a reunion with loved-ones."[30] The same article reports that the American audience in San Bernardino, California, chanted "¡Viva tu madre!" as a mysterious man from Seville knelt in front of the performers crying and opening his arms before running away without saying a word.[31] Sampelayo also describes the troupe's warm reception by the Spanish diaspora in Las Cruces, New Mexico, where a ninety-two-year-old elderly woman left her house for the first time in twenty years to see the performance.[32]

It is possible that these Spanish sources exaggerated or invented such positive receptions of Francoist propaganda in the United States to protect the Franco regime's reputation at home in Spain. But considering the proof we have of tremendous support for the Franco regime in conservative America during the first years of the Cold War, such cries of adulation for Franco during the Old Spanish Days Fiesta would not have been out of place. In any case, it is clear that pro-Franco journalists in Madrid wanted their readers to understand that Spain was no longer seen abroad as a backwater bridge to the Orient but a respected ally of the world's most powerful economy and military.

Both the American and Spanish news articles mentioned previously contradict the way historians have understood Francoist cultural diplomacy with the United States. Stehrenberger writes in her 2013 study that the enthusiastic reception of the Coros y Danzas at the Old Spanish Days festival was linked to the nineteenth-century "Spanish craze, the Spain of the archaic Others ... [that was common] among Europeans, US travelers, and art lovers."[33] However, evidence from the cited sources indicates that American interest in the Old Spanish Days festival was not always motivated by a desire to witness the culture of a distant foreign country; nor did the Coros y Danzas' tours in the Southwestern United States merely promote Spain as an exotic tourist destination. Instead, Californian journalists tended to express feelings of identification and nostalgia for a lost ancestral homeland. Francoist cultural politics became interwoven with local notions of race as white Hispanic and Anglo Americans attempted to exclude the legacy of Mexico and indigenous peoples from American Southwestern culture. This pattern became far more sinister in the Hispanophone Caribbean where white supremacist dictators and oligarchs contracted instructoras of the Sección Femenina's Department of Music to create propaganda for their own murderous regimes.

Gallegos and Andalusians in Cuba

Rivera and Sampelayo brought the Coros y Danzas to Cuba and the Dominican Republic during the early 1950s to promote solidarity between the old hub of the Spanish Empire and its former colonies in the Americas. Both of these Hispanophone Caribbean dictatorships shared white supremacist ideologies that fed into Francoist cultural politics. Spanish diplomats and foreign government officials contracted troupes of Coros y Danzas and individual instructoras of the Sección Femenina to tour the Caribbean, framing their repertoire of Spanish songs and dances as a shared, Hispanic cultural heritage. These musical collaborations helped maintain local conceptions of race and built much-needed international alliances

The dictator Fulgencio Batista (1901–1973), who came from a poor family with African and indigenous ancestry, was regarded as an outsider by Cuban society's white upper class. Although Batista created social programs and land-reform policies that were designed to benefit underprivileged Afro-Cubans, Havana's aristocracy maintained its racial and social hierarchy outside of Batista's office and the military.[34] After nearly three decades of Batista's turbulent political control as a military strong man (1933–1940), president (1940–1944), senator (1948–1952), and then president again (1952–1959), Afro-Cubans remained the island's most politically and economically oppressed demographic, and routine bigotry remained widely tolerated.[35] The Batista regime continued to allow the owners of hotels, nightclubs, and restaurants to prohibit non-white people from their establishments (except, of course, Batista himself). Over a third of Afro-Cubans were illiterate in the 1950s, and they made up the majority of the country's unemployed and incarcerated population.[36] Due to their difficult socioeconomic situation, Afro-Cubans rose to become some of the most prominent union leaders, adding a political dimension to the nation's racial hierarchy.[37] When confronted with the Cuban Revolution (1953–1959), Batista attempted to suppress all socialist activity and protect the hegemonic white elite.

The friendly relationship between Franco and Batista during the 1950s contrasted sharply with their antagonism a decade earlier. After Batista declared war on the Axis Powers in December 1941 following the example of Cuba's American allies, he closed the Spanish consulate, expelled Franco's representatives, and prevented Spanish immigrants living in Cuba from associating with Spain's Falangist party.[38] By the end of 1942, Batista attempted to persuade the United States to declare war on Francoist Spain, as explained in the *Time* magazine article "Plain Talk in Spanish," published on December 28 of that year:

> Cuba's shrewd, ebullient President Fulgencio Batista is no dilettante in power politics. He is a tough hombre who speaks his mind. Last week, after visiting with Washington dignitaries in the U.S., Batista said his piece about a pompous, would-be tough guy across the Atlantic. His theme: If the United Nations[39] go to war with Francisco Franco's Spain, Latin America will be on the United Nations' side. In Cuba, President Batista said, the only elements that would not applaud such a move are Cuban Falangists, now

being rounded up in droves as fifth columnists. Possibly there was some hyperbole in Batista's claim that an invasion of Spain would receive "a total ovation for the Allied cause throughout all Latin America." But, by being blunt, Batista expressed for the first time the sentiments of millions of good friends of democracy in the Western Hemisphere who are tired of apologies and flatteries for Franco.[40]

A decade later, Batista's hostility toward Francoist Spain was completely transformed by the new political landscape of the Cold War. After an eight-year hiatus from Cuban politics, Batista led a military coup in March 1952 to depose the centrist sitting president, Carlos Prío Socarrás (1903–1977). Batista's successful overthrow of Cuban democracy sparked the 26th of July Movement led by Fidel Castro (1926–2016), a revolutionary socialist from Cuba's political left with backing from exiled Spanish Republicans and the Soviet Union. Batista found himself in desperate need of anti-communist international allies, such as Franco, to help his dictatorship survive economically as he attempted to quash the guerrilla rebel fighters. Franco, on the other hand, wished to project an imperial vision of Spain within Cuba and garner international support for his brand of National Catholicism. The two far-right regimes would work together to halt the spread of the "red virus" throughout the "old" and "new" continents.

Spanish ambassador Juan Pablo de Lojendio (1906–1973) arrived in Havana almost immediately after Batista ousted Prío. This was the first time a Spanish diplomat had been on Cuban soil since the end of the Spanish Civil War.[41] By 1954, Batista closed the USSR embassy, officially suspended all of Cuba's socialist and communist press, and began persecuting exiled Spanish Republicans throughout the island. In return, Franco granted special trade benefits to Cuba by greatly reducing the taxes on tobacco and consolidating Spain's position as one of the first importers of Cuban goods.[42]

Of course, this new diplomatic alliance between Franco and Batista incited outrage in Cuba's leftist press. The communist newspaper *Noticias de hoy*, for example, described Franco as a "bloodthirsty Spanish tyrant," and the Franco-Batista partnership was portrayed as a surrender to foreign corporate exploitation.[43] As in the United States, Spanish diplomats had to contend with exiled Spanish Republicans and Lincoln Brigade members, as well as a large segment of the Cuban population that was deeply suspicious of Franco's previous dealings with Hitler's Germany. Spanish propagandists needed to reframe how the Franco regime was perceived in Cuba. Through ongoing cultural exchanges, diplomats hoped to portray Franco as the defender of a white Hispanic trans-Atlantic race defined by shared religion, language, culture, and "blood."

In October 1953, a Spanish diplomat in Havana, Javier Millan Astray, wrote to Rivera suggesting that the Coros y Danzas should tour Cuba. According to Millan Astray, the Coros y Danzas would be well received by Cubans, particularly Spanish immigrants and their Cuban-born descendants who may never have a chance to return to their motherland:

> The gratitude would be enormous and unforgettable due to the many Galicians, Asturians, Basques, Catalans, islanders, in a word, of all the components of the large Spanish Colony residing in America, of which most of them for economic reasons, others because of health, a few due to political ideologies, and most due to work-related obligations, will not see their beloved Spain for a long time or perhaps ever again.[44]

Rivera accepted Millan Astray's offer, organizing a two-and-a-half-month tour from early January to mid-March 1954 with 145 performers and instrumentalists in troupes from Castile and León, Aragon, Galicia, the Canary Islands, and Andalusia. The first performance in Cuba took place within the Spanish embassy, which had only recently reopened following the reconciliation between Batista and Franco (see figure 5.3). The following weeks of the tour were open to public ticket holders at Havana's largest and most well-known venues, including the Palacio de Los Deportes, Teatro Payret, and the Estadio de la Habana. Sponsored by Cuba's first lady, Martha Fernández Miranda, these performances were designed to raise money for impoverished Cuban children.[45]

The Cuban government was clearly enthusiastic about the venture; the performers were exempt from visa fees, and Cuba's national airline, Cubana de Aviación, paid for their airfare. The troupes arrived in Havana to the national anthems of Cuba and Spain being played by Cuba's Music Band of the General Staff of the Navy. Among those waiting on the tarmac were the Spanish ambassador to Cuba, Juan Pablo de Lojendio, the president of Cubana de Aviación, Cuban and Spanish businessmen, and representatives of cultural centers for Spanish immigrants and their descendants located throughout Havana (see figure 5.2).[46]

Since the tour coincided with her diplomatic visit to Argentina, Rivera made a brief appearance in Havana herself where she met with Batista,

Figure 5.2 Havana, Cuba, January 12, 1954. The ambassador of Spain Juan Pablo de Lojendio photographed at the airport of the Cuban capital with the troupes of Coros y Danzas from Andalusia, the Basque Country, and Canary Islands moments after his arrival in Havana. "Cartas de Madrid," *Excélsior-Habana*, January 21, 1954. Mundo-Habana MCD. AGA, Fondo de la Delegación Nacional de Sección Femenina, IDD (03)051.023, Caja 12/00647, exp. 4.

Fernández Miranda, and other Cuban officials. Referring to rumors of atrocities being committed by the Franco regime, Rivera told the Havana newspaper *Excelsior* that there was "no better way to destroy false legends" about Spain than to share its "songs and dances on the wide and beautiful Cuban stage."[47] Rivera said the tour would make Cuba and Spain "closer in a fraternal embrace."[48] Like in the southwest of the United States, this "fraternal embrace" would be achieved by celebrating the shared culture and history of an imagined transatlantic "Hispanic race."

In her effort to portray Cubans and Spaniards as belonging to a single race, Rivera chose young women to perform in the Coros y Danzas who had Cuban heritage. For example, Maruja Lopategui, a dancer from the troupe

BRILLANTE INAUGURACION DE LA EMBAJADA ESPAÑOLA

Con algunos integrantes de "Coros y Danzas de España", vemos en esta foto al Honorable Sr. Presidente de la República, mayor general Fulgencio Batista y señora Martha Fernández Miranda, a Su Eminencia el Cardenal Arteaga; al Embajador de España, Excmo. Sr. Marqués de Vellisca y la Marquesa de Vellisca; doctor Miguel Angel Campa, ministro de Estado; doctor Pedro Rodríguez Capote y otros.

Figure 5.3 A troupe of Coros y Danzas at the newly built Spanish embassy in Havana, including Fulgencio Batista (center, back row), Cardinal Manuel Arteaga y Betancourt (second to left, back row), Spanish Ambassador Pablo de Lojendio (third to the right, back row). "El gran acontecimiento de esta noche: el debut de Coros y Danzas de España," *Diario de la Marina*, January 15, 1954. MCD. AGA, Fondo de la Delegación Nacional de Sección Femenina, IDD (03)051.023, Caja 12/00647, exp. 4.

representing Castile and León, emigrated to Spain with her parents and her brothers as a child from the small rural town of El Cobre, Cuba. According to an interview in a Cuban periodical published by the Club Montaña for Spanish diaspora, when Lopategui heard about the possibility of returning to her place of birth, she "wept with emotion" and vowed to pray at the shrine of the Virgin Marry in Santiago de Cuba.[49] Such stories provided a vivid narration of the two Hispanic nations' cultural reconnection.

Much like the Coros y Danzas' visit to the Santa Barbara mission during their Southern California tour of 1950, the Cuban and Spanish media often discussed the performers' Catholic faith at length. During the day, when they were not rehearsing, the Spanish performers went to Mass and sang Gregorian chant for Havana's scholars of religious music. After a performance at the Colonia Montañesa, a club for Cantabrian immigrants and their descendants living in Havana, a club member wrote: "Since [the Coros y Danzas] are truly Christian in their training, they are joyful, with the healthy happiness of faith in God and in the country."[50] The Spanish troupes typically attended Mass in Havana's chapels moments before their performances, providing excellent photo opportunities for the conservative Cuban press.[51]

After the first few weeks in Havana's theaters, the rest of the performances took place in *sociedades españoles* (Spanish societies). These private clubs were founded by Spanish immigrants who had come to Cuba during the late nineteenth and early twentieth centuries.[52] Their migration was part of a massive exodus from Spain as the poor and working class tried to escape military service during the unpopular wars in Morocco and a depressed economy with little opportunity. The Spanish immigrants, who were mostly from Galicia, Asturias, and the Canary Islands, were usually not fluent in Castilian and arrived in Cuba impoverished, illiterate, and without a specific trade or skill.[53] The societies originally functioned as charities to help these immigrants find work and gain access to education and medical care. With the solidarity and help that the societies offered, many Galicians, Asturians, and Canarians managed to climb the nation's social ladder to enjoy a middle-class lifestyle. By 1961, the societies were enormous and politically influential, with over 55,000 members at the Centro Gallego (Galician Centre) and over 90,000 at the Centro Asturiano, for example.[54] Although the societies were originally intended to help immigrants and cultural minorities integrate into Cuban culture, they slowly became exclusive and racialized meeting places for well-to-do white Cuban citizens. Michael Kenny, an American anthropologist who visited the sociedades during the early 1960s, noted that

Negroes and Chinese are barred from entry to any of the Spanish associations but a few foreigners of European extraction are found in the membership books. In general, membership is limited to those born in Spain, their children and their grandchildren.[55]

The Spanish societies were owned and maintained by white elite subcultures that had grown to enormous proportions with outposts throughout the island. For these white Spanish expatriates and their descendants, the performances of the Coros y Danzas feed their desire to racially and culturally differentiate themselves from Afro-Cubans.

The visiting Coros y Danzas and Spanish diplomats saw the members of the Spanish societies as wealthy, influential leaders in Cuban society who could be easily won over by promoting solidarity through their shared white Hispanic identity. Consequently, the troupes of Coros y Danzas spent a great deal of time performing, socializing, and raising funds for their corresponding regional Spanish club in Havana. Following a performance by a Galician troupe in the Centro Gallego (Galician Centre) of Havana, the Spanish ambassador Juan Pablo de Lojendio said that he hoped Cubans and Spaniards would become more united and recognize the clubhouse as "a house of Spain and a house of Cuba too."[56] The Centro Gallego's president of culture, Juan Somoza Juame, added that "I do not know if I am more Cuban than Galician or more Galician than Cuban."[57] Shortly before the young Galician performers left Cuba, José López Vilaboy, the director of the Havana paper *Mañana* and the owner of Havana's Rancho Boyeros Airport, made an emotional last request: "the Galicians here beg you to go to the cemetery in Santiago [de Compostela] and kiss the graves of their parents, who they have left behind."[58] Such feelings of a Hispanic racial pride were certainly not restricted to the Spanish societies; during a dinner after a final performance at the Lions Club of Havana, an international charity organization, López Vilaboy gave another sentimental speech on the common ancestry and shared values between white Cubans and Spaniards. For López Vilaboy, to be Cuban was to have Spanish ancestry and uphold the religion and values of the first European conquerors in the Americas:

> But since the welcome comes so soon after the farewell, it would be good to tell you that when you are far away from Cuba, resting in your homes, your seductive performance will continue to live with us, it will not fade away, as the actions of the conquistadors who taught us to be noble did not fade away, nor that of the friars who urged us to raise our heads to heaven, because conquerors and priests were the rigorous and severe face of Spain.[59]

As the quotes above show, the distinctions between Cuban and Spanish national and racial identities seemed to blur throughout the 1954 tour.

The Cuban press advertised performances of the Coros y Danzas as "a genuine representation of Hispanic folklore" so that their repertoire may be interpreted as the cultural property of either nation.[60] Cuban newspapers and radio broadcasters referred to Spain using terms such as the "la Madre Patria" (the Motherland), or "the fruitful mother of nations, peoples, and civilizations."[61] After a public performance on February 2, a rather fanatical Cuban radio announcer commented on the historical, cultural, and racial ties between the two nations:

> Cubans and Spaniards all felt united by the irresistible power of a common, generous, and passionate blood. . . . They have made us experience the pride of belonging to this powerful race, which knows how to express in its dances and songs the sentiment of a people filled with virtues and greatness.[62]

This transcript describes a highly emotional scene in which Cubans and Spaniards behave like reuniting family members after a long separation. Reporters working for the conservative side of Cuban media seemed to silently lament the Desastre del 98, yearning nostalgically for Spanish colonial rule and the ideas of white Hispanic racial purity. In Spain, Franco's concept of a raza española was mostly defined by a shared religion, cultural tradition, and sentiment rather than biological connections.[63] In conservative Cuban media, however, being a member of Hispanidad could not be learned or acquired no matter how many generations a person's ancestors had lived in the Spanish-speaking world; rather, it was only inherited through blood.

Of course, the diplomats who were making these pledges of racial solidarity, such as the Cuban businessman López Vilaboy and the Spanish ambassador Lojendio, were keenly aware of the political and economic benefits that came with improved relations with their "blood-brothers and sisters" across the Atlantic. Besides opening new possibilities for trade, Spain's paternal relationship to Cuba would have relieved the national shame that lingered after the loss of Spain's few remaining colonies at the end of the Spanish-American War fifty-six years earlier. Cubans with Spanish ancestry, in theory, would look to their "mother country" for cultural and spiritual guidance as a means of affirming their whiteness.

Censorship within the Batista regime does not allow us to have a complete understanding of how the majority of Cuban citizens received the Spanish troupes. While some Cuban critics appeared to be persuaded by the instructoras' claims that certain Spanish songs and dances originated in the biblical cities of Tyre and Sidon "ten centuries before Christ," others were skeptical.[64] Moreover, immigrants from Spain often did not recognize such repertoire. The journalist Joaquín Aristigueta, a Spanish immigrant himself, described the reaction of Asturian immigrants during a performance at Havana's Universidad Santo Tomás:

> But the public needs some warnings, and I think it would be convenient to provide them for each number. Because I have heard Asturians comment, for example, that they had never seen dancing in Asturias like that which was performed by the pretty "neñas"[65] of the Asturian group of Coros y Danzas. And it is natural that, until now, they have not known these songs, melodies, and dances from the thirteenth century, or the fourteenth, or the sixteenth.[66]

On such occasions, the Spanish diplomats and instructoras of the Sección Femenina failed to adapt their propaganda to the Cuban public's idea of Spanish culture. The Sección Femenina's methods of collecting and reconstructing allegedly ancient songs and dances, as discussed in previous chapters, resulted in performances that were sometimes completely unfamiliar to communities of Spaniards living abroad who had not been indoctrinated with Francoist cultural propaganda.

The Spanish troupes faced more serious challenges in Cuba when they were confronted with anti-Franco sentiment from militants on both the political right and left. Such dynamics reflect how commonly accepted ideas of a monolithic communist Eastern Bloc, as presumed by the Truman Doctrine in the United States, for example, was shockingly myopic in the context of Cuba.[67] The notorious politician and strongman Rolando Masferrer (1918–1975) was a member of the Communist Party of Cuba and had fought alongside anti-fascist Americans in the Abraham Lincoln Brigade during the Spanish Civil War.[68] Despite his ongoing affiliation with the political left, Masferrer took on the double role of senator and hitman for the Batista regime during the 1950s. During the Cuban revolution, Masferrer organized and directed a parapolice group known as "Los Tigres" that tracked, terrorized, and assassinated Batista's political advisories, particularly Castro's socialist-leaning rebels. Working as a coeditor of the newspaper *El tiempo en Cuba*, the press of which was later demolished by Castro's victorious army, Masferrer denounced the atrocities being committed by the Franco regime. A columnist writing under the pseudonym "Crixo"[69] was vehemently against the tour of the Coros y Danzas in Cuba. "Crixo" portrays the Spanish ambassador, Lojendio, as a "pork butcher" while fervently denouncing the troupes of Coros y Danzas as fascist propaganda and enemies of both the Cuban and Spanish people:

> The tour of the "Coros y Danzas of Spain" on behalf of the tyrant Franco, as a means of capturing the sympathies of our people who have such deep democratic roots, has been a tremendous failure. What should have been an eminently popular show, in which the most wholesome of our people should have felt in their bones the echo of the beautiful and good Spanish people, our brothers in a thousand struggles for freedom, has only been the center of a reunion for the Francoist pork butcher that lives on our island. It was a secret to no one, much less the Spanish ambassador Lojendio . . . that our compatriots would have supported the show with their presence and their hearts, if [the Spaniards] had come to this country clean of the disgusting and repulsive veneer of Francoism.[70]

The reception of the Franco regime in Cuba during the mid-1950s was also deeply divided among Castro's revolutionaries, who perceived Francoist Spain with attitudes ranging from pragmatic tolerance to fervent animosity.[71] The bulk of anti-Franco sentiment lay with Spanish Republicans who had allied themselves with Castro. These exiles, who likely fought alongside Masferrer in Spain before becoming his enemies in Cuba, organized protests against the performances of the Coros y Danzas throughout the tour. The Casa de Cultura (House of Culture), a society founded to unite exiled Spanish Republicans with other anti-Francoists, tried to expose the true reality of life in Franco's Spain throughout the 1950s. Shortly before the Coros y Danzas' well-publicized tour of Cuba, the society sent anti-Francoist manifestos to all the Spanish regional centers. According to an anonymous columnist in the Casa de Cultura's main propaganda organ, the magazine *España republicana*, the flyers were "welcomed with lively satisfaction and clear signs of approval by all the Spaniards who saw it," although this seems like a gross exaggeration considering the positive reception of the Coros y Danzas in the columns written by members of these same societies quoted above.[72] Portraying the Coros y Danzas as merely a fascist "contrivance," the same article is accompanied by a cartoon of Franco with a swastika mustache acting as a puppeteer above the obscenely jerking bodies of the female dancers (see figure 5.4):

Franco: Les presento en Conjunto "Coros y Danzas de España"

Figure 5.4 A satirical cartoon showing the rejection of the Coros y Danzas. "Repulsa a los Coros y Danzas de la Falange," *España republicana*, January 23, 1954. MCD. AGA, Fondo de la Delegación Nacional de Sección Femenina, IDD (03)051.023, Caja 12/00647:

All of our compatriots support [the protesters'] energetic denunciation of this vile contrivance of the Franco regime that, after having plunged our people into a terrible situation of hunger, misery, and terror—a situation that obstructs the sources of their traditional joy and by no means creates a favorable atmosphere for singing and dancing—tries to take advantage of our rich folklore to gain the support of Spaniards in Cuba. . . . An example of this growing condemnation was what occurred at the Andalusian Center of Havana. Serving the Franco regime's grim purposes through its so-called artistic embassy, the directors of the Andalusian Center organized a reception for the members of the Falange's Coros y Danzas. While that reception was taking place, raucous cries against the criminal Franco regime rang out . . . which the daily press has had no choice but to mention, even though they have tried to distort its significance and downplay its importance.[73]

The columnist, who claims to be a Spanish immigrant, describes the jeers that were shouted at the Coros y Danzas while they were socializing at a diplomatic reception that took place the night after their arrival in Havana's Centro Andaluz, a club dedicated to Cubans with Andalusian ancestry. The columnist points out with irony that the musical traditions performed by the Coros y Danzas were precisely the kinds of customs that were dying out in Spain due to the hunger and terror produced by the Franco regime's economic policies and use of violence. Finally, the columnist comments on how the pro-Batista press omitted or glossed over the protests.

Although the excerpt from the above article is the only account of protests against the Coros y Danzas during their 1954 tour of Cuba, the furious tone of Cuban and Spanish officials at the same reception correspond with the politically volatile atmosphere described in the *España republicana*. For example, Juan Joaquín Otero (1893–1970) gave a fiery speech defending the Coros y Danzas at the Centro Andaluz on the very night that the protests supposedly took place. Joaquín Otero was a Galician poet and president of the Lions Club of Havana who had immigrated to Havana as a young man during the early twentieth century. While living in Cuba, he kept close connections to literary circles in Spain, eventually receiving the prestigious Order of Isabella the Catholic in 1955 from Franco himself for his contributions to Spanish-language poetry.[74] Joaquín Otero was one of the high-profile guests who attended the reception of the Coros y Danzas at the Centro Andaluz. In his welcoming speech, published in the Cuban periodical *Ecos de España* distributed among the nation's Spanish societies, Joaquín Otero attempts to strengthen relations between the Batista and Franco regimes by conflating the ongoing revolution in Cuba with the Spanish Civil War of the 1930s. According to Joaquín Otero, both wars were struggles between traditional Hispanic values and the "Mongol" hordes of invading Soviets. Joaquín Otero implies that Cubans can only be saved by a mutual love of their Hispanic cultural heritage, such as the repertoire performed by the Coros y Danzas:

The world sees in you [the Coros y Danzas] the noble morality of a people who . . . when they are unjustly besieged, when they are unjustly slandered and excommunicated, calmly re-examine their popular treasure, revive and purify it, go out and present it, even to [their] enemies, so that all the peoples of the world may be convinced that Spain, in such a climate of universal hatred or suspicion, of looming Mongol ferocity, or of gloomy and ruinous Western precaution, raises the honest flags of its most genuine traditions, and, in a display of generous and affectionate tranquility, goes out into the world to display the purity of its values.[75]

Such were the efforts of diplomats of the Batista and Franco regimes to foster solidarity between their dictatorships. The Franco regime's nostalgic imaginings of the old Spanish Empire helped maintain alliances with dictatorships across the Atlantic while at the same time shaping and perpetuating local views about race and nationalism. The soirées, private clubs, and dinner events provided ideal environments for the Franco regime to project its vision of a transatlantic Hispanidad.

But the Coros y Danzas spent a great deal of time and effort in Cuba preaching to the converted, particularly a wealthy, white, and conservative minority. Free, open-air performances, which were common practice in Spain, Morocco, and the United States, may have allowed the Coros y Danzas to target members of Cuba's politically unaffiliated working class. However, such locations in Cuba were either ignored or deliberately avoided. In Sampelayo's official summary of the tour written for Rivera, she offers some explanations as to why these decisions were made. Sampelayo writes that the Spanish ambassador in Havana did not give "any special attention" to the Coros y Danzas and never invited the 145 performers to dine at the embassy, as was customary in other nations.[76] On the one occasion when the Asturian troupe was asked to perform at the embassy, the Cuban press attaché was already waiting for them inside, as though the event were deliberately being given a low profile. Finally, the Spanish embassy did nothing to put the performers in direct contact with journalists and critics, an agreement that was made "probably with good intentions," according to Sampelayo. Given the volatile political environment in Cuba at the time, the Spanish diplomats may have believed that such public performances would have been too dangerous. Moreover, it is likely that Ambassador Lojendio and other diplomats thought performances for the island's working-class would have been a lost cause, possibly even provoking further unrest. The result was that the Coros y Danzas could only reach the majority of Cubans through television and radio, both of which were a rarity in Cuba and owned mostly by the economic elite.

The Coros y Danzas only visited Cuba once more to perform at the Casino Español in Havana in 1956. But no amount of cultural propaganda or political intervention from the part of the Franco regime or elsewhere was going to stop the colossal political and social transformations that had already begun to take place in Cuba since Batista's coup d'état. A decisive rebel victory on December 31, 1958, forced Batista to flee to the Dominican Republic, another nation that had political ties to the Franco regime and that was strongly influenced by the United States. Communications between Spain and Cuba did not end with Castro's victory. Perhaps due to Castro's wish to gain recognition within the Western Bloc, the Franco regime was tolerated in Havana, and the two governments continued to cooperate despite extreme ideological differences. It was only Lojendio's scandalous interruption of Castro's televised political address in 1960, followed by Castro's adoption of the Communist Party of Cuba in 1965, that effectively silenced Cuban-Spanish diplomatic relations until after Franco's death.

Sorority in the Dominican Republic

Barely three months after the 1954 tour of Cuba, Rivera turned her attention to another dictatorship in the Caribbean in which the political and economic elite were influenced by a similar brand of white chauvinism. On June 2, Rafael Trujillo Molina (1891–1961), the dictator of the Dominican Republic, visited Spain, the first Latin American head of government to do so since the Spanish Civil War. Amid the various banquets, tours, and expeditions of hunting parties, Franco and Rivera made sure their guest also had an opportunity to witness performances of the Coros y Danzas. Genuinely impressed by the troupes, Trujillo sought to recruit the Sección Femenina's music instructoras to the Dominican Republic to help build local music programs. The Spanish instructoras immersed themselves in Dominican racial politics to increase their chances of success in forging stronger cultural ties between the Franco and Trujillo regimes. This was no easy task, considering the extent to which the Trujillo regime went about rewriting Dominican history and altering the nation's musical culture.

Many aspects of Dominican social and racial politics resembled those of Cuba, where a racial divide was created between a Black, impoverished working class and a lighter-skinned elite. At the turn of the twentieth century, the border between the Spanish-speaking Dominican Republic and the Black, Francophone Haiti was mostly undefined. Rural farmers and traders living in the center of the island of Hispaniola enjoyed free movement and trade while speaking Creole, French, and Spanish interchangeably.[77] When Black Haitians and other non-Hispanic Black communities moved east from the interior of Hispaniola, they adapted to and influenced Dominican culture.[78] The white and lighter-skinned Dominican elite perceived this exchange as an economic and social threat and sought to distinguish themselves racially and culturally from their poorer, Black, Francophone neighbors at home and across the island in Haiti.[79] Using terms such as Dominicanidad (Dominican-ness) and antihaitianismo (anti-Haitianism), Dominican politicians and intellectuals reinforced anti-Haitian stereotypes, prejudices, and myths that had roots in the nineteenth century.[80]

When Trujillo seized power in 1930, Dominicanidad and antihaitianismo became central components of his regime's ideology.[81] Trujillo's newly founded Partido Dominicano (Dominican Party) hosted cultural programs and planned thousands of meetings, parades, and rallies to promote the dictator's idea of a white Dominicanidad.[82] Propaganda via radio and news articles portrayed Dominicans as belonging to a Hispanic and Catholic nation.[83] Trujillo portrayed the white, Catholic, and Hispanic raza dominicana (Dominican race) as being threatened by the Haitianizing influences of Afro-Caribbean culture.[84] In the Trujillo regime, Dominicanidad and Hispanidad were conflated with whiteness. Only Haitians were perceived to be as Black, while Dominicans were perceived as entirely of European descent (even if the actual ancestry of many "white" Dominicans was often far more complex!).[85] The regime outlawed all cultural and religious practices of African origin, deeming them "anti-Hispanic." Even the dictator himself, who came from a poor working family of a mixed Black and white background, occasionally wore makeup to lighten his complexion.[86]

Although the Trujillo regime's racist propaganda presented an international conflict between the Dominican Republic and Haiti, it was mainly utilized for domestic issues—Black laborers within the nation who opposed the regime were ostracized and portrayed as "foreign or un-Dominican."[87] The oppression of Haitians and Black Dominicans reached a horrific climax in October 1937 when Trujillo ordered the military to murder roughly fifteen thousand people of African ancestry living in the frontier zone.[88] This genocide was accompanied by a government program designed to encourage white immigrants, especially from Spain, to replace the population gap left by murdered and exiled Black Dominicans.

Music played a fundamental role in shaping and maintaining the Trujillo regime's racist ideology. The Dominican scholar and music critic Flérida de Nolasco (1891–1976) wrote that the nation's rural music traditions were derived from purely Iberian practices that had been corrupted and "Africanized" by Black slaves on the island of Hispaniola. According to Nolasco, "Dominican folk music cannot be but a derivation of Spanish music, adjusted to the environment, corrupted when it has fallen into inexpert hands, and sometimes contaminated with Black music, of savage stupidity."[89] This mission to cleanse Dominican music from the influence of Afro-Caribbean traditions was carried out in the nation's cultural programs. The Trujillo regime transformed the nation's popular songs and dances into symbols of whiteness and Dominicanidad, hiring professional composers to replace Afro-Caribbean elements in the national repertoire with Mexican rhythms.[90] Dominican music was thus "Hispanicized." Although this state-approved music soon became a staple of the nation's popular culture, the government needed official state troupes of singers and dancers who would standardize how this new repertoire was performed.

The Acción Feminista Dominicana, the "women's unit" of the Trujillo regime, was founded in 1931 and closely resembled the Sección Femenina of Franco's Spain. As in Spain, female instructoras of the Acción Feminista Dominicana were responsible for teaching young girls living in impoverished areas of the nation techniques for sanitation, literacy, and home economics.[91] In the 1940s, the Acción Femenista Dominicana gained an official role in the Dominican government and was renamed the Sección Femenina del Partido Trujillista adscrita al Partido Dominicano (Women's Section of the Trujillista Party attached to the Dominican Party).[92] A partnership developed between the Acción Feminista Dominicana and the Sección Femenina wherein the two organizations exchanged envoys to share and learn from each other's programs. A representative of the Sección Femenina traveled to the Dominican Republic as early as 1940 to attend a conference dedicated to the "Laws of Social Interest in the Era of Trujillo," a symposium that focused on the "present and future perspectives of pedagogical renovation within Dominican schools."[93] Later, in the mid-1950s, the Spanish Sección Femenina collaborated with the Sección Femenina del Partido Trujillista adscrita al Partido Dominicano to create music ensembles inspired by the Spanish Coros y Danzas.

When Trujillo witnessed a performance of the Coros y Danzas on his diplomatic visit to Spain in 1954, Alfonso Marqués de Merry del Val, the Spanish ambassador to the Dominican Republic, informed Rivera that the Dominican dictator was "greatly excited" by the women's performance. According to Merry del Val, Trujillo himself requested any available information on the troupes, especially reports and printed pamphlets regarding the Sección Femenina's research on Spanish musical folklore.[94] After several months of negotiations, the Dominican secretary of education and fine arts, Joaquín Balaguer (1906–2002), arranged for the Spanish Sección Femenina to send three of its "most experienced girls" to research Dominican traditional music and train new troupes of local Coros y Danzas.[95] According to the contract formulated by the Dominican government, the Spanish instructoras remained in the Dominican Republic "for the better part of the year" and were employed for $100 a month plus funds for accommodation and transportation.[96]

The newly trained Dominican ensembles were scheduled to give their first performance on December 20, 1955, for the beginning of the Trujillo regime's twenty-fifth anniversary. Known as La Feria de la paz y confraternidad del mundo libre (Celebration of Peace and Fellowship in the Free World), this celebration was the climax of a year-long fair that included spectacles, musical events, and parades.[97] The purpose of the fair was to raise awareness of the country's national products and resources while establishing the Dominican Republic as an attractive destination for tourism and foreign investments.[98] Much like the Franco regime, Trujillo wished to make the Dominican Republic an indispensable ally of the Western Bloc, capitalizing on the nation's strategic geographic location and agricultural capacity.

Before the Spanish instructoras could begin to train the Dominican ensembles, they needed to acquire a repertoire of Dominican music and dance. This is where the instructoras ran into a rather challenging situation; the traditional repertoire that was actually available in the Dominican countryside often did not align with Trujillo's idea of Dominicanidad. Any mistake on the part of the instructoras in their selection of Dominican repertoire could easily be perceived as an offense by Trujillo's government. In a cautionary letter to Rivera written before the instructoras' departure, Merry del Val wrote that the Dominican government was overly sensitive about the nation's cultural roots.[99] According to Merry del Val, this sensitivity within the upper echelons of the Dominican government stemmed from the fact that "there is very little folkloric background in this country."[100] In reality, the issue was not that the Dominican Republic lacked its own rural music traditions, but that the Trujillo regime perceived the vast majority of Dominican songs, dances, and traditional costumes as sounding or looking too Afro-Caribbean. The instructoras would spend very little time in the field transcribing musical traditions and collecting traditional costumes, as they often did in Spain, because the Trujillo regime was seeking to form a brand of Dominican culture that was not being practiced. In fact, Merry del Val informed Rivera that the Dominican authorities were "very interested in the resuscitation of a typical national dress that I have not been able to confirm ever actually existed."[101]

To help negotiate this complex diplomatic situation, Merry del Val informed Rivera that only those instructoras who possessed "exceptional prudence and wisdom" should be selected for the mission.[102] The Spanish ambassador was keen to receive music instructoras who would quickly grasp the Trujillo regime's concept of Dominicanidad so as not to contradict the discriminatory policies of the Dominican government. In fact, Merry del Val told Rivera of such a scandal that had occurred the previous year. When the Dominican state secretary for education and fine arts hired an independent French specialist to collect the traditional songs and costumes of the nation, the young woman traveled to Haiti for part of her research.[103] Of course, the repertoire and traditional clothing she found there were rejected by the Dominican authorities for being too much inspired by the French Afro-Antilles. Consequently, when the first Spanish instructora arrived in the Dominican Republic in the summer of 1955, the Spanish ambassador likely provided her with a statement similar to the one that he included in his letter to Rivera on March 25:

> Afro-Antillean [culture] does not have any historical basis in Santo Domingo where, during the last years of our sovereignty [before the Haitian occupation of 1822–1844], there were only about 15,000 black slaves, and the vast majority of the population was of Spanish origin.[104]

The instructoras of the Spanish Sección Femenina helped the Trujillo regime create a distinctly "Hispanicised" version of Dominican rural musical traditions and costumes. In fact, Merry del Val persuaded the Spanish instructora to copy sketches of traditional clothing from engravings and drawings of the late eighteenth and nineteenth centuries found in the Biblioteca Nacional in Madrid and the Archivo General de Indias in Seville before they had even reached the Caribbean.[105] While still in Spain, instructoras prepared material specifically from the Canary Islands, Andalusia, Asturias, and Galicia where, according to Merry del Val, the majority of Dominican families originated.[106] However, instead of exhibiting this repertoire as the musical folklore of Spain—as they did during their missions of cultural diplomacy throughout the United States and Europe— the instructoras presented their findings as being wholly Dominican. Once the instructoras arrived in the Caribbean, Merry del Val directed them to focus on the inland regions that had a "clear Spanish tradition," such as Cibao, Mao, and the area around Santiago de los Caballeros.[107] If these locations provided insufficient musical material, Merry del Val asked the instructoras to adapt melodies and costumes from Cuba and Puerto Rico in place of the more African-influenced repertoire found in the Dominican Republic.[108] Rather than seek out or create uniquely Dominican traditional music and costumes, Merry del Val encouraged the instructoras to concoct a blend of melodies and costumes from around the Spanish-speaking Caribbean, which, he said, were all "very similar." For the Trujillo regime, forming connections with an international Hispanic community outweighed developing a distinct national culture.

The Spanish Sección Femenina helped to perpetuate the Trujillo regime's idea of Dominicanidad by replacing Dominican music with Spanish repertoire and training state dance ensembles. As with the Spanish societies in Cuba, these collaborations were designed to help the white elite in the Dominican Republic confirm their ancestral connections to Europe while the Franco regime gained another ally across the Atlantic. As mentioned earlier, one of the goals of cultural diplomacy is to foster a sense of "common interests and values and feelings of mutuality" with the members of the host nation.[109] The Sección Femenina's representation of Hispanidad in the Dominican Republic was driven by the Franco regime's desire to foster an international network of Hispanic peoples with a shared history, culture, and a set of common geopolitical interests.

With changing international pressures after the fall of the Axis powers in 1945, Rivera and the instructoras of the Sección Femenina learned to adapt their representation of Hispanidad around the world for the sake of colonial influence and cultural diplomacy, even if these adjustments occasionally challenged how they defined their idea of raza española at home.

Several complications created these different narrations of Hispanidad. Within Spain, the Sección Femenina associated itself with Queen Isabella I of Castile and the "heroes" of the Reconquista who purged the peninsula of the "impurities" of Moorish civilization. This nostalgia for Spanish imperialism and traditional Catholic values strengthened the cultural ties between the Franco regime and the Sección Femenina's Hispanic hosts in the United States and the Caribbean. In the Spanish Protectorate, however, the instructoras celebrated ancient Islamic Iberia as a cultural bridge between Spain and Morocco, and the women of the Coros y Danzas became direct cultural heirs of medieval al-Andalus. Within the United Kingdom and France, the Sección Femenina adjusted the gender distribution of the Coros y Danzas while on international tours, a decision that coincided with disapproving articles written by British critics and musicologists who thought the all-female ensembles were inauthentic representations of Spanish traditional dance. Meanwhile, the women were often required to attend events involving alcohol and unruly male diplomats—situations that not only contradicted the Sección Femenina's conceptions of Catholic morality but also put the performers at risk of sexual abuse.

As the Sección Femenina developed their role as cultural diplomats, it was necessary for the Coros y Danzas' portrayal of Spanish history, gender roles, and music to become more malleable in order to negotiate the Franco regime's delicate international position. All the Sección Femenina's portrayals of Hispanidad were designed, with varying degrees of success, to help the Franco regime transform its international image and negotiate a new political role for itself in a world from which Spain had been alienated since 1939.

Reflections

Throughout this book, I have examined how various networks of artists, politicians, and entrepreneurs adapted ideas of raza española and
Hispanidad to suit different political circumstances during the first two
decades of the Franco regime. After the regime transitioned from a supporter
of Nazi Germany to an ally of the Western Bloc, Spanish propagandists developed multiple national identities to suit Spain's new and diverse geopolitical relationships. These narrations were based on imagined readings of a
common Hispanic past that linked the officials of the Franco regime with
various cultural groups within Spain and abroad.

I have shed light on the Sección Femenina's important but overlooked role
in facilitating Spain's regional, colonial, and diplomatic relationships. First,
I examined how the Sección Femenina claimed to save Spanish folk music
from the corrupting influences of modern cosmopolitanism and foreign political ideologies. The instructoras staged their repertoire as part of a genuine
Spanish culture that had been resurrected from the distant past, while the
young women themselves were enshrined in Catholic conceptions of virtue.
Rivera and her instructoras presented the performers in the troupes of Coros
y Danzas as untrained volunteers, plucked from their native villages to share
their music and dance traditions. But in truth, most of the women who made
up these troupes were from middle-class families and only encountered
most of this repertoire via the cultural programs of the Franco regime. These
officials appropriated or invented regional musical traditions to express
Francoist conceptions of race, gender roles, and Spanish history. The Sección
Femenina's idealization of Spanish peasantry helped the Franco regime perpetuate myths of a national character and work ethic. From the beginning
of the Cold War, Rivera, the instructoras, and Spanish diplomats used these
well-trained performing troupes to make use of political climates around
the world.

According to sociologists such as Lawrence and Boym, nation-states
emerge when self-proclaimed ethnic groups decide that it is in their interest
to govern themselves.[1] But determining the ways in which an ethnic group
defines itself can be highly problematic; individual actors, even under the

patronage of a ruthless dictatorial regime, may express multiple and conflicting identities of nationhood according to their own political objectives. Despite the Franco regime's massive censorship and propaganda campaigns, definitions of raza española and Hispanidad were open to interpretation by various musicians, impresarios, and government officials both in Spain and abroad. A flexible definition of race was useful for those in power, enabling the dictatorship to simultaneously confront regional divisions, define and reinterpret gender roles, and negotiate Spain's new political role in the Cold War era.

The divides between the regime's various narratives of raza española and Hispanidad were extremely permeable; different ideas of race were not confined to their geopolitical contexts but were often found alongside those that the regime directed toward Spaniards at home. The numerous articles published in Spanish newspapers concerning the Coros y Danzas' tours in Morocco and the West reveal that it must have been common knowledge among politically aware Spaniards that the regime's dominant domestic ideology of National Catholicism was being changed overseas for political gain. The Franco regime was a bureaucratic authoritarian state tempered by a complex internal network of oligarchs competing for power and with divergent, and at times opposing, political objectives. The more we understand the microhistories of individual agents acting in the Franco regime's name, the more we find that the regime's dominant narrations of race at home existed alongside other diverging national narratives.

However, there is one common thread that ties together the Sección Femenina's various representations of the raza española and Hispanidad: the instructoras created different notions of race using narratives of Spanish cultural diaspora. Whether they were bringing rural traditions to city centers, restoring myths of a brotherhood between ancient Muslims and Christians of al-Andalus, or reviving the dances of seventeenth-century Spanish colonists in the Americas, the Sección Femenina represented rural Spain as the mother (or father) nation to the communities in which they were performing. When abroad, the Sección Femenina created cultural and emotional connections with foreign publics by providing origin stories that fed into local narratives concerning race.

Perhaps one of the most important contributions of this book is that it provides a background context for the repertoire and performance practices of a large number of ensembles in Spain today. I have no desire to subject the modern Coros y Danzas to some kind of authenticity test; traditions must be invented sometime, somewhere, even if they are not as old as their practitioners claim. However, the context in which traditions are formed can be important, especially if the context has a significant impact on how a group of people continues to define itself. As I mentioned in the Introduction, many of the ensembles of Coros y Danzas studied in this book are still functioning today, having outlasted the Sección Femenina and the Franco regime itself. While some of the modern Coros y Danzas are made up of youth, many others have been dancing, singing, or otherwise involved with these ensembles long before Spain's transition to democracy. In fact, one director of a prominent Andalusian ensemble with whom I have been in correspondence told me with pride that she founded the troupe in the 1960s when she was an instructora of the Sección Femenina. The significance of this research is heightened by growing support for the far-right political party, Vox, and continued fascist demonstrations throughout the nation. Based on the interactions I have had with citizens of Andalusia who are familiar with the Coros y Danzas, some of these modern troupes maintain connections to far-right politics. More research is needed to determine how these ensembles, created and curated by messengers of Francoist and Falangist propaganda, continue to carry cultural weight in twenty-first-century Spain. The same can be said for the Sección Femenina's influence on the music programs of foreign nations, particularly the Dominican Republic and Morocco.

There are several other ways in which research on the Sección Femenina and its cultural policies may be expanded. First, a more in-depth study is needed of the Sección Femenina's representation of Spain's regional cultures outside of Andalusia, especially in the regions with separate native languages such as Catalonia, the Basque Country, and Galicia. Although this book touches upon the ways in which the music instructoras represented non-Castilian languages, it is not an exhaustive analysis of the available material that is likely held in the local provincial archives throughout these regions. Further research in local archives could reveal more about the contradictory ways in which the Sección Femenina defined these non-Castilian cultures, and how their programs may have influenced peripheral nationalisms in Spain today. Similarly, further research is needed on what appears to be the extensive education system run by the Sección Femenina for Muslim children living in the Spanish Protectorate. Of particular importance would be the way in which Moroccan repertoire and the Arabic language were presented by Coros y Danzas stationed in Tétouan, Ceuta, and Melilla. Finally, research in the state archives of the Dominican Republic and Cuba may yield additional information on Sección Femenina's musical collaboration with foreign women's organizations.

Rules of the National Competition of Coros y Danzas

La organización de los grupos de coros y Danzas data del año 1939, se organizan con el fin de conservar y recoger las auténticas danzas y canciones expuestas a desaparecer.

Para realizar esta labor se empezaron a formar grupos de Coros y Danzas en todas las provincias y sus locales, formados por camaradas de la Sección Femenina que se encuadraron y se encuadran voluntariamente en este servicio.

Se realizan inspecciones a los pueblos donde se sabe hay danzas y canciones interesantes a punto de desaparecer.

Una vez resurgido el baile se procura vuelva a arraigar en el pueblo y quede en él para siempre.

La edad de las muchachas que forman los grupos no puede ser superior a 28 años, pues es natural que pasada esta edad la agilidad, salvo casos extraordinarios, no es la misma ni la resistencia tampoco es igual.

Para estimular la organización de grupos nuevos y la recogida de danzas y canciones la Regiduría Central de Cultura de la Delegación Nacional [sic] de Sección Femenina convoca unos Concursos Nacionales en los que participan todos los grupos.

Prestas de la que se compone el concurso

1a Prueba Llamada Provincial. En esta primera prueba concurren los grupos de una mismo provincial o sea que se celebra la competición entre los pueblos de cada provincial. De esta primera competición quedan seleccionados un grupo de coro y otro de danza de Sección Femenina y otro de Coro y otro de danza de Juventudes.

2a Prueba Regional. En esta segunda prueba concurren los grupos seleccionados en cada provincial correspondientes a una misma región y quedan igualmente seleccionados por cada Región dos grupos de Coro, uno de Sección Femenina y otro de Juventudes y otros dos de danzas, uno de Sección Femenina y otro de Juventudes. Los grupos de danzas de Sección Femenina que quedan vencedores en esta Segunda Prueba Regional pasan directamente a la Prueba Final.

Esto lo hacemos porque es completamente imposible incluir en una Prueba de Sector grupos de Danzas de varias Regiones cuyas características son a veces puestas y de gran contraste, por lo que se deja su clasificación para la Prueba Final.

3a Prueba de Sector. A esta 3a Prueba de Sector concurren solamente los grupos de Coros de Sección Femenina y Juventudes y los de Danza de Juventudes.

Para ellos se dividen las regiones de España en cuarto Sectores, en cada una de ellos concurren las Regiones que les integran. De esta forma quedan seleccionados cuatro Coros de Sección Femenina y cuatro de Juventudes, y cuatro Grupos de Danzas de Juventudes.

Prueba Final. En esta última Prueba concurren: los cuatro grupos de Coros de Sección Femenina que quedaron seleccionados en la Prueba de Sector, igualmente los cuatro Coros de Juventudes y los cuatro Grupos de Danzas de Juventudes. Mas todos los grupos de Danzas de Sección femenina que quedaron clasificados en las Pruebas regionales.

Jurados

Los Jurados para clasificar estas pruebas se designan entre las autoridades musicales más competentes para juzgar las diferentes pruebas.

¿Que deben juzgar ante todo?

Canciones. Con respecto a éstas su autenticidad y pureza folklórica, afinación, dicción, interpretación del programa y dirección de la Instructora que dirige el Coro.

Danzas. Con respecto a las Danzas su autenticidad y pureza folklórica, interpretación, ejecución, ritmo, etc.

Trajes. Su autenticidad, si son antiguos, propiedad de aderezos, peinados, calzado de los trajes son copiados, su fidelidad en la copia tanto en colorido, telas, hechuras, etc.

La realización de estos Concursos no está llevando a una magnífica conclusión; el resurgimiento total y revalorización de todo nuestro arcaico folklore. Habiendo sacado del olvido verdaderos tesoros de nuestro folklore moderno.

La estadística adjunta indica el movimiento siempre "*in crescendo*," tanto de grupos como de participantes.

Dirección de los grupos

La dirección de estos grupos las lleva Instructoras de Sección Femenina de Música y Danzas que para realizar su misión, se capacitan en cursos espaciales que periódicamente organiza la Regidora de Cultura. Ellas son la que se desplazan a los pueblos para investigar y recoger toda su pureza la canción o danza expuesta a desparecer, o que desaparecen ante la invasión de lo moderno del despego a lo antiguo y tradicional.

Actividades

Los grupos de Coros y Danzas tienen una actividad continuada dentro de la Península, continuamente son solicitadas para actuar en los diversos congresos internacionales que se celebran en España, Actos Culturales, etc.

Viajes al extranjero

Para los viajes al extranjero se tienen muy en cuenta los siguiente:

Selección de Grupos. Aquellos que alcanzaron los primeros lugares en los Concursos Nacionales y cuya actividad en la Península le hace ser acreedor a esta selección.

Programas

Una vez reconocido el número de grupos que van a desplazarse y que grupos son los seleccionados se confeccionan varios programas de canciones, y danzas para actuaciones de tres o tres horas y media divididas en dos parten con su pequeño descanso intermedio.

En estos programas se procura siempre abarcar los más característicos de nuestro folklore Nacional.

Agrupaciones o federación nacional de conjuntos de danzas y bailes populares

Fines u objetivos principales

1. Aunar los esfuerzos y voluntades de cuantas personas y asociaciones amantes y propulsores de nuestras típicas danzas se hallan en las provincias de toda España, para estudiar y alcanzar con mayor rapidez y eficacia, los medios conducentes a procurar la persistencia más dilatada posible en nuestros pueblos y aldeas, de la práctica de los bailes y danzas tradicionales, práctica que, como es bien sabido, decae más cada día en tale lugares de origen.

2. Lograr con la unión, asimismo, la necesaria fuerza moral, para suscitar en el ánimo de las autoridades oficiales y del Estado, la persuasión de amparar por su parte y ayudar con la generosidad que requiere y merece, la empresa señalada en el anterior aparatado.

3. Conseguir, por las mismas razones, que, dentro de la ayuda y protección susodicha, sean incluidas las que permitan a las asociaciones o *grupos* de las provincias que, a la vez que atienden al referido *empeño*, están por si mismos constituidos en practicantes activos y exhibidores, de nuestras danzas folklóricas, permitan les, decimos, moverse con facilidad y costearse los gastos en los periódicos desplazamientos que para el estudio, captación y recogida de tales danzas, así como para la vigilancia y control del desarrollo y buena marcha de la empresa indicada, han de realizar, forzosamente, a los pueblos y espacios rurales.

4. Estar en contacto continuo los *grupos* de toda España, para comunicarse recíprocamente los problemas y anhelos que, por separado, o ya a la colectividad, en parte, o en bloque, puedan afectar o sentir a los que, por la unión precisamente, cabe hallar remedio y dar satisfacción con facilidad y prontitud mayores, que en el caso de no existir tal unión.

5. Poder reunirse en Congreso, una vez al año, y en una ciudad de España, que cada año se señalaría, las representaciones directivas de los grupos, para intercambiar ideas, impresiones y noticias sobre las cuestiones, que a todos importan, y estudiar a la par, los variados aspectos que se relacionan con la vida social y artística de las agrupaciones, los trabajos y actividades que desarrollan y el modo como se desenvuelve y marcha en los medios aldeanos de las respectivas provincias, el empeño de lograr, la persistencia o vigorización de las tradiciones del baile y la danza. Y con ésto [*sic*?], el tomar los acuerdos pertinentes, para las soluciones, me joramientos [*sic*?], desenvolvimientos, etc. de los asuntos e ideas que en la reunión se expresan o propongan.

6. Promover y fomentar, tanto en España como en el Extranjero, las actuaciones y exhibiciones públicas de los grupos de todas las provincias. Con la propuesta unión, se impone y es factible, lo que sin la misma resultó siempre problemático; el que

por igual y de continuo, tengan todos los *grupos*, nacionales la posibilidad de actual en los escenarios de nuestra nación y del extranjero, siguiendo un régimen alternativo, mediante el cual, las actuaciones se efectuarán distribuyéndose entre todos equitativamente y en pie de igualdad.

7. Obtener un conocimiento exacto no solo de los grupos y conjuntos folklóricos de danza que hay constituidos en España o que pueden constituirse, sino además, y sobre todo, cuales son y donde se hallan los que por la calidad y excelencia de sus ejecuciones y arte, por su perfección, en una palabra, pueden ser seleccionados para actuaciones de *representación* o de excepcional *lucimiento* en ocasiones de concursos internacionales, festejos de gran altura artística, especiales solemnidades, homenaje y recreación a personajes, visitantes y viajeros próceres. etc. etc.

8. Posibilidad grande y eficaz medio de ayuda para el mejor conocimiento y catalogación efectiva de las danzas populares españolas por los informes *más copiosos* que al respecto pueden allegarse con la colaboración unificada de los componentes todos de la Federación.

*"Normas principales que siguen los grupos de coros y danzas." ES-AGA, 51.023 Caja 103.

International Tours of the Coros y Danzas (1947–1952)

The following information was taken from *Alcance y Acción de la Sección Femenina* (Madrid, 1952), 69–70. ES-AHP Málaga, Caja 1683, no. 29492.

1947 Tour

United Kingdom

The Coros y Danzas' first international tour was to the Llangollen International Festival of Folklore in Wales, 1947. Two groups participated, representing provinces in Andalusia (Seville) and the Basque country (San Sebastian).

1948 Tours

United Kingdom

Three troupes of Coros y Danzas returned to the Llangollen International Festival in 1948 in Wales. The regions of Andalusia (Córdoba) and Castile and León (Segovia) were represented, along with El Ferrol del Caudillo, a city in Galicia named after "the Dictator" (Franco).

Argentina, Brazil, Portugal

Eleven troupes of Coros y Danzas performed for the president Juan Perón and his wife Eva Perón (Argentina) and the dictator António de Oliveira Salazar (Portugal). This tour was represented by eleven troupes: Vigo (Galicia), La Coruña (Galicia), Olviedo (Asturias), Bilbao (Basque Country), Logroño (La Roja), Zaragoza (Aragon), Lerida (Catalonia), Caceres (Extremadura), Seville (Andalusia), Malaga (Andalusia), Santa Cruz de Tenerife (Canary Islands).

1949 Tours

United Kingdom

Three troupes of Coros y Danzas competed in the Llangollen International Folklore Festival in Wales for the third time, represented by Carlet (Valencia), Logroño (La Roja), and Caceres (Extremadura).

France

Two troupes of Coros y Danzas competed in the Biarritz Festival of Folklore in Nice, represented by Málaga (Andalusia), and Vigo (Galicia).

France

One troupe of Coros y Danzas competed in the Amélie-les-Bains International Festival of Folklore, represented by Seville (Andalusia).

Switzerland

Four troupes of Coros y Danzas competed in the Lausanne Festival of Folklore, represented by Barcelona (Catalonia), La Coruña (Galicia), and Cádiz (Andalusia).

French Protectorate in Morocco

One troupe of Coros y Danzas performed in the Festival of Rabat, represented by Cádiz (Andalusia).

Italy

Two troupes of Coros y Danzas competed in the International Festival of Folklore in Venice, organized by Ralph Vaughan Williams, represented by Zaragoza (Aragon) and Salamanca (Castile y León).

Peru, Chile, Ecuador, Panama, Colombia, Venezuela, Dominican Republic, Haiti, Puerto Rico

In its second tour of Latin America, eleven troupes of Coros y Danzas perform, represented by Ponte Vedra (Galicia), Torrelavega (Cantabria), San Sebastián (Basque

Country), Huesca (Aragon), Blanes (Catalonia), Astorga (Castile y Leon), Segovia (Castile y Leon), Cieza (Murcia), Palma de Mallorca (Canary Islands), Badajoz (Extremadura), and Córdoba (Andalusia).

1950 tours

Greece, Egypt, Turkey, Lebanon, Jerusalem

Seven troupes performed represented by Santiago de Compostela (Galicia), Olivenza (Extremadura), Granada (Andalusia), San Sebastián (Basque Country), Tarragona (Catalonia), Teruel (Aragon), and Valladolid (Castile y León).

Italy

Five troupes performed in Rome represented by Sitges (Catalonia), Huelva (Andalusia), Palencia (Castile y León), Ruente (Cantabria), and Cheste (Valencia).

French Protectorate of Morocco

Two troupes performed in Casablanca represented by Cádiz (Andalusia) and Tétouan (Spanish Protectorate).

Portugal

Two troupes performed, represented by Badajoz (Extremadura) and Huesca (Andalusia).

United States of America

Three troupes performed in Los Angeles (Hollywood Bowl) and Santa Barbara (Old Spanish Days Fiesta), represented by Málaga (Andalusia) and Zaragoza (Aragon).

1951 Tours

France, Belgium, Italy

Eight troupes performed, representing Bilbao (Basque Country), Caceres (Extremadura), Castellon (Valencia), Lerida (Catalonia), Logroño (La Rioja), Madrid, Zaragoza (Aragon), and Cádiz (Andalusia).

Tangier International Zone

Three troupes performed in the Semana de Tánger, represented by Cádiz (Andalusia), Málaga (Andalusia), and Madrid.

1952 Tours

United Kingdom, France, Belgium, Holland, Germany, Switzerland

Ten troupes performed, representing Teruel (Aragon), El Ferrol de Caudillo (Galicia), Oviedo (Asturias), Santander (Cantabria), Barcelona (Catalonia), Palma de Mallorca (Canary Islands), Palencia (Castile y León), Zamora (Castile y León), Madrid, and Granada (Andalusia).

Between 1953 and 1975 the Coros y Danzas frequented the following additional nations along with those already mentioned: Austria, Canada, Colombia, Cuba, Equatorial Guinea, Ireland, Japan, Latvia, Mexico, Monaco, and Palestine.

Notes

Introduction

1. Ana Ordaz, "El Valle de los Caídos registra una cifra record de visitantes," *El Diario*, September 8, 2018, https://www.eldiario.es/sociedad/valle-caidos-registro-agosto-visitantes_1_1955312.html.
2. Antonio Cazorla-Sánchez, "From Anti-Fascism to Humanism: The Spanish Civil War as a Crisis of Memory," in *Memory and Cultural History of the Spanish Civil War: Realms of Oblivion*, ed. Aurora Gómez Morcillo (Leiden: Brill, 2013), 32; Juan Pablo Fusi Aizpúrua, "El franquismo: la etapa totalitaria (1939–1959)," in *España: sociedad, política y civilización (siglos XIX–XX)*, ed. Jover Zamora and José María (Madrid: Areté, 2001), 728; Michael Richards and Chris Ealham, "History, Memory and the Spanish Civil War: Recent Perspectives," in *The Splintering of Spain: Cultural History and Spanish Civil War, 1936–1939*, ed. Chris Ealham and Michael Richards (Cambridge: Cambridge University Press, 2005), 3.
3. Fundación Nacional Francisco Franco, April 7, 2021, https://fnff.es/.
4. Omar Encarnación, *Democracy without Justice in Spain: The Politics of Forgetting* (Philadelphia: University of Pennsylvania Press, 2014), 3.
5. Ibid., 2.
6. Omar Encarnación, "Reconciliation after Democratization: Coping with the Past in Spain," *Political Science Quarterly* 123, no. 3 (2008): 437.
7. Ulrike Capdepón, "Challenging the Symbolic Representation of the Franco Dictatorship: The Street Name Controversy in Madrid," *History and Memory* 32, no. 2 (Spring/Summer 2020): 100–130.
8. Federación de Asociaciones de Coros y Danzas de España (FACYDE). Accessed November 9, 2018, http://www.danza.es/danza.es/guia-danza/asociaciones/.
9. "los mejores guardianes y difusores de la música y la danza tradicional española, además de unos importantes embajadores de nuestro folklore por todo el mundo, alcanzando un gran prestigio nacional e internacional por su demostrada seriedad y calidad artística." Federación de Asociaciones de Coros y Danzas de España (FACYDE). Accessed November 9, 2018, http://www.danza.es/danza.es/guia-danza/asociaciones/.
10. The website for the Coros y Danzas *de Granada*, for example, provides the following history of their organization: "The recovery, conservation and dissemination of folklore from different regions of our country was the main objective for provincial and local groups of Choirs and Dances of Spain, created from 1939, within the Female Section of the National Movement. Back during the 40s [music instructoras] began to form groups in different locations throughout our province [Granada], where

they researched, recovered, and taught dances that were still performed by elders in the community. . . . With the political changes [in the 1970s], the coming of democracy, and the disbandment of the Sección Femenina, the troupes of Coros y Danzas were at risk of disappearing. But the members intervened and formed their own cultural associations, allowing the work of recovery, conservation, and dissemination of Spanish folklore to continue to this day"; "*La recuperación, conservación y difusión del folclore de las diferentes regiones de nuestro país fue la tarea primordial de los grupos provinciales y locales de Coros y Danzas de España, creados a partir de 1939, dentro de la Sección Femenina del Movimiento Nacional. Allá por los años 40 comienzan a formarse los grupos de las diferentes localidades de nuestra provincia, en los cuales se realizaban las labores de investigación, recuperación y transmisión de danzas que todavía ejecutaban los mayores. . . . Con la transición política, la llegada de la democracia y la desaparición de la Sección Femenina, los Grupos de Coros y Danzas corrieron el riesgo de desaparecer. Fue la intervención de sus miembros, que se constituyeron en asociaciones culturales, lo que permitió que la labor de recuperación, conservación y difusión del folclore español prosiguiera su curso.*" Asociación de Coros y Danzas de Granad, accessed November 1, 2018, http://www.corosydanzasgranada.es/aboutus.html.

11. It is crucial that more research be conducted on how this repertoire, created by messengers of fascist propaganda, continues to bear cultural weight in modern-day Spain after the Franco regime. Based on the few interactions I have had with citizens of Andalusia who are familiar with the Coros y Danzas, a significant number of these modern troupes seem to have connections to far-right politics.

12. Previous studies on the Sección Femenina have focused on official correspondences, speeches, and circulars. These sources, however, do not reveal how these complex power dynamics played out on the ground. Microhistories of individual actors recorded in documents I consulted in the Archivo General de la Administración (AGA) in Madrid and provincial archives throughout Spain show us that the Sección Femenina's power was constantly challenged by male officials of the Spanish government, foreign agents, and impresarios who maintained very different gender ideologies and conceptions of sexual morality. When we catch glimpses of how the Sección Femenina's programs were being interpreted and experienced, a power struggle emerges between male and female Spanish officials that was far more volatile than what previous studies suggest. The most significant studies on the Sección Femenina include the following: Inbal Ofer, "Historical Models, Contemporary Identities: The Sección Femenina of the Spanish Falange and Its Redefinition of the Term 'femininity,'" *Journal of Contemporary History* 40, no. 4 (2005): 663–674; Inbal Ofer, *Señoritas in Blue: The Making of a Female Political Elite in Franco's Spain* (Portland: Sussex Academic Press, 2009); Eva Moreda Rodríguez, "'La mujer que no canta no es . . . ¡ni mujer española!': Folklore and Gender in the Earlier Franco Regime," *Bulletin of Hispanic Studies* 89, no. 6 (2012): 627–644.

13. José Álvarez-Junco, *Mater Dolorosa: La idea de España en el siglo XIX* (Madrid: Taurus, 2001), 45.

14. Ibid.

15. Gemma Pérez Zalduondo, "Racial Discourses in Spanish Musical Literature, 1915–1939," in *Western Music and Race*, ed. Julie Brown (Cambridge: Cambridge University Press, 2007), 213; Matthew Machin-Autenrieth, *Flamenco Regionalism and Musical Heritage in Southern Spain* (London and New York: Routledge, 2017), 80.

16. Pérez Zalduondo, "Racial Discourses in Spanish Musical Literature," 213.

17. William Washabaugh, "The Politics of Passion: Flamenco, Power and the Body," *Journal of Musicological Research* 15, no. 1 (1995): 94; Jonathan Holt Shannon, *Performing al-Andalus: Music and Nostalgia across the Mediterranean* (Bloomington: Indiana University Press, 2015), 128.

18. Joaquim Homs, *Roberto Gerhard and His Music* (Sheffield: Anglo-Catalan Society, 2000), 25, 31; Eva Moreda Rodríguez, *Music and Exile in Francoist Spain* (London: Routledge, 2016), 165.

19. Samuel Llano, *Whose Spain?: Negotiating Spanish Music in Paris, 1908–1929* (New York: Oxford University Press, 2013), 3.

20. Pérez Zalduondo, "Racial Discourses in Spanish Musical Literature," 208; Álvarez-Junco, *Spanish Identity in the Age of Nations*, 246.

21. Álvarez-Junco, *Spanish Identity in the Age of Nations*, 248.

22. Ibid.

23. Ibid., 111.

24. Ibid.

25. Isabelle Rohr, "Productive Hatreds: Radical Segregationist Discourses and the Making of Francoism," in *Interrogating Francoism: History and Dictatorship in Twentieth-Century Spain*, ed. Helen Graham (London: Bloomsbury, 2016), 100.

26. Lorenzo Delgado Gómez-Escalonilla, *Imperio de papel: Acción cultural y política exterior durante el primer franquismo* (Madrid: Consejo superior de investigaciones científicas, 1992), 48; Lorenzo Delgado Gómez-Escalonilla, *Diplomacia franquista y política cultural hacia Iberoamerica, 1939–1953* (Madrid: Consejo superior de investigaciones científicas, 1988), 17; Stephen Ambrose, *Rise to Globalism: American Foreign Policy since 1938* (New York: Penguin, 1988), 175.

27. Geoffrey Jensen, *Irrational Triumph: Cultural Despair, Military Nationalism, and Ideological Origins of Franco's Spain* (Reno: University of Nevada Press, 2002), 84.

28. Pérez Zalduondo, "Racial Discourses in Spanish Musical Literature," 208; Llano, *Whose Spain?*, 52.

29. Álvarez-Junco, *Spanish Identity in the Age of Nations*, 296; Pérez Zalduondo, "Racial Discourses in Spanish Musical Literature," 208.

30. Jensen, *Irrational Triumph*, 84.

31. Llano, *Whose Spain?*, 53.

32. Federico Romero Salvadó, "Building Alliances against the New?: Monarchy and the Military in Industrializing Spain," in *Interrogating Francoism: History and Dictatorship in Twentieth-Century Spain*, ed. Helen Graham (London: Bloomsbury, 2016), 49.

33. Martin Blinkhorn, *Fascism and the Right in Europe, 1919–1945* (Harlow: Longman, 2000), 78.

34. Ibid.; Shlomo Ben-Ami, *Fascism from Above: The Dictatorship of Primo de Rivera in Spain, 1923–1930* (Oxford: Oxford University Press, 1983), 104–106.

35. Stanley Payne, *The Franco Regime: 1936–1975* (Madison: University of Wisconsin Press, 1987), 28.

36. Ibid., 29.

37. Luis Moreno Fernández, *The Federalization of Spain* (London: Routledge, 2001), 56; Maria Thomas, "Twentieth-Century Catholicisms: Religion as Prison, as Haven, as 'Clamp'," in *Interrogating Francoism: History and Dictatorship in Twentieth-Century Spain*, ed. Helen Graham (London: Bloomsbury, 2016), 31; Gómez-Escalonilla, *Imperio de papel*, 122.

38. Thomas, "Twentieth-Century Catholicisms," 31.

39. Ana Aguado, "Citizenship and Gender Equality in the Second Spanish Republic: Representations and Practices in Socialist Culture (1931–1936)," *Contemporary European History* 23, no. 1 (2014): 96, 105.

40. Gómez-Escalonilla, *Imperio de papel*, 122; Moreno Fernández, *The Federalization of Spain*, 56.

41. Thomas, "Twentieth-Century Catholicisms," 36; Helen Graham, "Reform as Promise and Threat: Political Progressives and Blueprints for Change in Spain, 1931–6," in *Interrogating Francoism: History and Dictatorship in Twentieth-Century Spain*, ed. Helen Graham (London: Bloomsbury, 2016), 82–83; Moreno Fernández, *The Federalization of Spain*, 54; Gómez-Escalonilla, *Diplomacia franquista y política cultural hacia Iberoamérica*, 28.

42. Payne, *The Franco Regime*, 35.

43. Ibid., 36.

44. Aguado, "Citizenship and Gender Equality in the Second Spanish Republic," 104.

45. Samuel Pierce, "The Political Mobilization of Catholic Women in Spain's Second Republic: The CEDA, 1931–6," *Journal of Contemporary History* 45, no. 1 (2010): 77.

46. Pierce, "The Political Mobilization of Catholic Women in Spain's Second Republic," 96.

47. Ibid., 77.

48. Ibid., 78; Aguado, "Citizenship and Gender Equality in the Second Spanish Republic," 106.

49. Pierce, "The Political Mobilization of Catholic Women in Spain's Second Republic," 79.

50. Ibid., 74.

51. In 1934, the Falange Española merged with the less-funded but politically similar Juntas de Ofensiva Nacional Sindicalista (Spanish Phalanx of the Councils of the National Syndicalist Offensive).

52. Thomas, "Twentieth-Century Catholicisms," 35; Florentino Portero, *Franco aislado: La cuestión española (1945–1950)* (Madrid: Aguilar, 1989), 27.

53. José Antonio expressed his conception of national unity by coining the phrase "una unidad de destino en lo universal" ("a unity of destiny in universal affairs").

54. Payne, *The Franco Regime*, 58.

55. Ibid., 219–220.

56. Ibid., 58

57. For a detailed study of the humanitarian crimes that took place during the Spanish Civil War, see Paul Preston, *The Spanish Holocaust: Inquisition and Extermination in Twentieth-Century Spain* (London: Harper Press, 2012).

58. Payne, *The Franco Regime*, 219–20.

59. Florentino, *Franco aislado*, 27.

60. Payne, *The Franco Regime*, 199; Thomas, "Twentieth-Century Catholicisms," 28; Jensen, *Irrational Triumph*, 166; Pérez Zalduondo, "Racial Discourses in Spanish Musical Literature," 208, 216.

61. Thomas, "Twentieth-Century Catholicisms," 28, 36; Jensen, *Irrational Triumph*, 166; Payne, *The Franco Regime*, 199; Pérez Zalduondo, "Racial Discourses in Spanish Musical Literature," 208, 216, 218.

62. Richards, *A Time of Silence*, 47; Loren Chuse, *The Cantaoras: Music, Gender and Identity in Flamenco Song* (New York: Routledge, 2003), 104; Daniela Flesler, *The Return of the Moor* (West Lafayette, IN: Purdue University Press, 2008), 58; Moreda Rodríguez, "'La mujer que no canta no es . . . ¡ni mujer española,'" 630; Fusi Aizpúrua, "El franquismo," 727.

    Núñez Seixas, "Nations in Arms against the Invader: On Nationalist Discourses during the Spanish Civil War," in *The Splintering of Spain: Cultural History and the Spanish Civil War, 1936–1939*, ed. Chris Elham and Michael Richards (Cambridge: Cambridge University Press, 2005), 55; Juan Carlos Losada Malverez, *Ideología del ejército Franquista (1939–1959)* (Madrid: Selección Fundamentos, 1990), 286; Graham, "Introduction," 3; Isabelle Rohr, "Productive Hatreds: Radical Segregationist Discourses and the Making of Francoism," in *Interrogating Francoism: History and Dictatorship in Twentieth-Century Spain*, ed. Helen Graham (London: Bloomsbury, 2016), 99.

63. Thomas, "Twentieth-Century Catholicisms," 28, 35; Graham, "Introduction," 4; Juan Pablo Fusi Aizpúrua, "El franquismo: la etapa totalitaria (1939–1959)," in *España: sociedad, política y civilización (siglos XIX–XX)*, ed. Jover Zamora and José María (Madrid: Areté, 2001), 727; Gómez-Escalonilla, *Diplomacia franquista y política cultural hacia Iberoamérica*, 57; Rohr, "Productive Hatreds," 99.

64. Rohr, "Productive Hatreds," 99–102; Graham, "Introduction," 4.

65. Rúben Serém, "A Coup against Change: Repression in Seville and the Assault on Civilian Society," in *Interrogating Francoism: History and Dictatorship in Twentieth-Century Spain*, ed. Helen Graham (London: Bloomsbury 2016), 117; Jensen, *Irrational Triumph*, 167; Richards, *A Time of Silence*, 6; Thomas, "Twentieth-Century Catholicisms," 28, 35; Rohr, "Productive Hatreds," 99, 102.

66. Eric Calderwood, *Colonial al-Andalus* (Cambridge: Cambridge University Press, 2018).

67. Ibid., 170.

68. Moreno Fernández, *The Federalization of Spain*, 56; Rohr, "Productive Hatreds," 104.

69. Rohr, "Productive Hatreds," 104; Moreno Fernández, *The Federalization of Spain*, 13, 56; Chuse, *The Cantaoras*, 103.

70. Moreno Fernández, *The Federalization of Spain*, 56.

71. Richards, *A Time of Silence*, 9.

72. Jean Grugel, *Franco's Spain* (London: Arnold, 1997), 139; Moreno Fernández, *The Federalization of Spain*, 56.

73. Carmen Ortíz García, "The Uses of Folklore in the Franco Regime," *Journal of American Folklore* 112, no. 446 (1998): 479–496; Moreda Rodriguez, "La mujer que no canta no es . . . ¡ni mujer española!," 637.

74. Ortíz García, "The Uses of Folklore in the Franco Regime," 481; Moreda Rodriguez, "La mujer que no canta no es . . . ¡ni mujer española!," 637.

75. Moreda Rodriguez, "La mujer que no canta no es . . . ¡ni mujer española!," 637.

76. Portero, *Franco aislado*, 65; Francisco Sevillano Calero, *Propaganda y medios de comunicación en el franquismo (1936–1951)* (Alicante: Universidad de Alicante, 2003), 101; Juan Linz, "An Authoritarian Regime: Spain," in *Cleavages, Ideologies, and Party Systems: Contributions to Comparative Political Sociology*, ed. Erik Allardt and Yrjö Littunen (Helsinki: Transactions of the Westermaark Society, 1964), 323; Grugel, *Franco's Spain*, 139.

77. Grugel, *Franco's Spain*, 139.

78. Linz, "An Authoritarian Regime," 315.

79. Ibid., 315.

80. Ibid., 292.

81. Ibid., 292.

82. Ibid., 322.

83. Ibid., 294.

84. Ibid., 294.

85. Judith Butler, *Gender Trouble: Feminism and the Subversion of Identity* (New York: Routledge, 1999), 163; Aguado, "Citizenship and Gender Equality in the Second Spanish Republic," 97; Joan Scott, "Gender: A Useful Category of Historical Analysis," *American Historical Review* 91, no. 5 (1986): 1059; Eric Hobsbawm, *The Invention of Tradition* (Cambridge: Cambridge University Press, 2012).

86. Paul Lawrence, *Nationalism: History and Theory* (Harlow: Pearson Education, 2005), 44; Philip Bohlman, "Music before the Nation, Music after Nationalism," *Musicology Australia* 31, no. 1 (2009): 83.

87. For example, Benito Mussolini linked the supposed "Italian race" to ancient Rome, although the contemporary nation of Italy had only been unified since 1861. Jean-Marie Le Pen, former leader of France's far-right National Front, claimed in 1991 that a French "race" was born with the baptism of Clovis in 496 and has continued to carry the "inextinguishable flame that is the soul of France for almost one thousand five hundred years." As late as the 1860s, however, government censuses show that almost a quarter of the population did not speak French. See Lawrence, *Nationalism*, 44.

88. Svetlana Boym, *The Future of Nostalgia* (New York: Basic Books, 2001).

89. Ibid., 37.

90. Ibid.

91. Eckehard Pistrick, *Performing Nostalgia: Migration, Culture and Creativity in South Albania* (Farnham and Burlington: Ashgate, 2015), 36.

92. Ibid.

93. In Chapter 5 of her book *Russian Music and Nationalism*, Marina Frolova-Walker examines how individual composers and folklorists during the early twentieth century developed idealized representations of Russian peasantry into symbols of the

nation's epic past. Collectors of folksong strove for a "rebirth" of the nation's traditional rural cultures while perpetuating myths of a national history and character. These folklorists used musical portrayals of Russia's rural societies to shape a historical narrative of an "original pristine" Russian folk culture uncontaminated by the "corrupting" influences of the West. See Marina Frolova-Walker, *Russian Music and Nationalism from Glinka to Stalin* (New Haven, CT, and London: Yale University Press, 2007).

94. Antonio Cazorla Sánchez, *Fear and Progress: Ordinary Lives in Franco's Spain, 1939–1975* (Chichester: Wiley-Blackwell, 2010), 13.

95. Ibid.

96. Ibid.

97. Cynthia Schneider, "Cultural Diplomacy: Hard to Define, but You'd Know It If You Saw It," *Brown Journal of World Affairs* 13, no. 1 (2006): 191; Andrew Justin Falk, *Upstaging the Cold War: American Dissent and Cultural Diplomacy, 1940–1960* (Amherst: University of Massachusetts Press, 2011), 7; Jessica Gienow-Hecht and Mark Donfried, "The Model of Cultural Diplomacy: Power, Distance, and the Promise of Civil Society," in *Searching for a Cultural Diplomacy*, ed. Jessica Gienow-Hecht and Mark Donfried (New York: Berghahn, 2010), 13.

98. Joseph Nye, "Public Diplomacy and Soft Power," *Annals of the American Academy of Political and Social Science* 616, no. 1 (2008): 94.

99. Danielle Fosler-Lussier, *Music in America's Cold War Diplomacy* (Oakland: University of California Press, 2015), 3.

100. Ibid., 3.

101. Ibid., 8; Damien Mahiet, Mark Ferraguto, and Rebeckah Ahrendt, "Introduction," in *Music and Diplomacy from the Early Modern Era to the Present*, ed. Damien Mahiet, Mark Ferraguto, and Rebeckah Ahrendt (Basingstoke: Palgrave Macmillan, 2014), 2, 6.

102. Clare Croft, *Dancers as Diplomats: American Choreography in Cultural Exchange* (Oxford: Oxford University Press, 2015), 4, 7.

103. Jessica Gienow-Hecht, "What Are We Searching For?: Culture, Diplomacy, Agents, and the State," in *Searching for a Cultural Diplomacy*, ed. Jessica Gienow-Hecht and Mark Donfried (New York: Berghahn, 2010), 10.

104. Karen Johnson-Cartee and Gary Copeland, *Inside Political Campaigns: Theory and Practice* (Westport, CT, and London: Praeger, 1997), 94.

105. Ibid., 94.

106. Ibid., 93.

Chapter 1

1. Carmen Miedes was later made into an official martyr of Nationalist Spain.

2. The description of this scene is derived from photos of the IV Consejo Nacional de la Sección Femenina (IV National Council of the Women's Section) held in the Archivo Regional de la Comunidad de Madrid. ES-ARCM 28079 201 .001 .45630.9.

3. (All translations are by the author unless otherwise specified.) "Para que un pueblo se salve hace falta que alguien se sacrifique, porque las grandes cosas se consiguen con grandes renuncias. Vosotras habéis visto cómo para ganar la guerra han hecho falta miles y miles de muertos. . . . Y aunque de momento tengamos que llevar una vida incómoda, casi retirada, impropia de nuestra edad, a lo largo nos cabrá la gloria de haber contribuido a engrandecer a España . . . todas las mujeres afiliadas podrán tener los conocimientos más elementales de cultura, sabrán del cuidado de los hijos, del arreglo y de la higiene de la casa, y por medio de la Hermandad llegarán a ellas también los conocimientos para el cuidado y selección de animales domésticos, de labores artesanas y de productos de la tierra. . . . Y así, después de todo esto, podremos ofrecerle al Caudillo, al cabo de un año, una labor realizada en cada pueblo de España, una labor, como os decía al principio, realizada de verdad en cada mujer y en cada hogar de la Patria. Camaradas: Por Franco, ¡arriba España!" Pilar Primo de Rivera, "Mensaje a las jefes locales (1940)," in *Discursos, circulares, escritos* (Madrid: Gráficas Afrodisio Aguado, 1943), 31–32.

4. Isabelle Rohr, "'Productive Hatreds': Radical Segregationist Discourses and the Making of Francoism," in *Interrogating Francoism: History and Dictatorship in Twentieth-Century Spain*, ed. Helen Graham (London: Bloomsbury, 2016), 104.

5. Ibid.; Inbal Ofer, "Fragmented Autobiographies: A Style of Writing or Self-Perception? The Case of Pilar Primo de Rivera," *Iberoamericana* 9, no. 3 (2003): 39; Ofer, *Señoritas in Blue*, 28, 55.

6. Rohr, "Productive Hatreds," 104.

7. Ofer, "Historical Models, Contemporary Identities," 663.

8. Angela Flynn, *Falangist and National Catholic Women in the Spanish Civil War (1936–1939)* (New York: Routledge, 2020).

9. Elizabeth Harvey, "International Networks and Cross-Border Cooperation: National Socialist Women and the Vision of a 'New Order' in Europe," *Politics, Religion & Ideology* 13, no. 2 (2002): 150.

10. Ibid.

11. "savia fecunda," "Congreso internacional de la mujer: La Mujer alemana." ES-AGA, (03)051.023, Caja 1086.

12. "formar hombres físicamente sanos." "Congreso internacional de la mujer: La Mujer alemana." ES-AGA, (03)051.023, Caja 1086.

13. "La mujer alemana contribuye a la nacionalización del pueblo alemán explicando, propagando é incubando la doctrina Nacional Socialista á las futuras madres. De esta educación nacional se ocupa principalmente la N.S. Frauenschaft: organiza conferencias y tiene su servicio de propaganda (prensa, radio, film). . . . Estudiando la magnífica labor desarrollada por las organizaciones de la Frauenschaft y N.S.V. se puede apreciar el patriotismo y puro socialismo que inspira y mueve a la mujer alemana que la anima para llevar a cabo una obra que la honra, revela todas sus capacidades y la intensidad é integridad con que trabaja y confirma sus ideales encerrados en la doctrina nacionalista." Ibid.

14. Harvey, "International Networks and Cross-Border Cooperation," 150; Moreda Rodríguez, "La mujer que no canta no es . . . ¡ni mujer española!," 630.

15. Ofer, "Historical Models, Contemporary Identities," 663; Aurora Morcillo, *The Seduction of Modern Spain: The Female Body and the Francoist Body Politics* (Lewisburg, PA: Bucknell University Press, 2010), 92.

16. "Para aquellos que sostienen la errónea impresión de que en España, la mujer 'sólo sirve en la cocina,' para quienes siguen viendo una España de serrallos y de mujeres 'esclavas del matrimonio,' esta magnífica mujer que ha dedicado subida entera a la reivindicación de la mujer española." Francisco Mota, "Asi Canta y Baila España: la Canción Tradicional," *Mañana—Habana*, January 12, 1954. ES-AGA, (03)051.023 12-00647-00004-0177.

17. "sepáis llevar perfectamente una Jefatura local, con sus ficheros, sus estadísticas y sus archivos; toda esta cosa prosaica y pesada, pero indispensable, y para daros un nivel de cultura superior al de las demás mujeres del pueblo, con el fin de que podáis vosotras, decorosamente, tratar con las autoridades y jerarquías locales, con las que, por razón de vuestro cargo, tenéis que estar en continuo contacto." Rivera, "Mensaje a las jefes locales (1940)," 31–32.

18. Concepción Carbajosa Menéndez, *Las profesoras de educación física en España: historia de su formación (1938-1977)* (Oviedo: Universidad de Oviedo, 1999), 13; Ofer, *Señoritas in Blue*, 28–38.

19. Morcillo, *The Seduction of Modern Spain*, 92; Moreda Rodríguez, "La mujer que no canta no es . . . ¡ni mujer española!," 630; Wayne Bowen, "Pilar Primo de Rivera and the Axis Temptation," *The Historian* 67, no. 1 (2005): 62; Ofer, *Señoritas in Blue*, 60.

20. Sección Femenina, "Alcance y acción de la Sección Femenina," (Madrid: Industrias Graficas Magrit, 1953), 3–4. ES–AHP Málaga, Caja 1683, no. 29492.

21. Carbajosa Menéndez, *Las profesoras de educación física en España*, 13.

22. Luis Sárez Fernández, *Cronica de la Sección Femenina y su Tiempo* (Madrid: Asociación Nueva Andadura, 1993), 31; Ofer, "Historical Models, Contemporary Identities," 667.

23. "Con espíritu misionero y nacionalsindicalista, iréis llevando por todas las tierras que conquistan los soldados de Franco el calor y la hermandad de nuestra doctrina." Pilar Primo de Rivera, "Circular de 15 de octubre de 1938," in *Discursos, circulares, escritos* (Madrid: Gráficas Afrodisio Aguado, 1943), 64.

24. "Pero de una manera callada, sin exhibiciones y sin discursos, porque esas cosas no son propias de mujeres, sino, sencillamente, como lo hizo Teresa." Ibid.

25. Xosé-Manoel Núñez Seixas, "Nations in Arms against the Invader," in *The Splintering of Spain: Cultural History and the Spanish Civil War, 1936-1939*, ed. Chris Elham and Michael Richards (Cambridge: Cambridge University Press, 2005), 55.

26. Ofer, "Historical Models, Contemporary Identities," 668; Suárez Fernández, *Crónica de la Sección Femenina y su tiempo*, 31.

27. Kathleen Richmond, *Women and Spanish Fascism: The Women's Section of the Falange, 1934-1959* (London: Routledge, 2003), 42–45.

28. Ofer, "Historical Models, Contemporary Identities," 669.

29. Ibid.; Juan Linz, "An Authoritarian Regime: Spain," in *Cleavages, Ideologies, and Party Systems: Contributions to Comparative Political Sociology*, ed. Erik Allardt and Yrjö Littunen (Helsinki: Transactions of the Westermaark Society, 1964), 323.

30. Ofer, "Historical Models, Contemporary Identities," 668.

">154 NOTES

54 NOTES

31. Gemma Pérez Zalduondo, "De la tradición a la vanguardia: música, discursos e instituciones desde la Guerra Civil hasta 1956," in *Historia de la música en España e Hispanoamérica*, ed. Alberto Gómez Lapuente (Ciudad de México: Fondo de Cultura Económica, 2009), 110; Carmen Ortíz García, "The Uses of Folklore in the Franco Regime," *Journal of American Folklore* 112, no. 446 (1999): 492; Josep Martí Pérez, "Folk Music Studies and Ethnomusicology in Spain," *Yearbook for Traditional Music* 29 (1997): 107–140.

32. Ortíz García, "The Uses of Folklore in the Franco Regime," 492.

33. Gemma Pérez Zalduondo, "Racial Discourses in Spanish Musical Literature, 1915–1939," in *Western Music and Race*, ed. Julie Brown (Cambridge: Cambridge University Press, 2007), 218.

34. Beatriz Martínez del Fresno, "Women, Land and Nation: The Dances of the Falange's Women's Section in the Political Map of Franco's Spain (1939–1952)," in *Music and Francoism*, ed. Gemma Pérez Zalduondo and Gan Quesada (Turnhout: Brepols, 2013), 99–126; Pérez Zalduondo, "Racial Discourses in Spanish Musical Literature," 218.

35. Martínez del Fresno, "Women, Land and Nation," 107; Jean Grugel, *Franco's Spain* (London: Arnold, 1997), 139.

36. Jazz, however, continued to be used at events hosted by Spanish politicians even though any composition in a foreign language was officially banned in 1942 by the vice-secretary of popular education. See Iván Iglesias, "Swinging Modernity: Jazz and Politics in Franco's Spain (1939–1968)," in *Made in Spain: Studies in Popular Music*, ed. Sílvia Martinez and Héctor Fouce (New York: Routledge, 2013), 102.

37. Moreda Rodriguez, "La mujer que no canta no es . . . ¡ni mujer española!," 637.

38. *Cuplé*: a popular song that developed in urban cabarets during the nineteenth century and became associated with the Second Republic. Martínez del Fresno, "Women, Land, and Nation," 107; Fernando Martínez López and Miguel Gómez Oliver, "Political Responsibilities in Franco's Spain," in *Memory and Culture of the Spanish Civil War: Realms of Oblivion*, ed. Arora Morcillo (Leiden and Boston: Brill, 2013), 107; Eva Moreda Rodríguez, *Music Criticism and Music Critics in Early Francoist Spain* (New York: Oxford University Press, 2016), 110.

39. In addition to the present book, Casero-García's *La España que bailó con Franco* (2000) is the only study to date that gives us a detailed account of how the Sección Femenina collected, taught, and performed local Spanish songs and dances. Since Casero-García's publication in 2000, a mountain of material from the Sección Femenina's Department of Music has been donated to national and provincial archives throughout Spain. These include travelogues, personal letters, and manuscripts of musical transcriptions. This new era of transparency allows us a glimpse into the personal experiences of the performers, the power dynamics between male politicians and female administrators, and the way the instructoras adapted their repertoire to an international, cosmopolitan audience. See Estrella Casero-García, *La España que bailó con Franco: Coros y Danzas de la Sección Femenina* (Madrid: Editorial Nuevas Estructuras, 2000), 84.

40. Casero-García, *La España que bailó con Franco*, 90.

41. Ibid.
42. Ibid., 86; Ortíz García, "The Uses of Folklore in the Franco Regime," 482; Manuel García Mateos, *Danzas populares de España* (Madrid: Sección Femenina del Movimiento, 1971), i.
43. Moreda Rodriguez, "La mujer que no canta no es . . . ¡ni mujer española!," 637.
44. Martínez del Fresno, "Women, Land and Nation: The Dances of the Falange's Women's Section in the Political Map of Franco's Spain (1939–1952)," in *Music and Francoism*, ed. Pérez Zalduondo and Gan Quesada (Turnhout: Brepols, 2013), 111.
45. "aspiramos a descorrer el velo de tantos problemas como encierran nuestro folk-lore y del estudio científico de nuestro pasado musical; aspiramos a despertar en nuestro país vocaciones para tales estudios, y a merecer estima mundial por nuestro patrimonio tan rico como ignorado." Higinio Anglés i Pàmies, "Introducción," *Anuario Musical* 1, no. 1 (1946): 3.
46. "No estamos en presentica de un movimiento folklorista entendido como trabajo de erudición. Se trata de algo más sencillo pero más vital e importante." Benito García de la Parra, *Cancionero español (Cuadro tercero)*, (Madrid, c. 1940), i.
47. Ibid.
48. "Whereas men's pursuit of knowledge is commensurate with masculine prowess of the mind, women's reproductive and nurturing functions (menstruation, gestation, lactation) derive from feminine obeisance to the body. Whereas masculinity's mental capacity is manifest in reason, femininity's subjection to the body is associated with susceptibility to feeling. Whereas masculinity produces culture, femininity is bound to nature." Lucy Green, *Music, Gender, Education* (New York: Cambridge University Press, 1997), 14; See also Ellen Koskoff, *A Feminist Ethnomusicology: Writings on Music and Gender* (Urbana: University of Illinois Press, 2014), 81.
49. Maruja Sampelayo always signed her letters and was addressed with the given name Maruja, the diminutive of María.
50. Santiago López-Ríos Moreno and Antonio Juan González Cárceles, *La facultad de filosofía y letras de Madrid en la Segunda República: arquitectura y universidad durante los años 30* (Madrid: Sociedad Estatal de Conmemoraciones Culturales, 2008), 483. Retrieved on October 1, 2019, from http://eprints.ucm.es/8782/1/view.php.pdf.
51. "Relación de danzas para Rabat." ES-AGA, (03)051.023 caja 1460 top. 23/ 25.406–30.103.
52. "unidad de destino en lo universal." Pilar Primo de Rivera, *4 discursos de Pilar Primo de Rivera* (Barcelona: Editora Nacional, 1939), 35; Cécile Stephanie Stehrenberger, "Folklore, Nation, and Gender in a Colonial Encounter: Coros y Danzas of the Sección Femenina of the Falange in Equatorial Guinea," *Afro-Hispanic Review* 28, no. 2 (2009): 235.
53. "No es necesario un número determinado, bastan que sean parejas." "Fandango 'El Gazpacho'"; "El Cangrejo"; "Piconera (Maja gaditana)," ES-AHP Cádiz, Caja 13324, no. 3.
54. This policy changed in the early 1950s for reasons that will be explored later in Chapter 2.

55. "Es natural que pasada esta edad la agilidad, salvo casos extraordinarios, no es la misma ni la resistencia tampoco es igual." "Normas principales que siguen los grupos de coros y danzas," ES-AGA, 51.023 Caja 103.

56. "universitarias, campesinas, empleadas e hijas de familia, sin distinción de clases, unidas solo en su común deseo de servir a España mostrando al mundo la belleza de sus canciones y sus danzas." Script used during a radio broadcast from February 2, 1954. ES-AGA, (03)051.023 Caja 1460 top. 23/25.406–30.103.

57. "Documentos de actividades de la Sección Femenina," ES-CDMA, Fondos de la Sección Femenina R.30.809.

58. "The girls were free this morning. Some went to shop and others went to the beach." "Las chicas tuvieron libre por la mañana. Unas se fueron de compras y otras a la playa." "Informe del viaje a Tánger de los grupos de Coros y Danzas de Madrid, Málaga y Cádiz efectuado en los días 8 al 13 de Julio de 1951." AGA Caja 1460 top. 23/25.406–30.103.

59. For example, the twenty-six-year-old Dolores Rodríguez attained a signature from her father before she toured in Amélie-les-Bains, France, in 1955. AGA (03)051.023 Caja 1460 top. 23/25.406–30.103

60. "El grupo tiene como principal defecto un exceso de soberbia, tal vez propio del carácter bilbaíno que se cree superior al resto de España, sin querer separatistas, sin embargo fueron mejorando durante el viaje incorporándose más al resto de la expedición y demostrando más disciplina en todo." "Informe sobre los grupos que han realizado el viaje a la Argentina 1948," ES–AGA, (03)051.023, Caja 1460 top. 23/25.406–30.103

61. "solo gira en torno a las necesidades de los hombres. . . . y así no haremos exhibiciones públicas, que no son el lugar de una mujer, o argumentos desagradables." Rivera, *4 discursos*, 22.

62. The Delegación Nacional del Frente de Juventudes was a political-administrative body of the FET y de las JONS created in 1940 for the political indoctrination of Spanish youth according to the principles of the Movimiento Nacional. "Programa de los Coros y Danzas," ES-AHP-Málaga, S.1724, Caja 29533. For more on the Frente de Juventudes, see Antonio Alcoba, *Auge y ocaso del Frente de juventudes* (Madrid: San Martin, 2002).

63. "Normas principales que siguen los grupos de Coros y Danzas," AGA Caja (03)051.023, Caja 1460 top. 23/25.406–30.103.

64. "se designan entre las autoridades musicales más competentes." "Normas principales que siguen los grupos de coros y danzas," AGA Caja (03)051.023, Caja 1460 top. 23/25.406–30.103.

65. "Informe de la Delegación Nacional de la Sección Femenina: Regiduría Central de Cultura," ES-AGA 12-00546-005.

66. Timothy Dewaal Malefyt, "'Inside' and 'Outside' Spanish Flamenco: Gender Constructions in Andalusian Concepts of Flamenco Tradition," *Anthropological Quarterly* 71, no. 2 (1998): 64; Michelle Heffner Hayes, *Flamenco: Conflicting Histories of the Dance* (Jefferson, NC: McFarland & Co, 2009), 41.

67. For the present book, I directly refer to eighty-four song, dance, and dress files, most of which are held in Madrid's Biblioteca Nacional.

68. As discussed at the Concluding Remarks, these files still provide the repertoire for modern groups of Coros y Danzas throughout Spain, many of whom proudly trace their lineage to the Sección Femenina.

69. Casero-García, *La España que bailó con Franco*, 91.

70. See ES-BNE: M.SEC.FEM./26/3; M.SEC.FEM./26/6; M.SEC.FEM./26/8; Jaén BNE: M.SEC.FEM./28/8.

71. For example, the musicians Manuel del Águila from Almería and Vicente Sarasa from Cádiz helped their local instructora by recording songs on tape for her to transcribe. See: ES-BNE; M.SEC.FEM./24/5; M.SEC.FEM./24/35; M.SEC.FEM./24/36.

72. "afinación, dicción, interpretación." "Normas y principales que siguen los grupos de Coros y Danzas," AGA Caja (03)051.023, Caja 1460 top. 23/25.406–30.103.

73. "muy afinadas." Regidora Central de Cultura: Informe. ES-AGA, 12-00546-004.

74. "Pronunciación muy floja y desiguales." "Regidora Central de Cultura: Informe." ES-AGA, (03)051.023, 12-00546-026.

75. Daniel Jordan, "Sección Femenina: Documenting and Performing Spanish Musical Folklore during the Early Franco Regime (1939–1953)," *Music and Letters* 101, no. 3 (2020): 544–566.

76. "La alegría y sencillez la convierten en un sentimiento artístico de gran valor." "El niño hermoso," ES-AHP Cádiz, Caja 13327.

77. "la sal de la tierra." "Alegría," ES-AHP Cádiz, Caja no. 13326, no. 3, Tomo I, #5345.

78. "Melodía ingenua, fácil y graciosa." "Terrenilla está bordando," ES-BNE, M.SEC. FEM./26/16.

79. William Washabaugh, *Flamenco: Passion, Politics and Popular Culture* (Oxford: Berg, 1996), 110.

80. "Cursos de Música y danza; Relación de cursos música de 1938 a 1968," ES-AGA, 3.51.23.12 Caja 1087.

81. "This . . . song is very poor and very badly harmonized"; "Esta . . . canción está muy pobre y muy mal armonizada." "Informe," ES-AGA, 3.51.23.12-00546-074.

82. "pueden ser hombres y mujeres o mujeres solas." "Fandango de Grazalema"; "Tanguillo del cangrejo," ES-AHP Cádiz, Caja 13327.

83. "Se adapta muy bien para bailarlo niñas por su ingenuidad y sencillez de movimiento." "Peteneras clásicas" ES-AHP Cádiz, Carpeta num. 4, Libro 1.

84. As we shall see in Chapter 3, men were added to ensembles of Coros y Danzas in 1952 only after intense criticism while touring abroad.

85. Stehrenberger, "Folklore, Nation, and Gender in a Colonial Encounter," 232.

86. Ferrol is a city in the region of Galicia that was officially renamed "Ferrol del Caudillo" during the Franco regime because it was the dictator's birthplace.

87. The Instituto de España was a Francoist organization that was intended to manage and promote Spanish academia across the humanities. In London, the Instituto de España was chiefly responsible for organizing Spanish-language courses. See Margarita Díaz-Andreu García, *Archeological Encounters: Building Networks of Spanish and British Archaeologists in the 20th Century* (Newcastle: Cambridge Scholars, 2012), 156.

88. "Londres 1947." ES-AGA, (03)051.023 Caja 1460 top. 23/25.406–30.103.

89. "Desde ese momento todas notamos el trato poco natural." Ibid.

90. "le dije que creía eran ellos los que tenían que pensar como nos iban a llevar pues aquella no era una fiesta a la que habíamos asistido particularmente y por gusto sino que era una fiesta que les dábamos como representantes de España y que sobre todo ser señoritas la cortesía masculina obligaba a llevarnos a casa a los huéspedes horas de la noche. . . . Bastante rápidamente nos trajo los taxis diciéndoles a las camaradas que les pagaran. Nuestra violencia ante esto fue lo que ni siquiera pude incomodarme y si lo único que pude decirles fue lo que eran muy despreciados de quienes éramos y llegar al Convento les mandaría los taxis al Instituto para que abonaran su importe." Ibid.

91. "Informe del viaje a Tánger de los grupos de coros y danzas de Madrid, Málaga y Cádiz efectuado en los días 8 al 13 de Julio de 1951," ES-AGA, (03)051.023 Caja 60, (Grupo 7, no. 1).

92. This festival will be discussed in more detail in Chapter 3.

93. "Informe del viaje a Tánger de los grupos de coros y danzas de Madrid, Málaga y Cádiz efectuado en los días 8 al 13 de Julio de 1951," ES-AGA, (03)051.023 Caja 60, (Grupo 7, no. 1).

94. "muy alocado." Ibid.

95. "Primero me dijeron (esto durante el camino) que llevaban a las chicas a la feria solo para que las viera la gente y saludaran desde un tablado, pero una vez allí a querían que bailaran. Yo las defendí lo que pude porque el procedimiento de llevarlas derechas del puerto a bailar a unas chicas que además venían mareadas me parecía inhumano, pero cuando a fuerza de ruego yo estaba ya casi dispuesta a ceder, resultó que se subieron al tablado unos flamencos profesionales y entonces ya me negué en rotundo a que bailaran las nuestras, explicando a aquellos señores que teníamos por norma el no hacerlo junto con otros organismos o con profesionales. Entonces ya desistieron." Ibid.

96. "un sitio muy chic, con piscina, pista de baile, mesitas, bonita iluminación etc. etc." Ibid.

97. "Muy agradable ir a cenar y pasar el tiempo, pero no a la hora de hacer una demostración de Coros y Danzas." Ibid.

98. "When the place [a troupe] is going to is unknown, a knowledgeable person must be assigned before the arrival of Choirs and Dances. This time it was Fernando Fuentes, but that did not work. It has to be someone from the Women's Section." "Cuando el lugar a que se va es desconocido debe destacarse una persona entendida, antes de la llegada de Coros y Danzas. Esta vez ha ido Fernando Fuentes pero eso no sirve. Tiene que ser alguien de la Sección Femenina." Ibid.

99. Antonio Cazorla Sánchez, *Fear and Progress: Ordinary Lives in Franco's Spain (1939–1975)* (Chichester: Willey-Blackwell, 2010), 64; Morcillo, *The Seduction of Modern Spain*, 92.

100. Morcillo, *The Seduction of Modern Spain*, 92.

101. Koskoff, *A Feminist Ethnomusicology*, 79.

102. Ibid., 86.

103. Tola Korian, "The Venice Festival: Some Impressions of a Visitor," *Journal of the International Folk Music Council* 2, no. 20 (1950): 3.
104. Editorial, *Journal of the International Folk Music Council* 2, no. 20 (1950): 1.
105. Korian, "The Venice Festival," 3.
106. Participating countries included Austria, Belgium, Canada, Denmark, France, Germany, Indonesia, the Republic of Ireland, Israel, Italy, Netherlands, Norway, Spain, Sweden, Switzerland, Turkey, United Kingdom, and United States of America. See "Report of the Second Meeting of the General Conference Held in Conjunction with the International Folk Music Festival and Congress in Venice." Retrieved on February 11, 2021, from https://ictmusic.org.
107. Korian, "The Venice Festival," 3.
108. Pamphlet, "First International Folk Music Festival," ES-AGA, (03)051.023 Caja 1460 top. 23/25.406–30.103.
109. Editorial, "Some Reflections on the Venice Festival and Congress," *Journal of the International Folk Music Council* 2, no. 20 (1950): 2.
110. Letter from Karpeles to Rivera, March 24, 1949, (03)051.023 Caja 1460 top. 23/25.406–30.103.
111. "Eisteddfod" is a Welsh competitive arts festival. Letter from Karpeles to Rivera, August 16, 1949. (03)051.023 Caja 1460 top. 23/25.406–30.103.
112. Ibid.
113. Letter from Karpeles to Rivera, August 16, 1949, (03)051.023 Caja 1460 top. 23/25.406–30.103.
114. Lauren Chuse, *The Cantaoras: Music, Gender, and Identity in Flamenco Song* (New York: Routledge, 2003), 267.
115. Letter from Karpeles to Rivera, August 11, 1949, (03)051.023 Caja 1460 top. 23/25.406–30.103.
116. "Report of the Second Meeting of the General Conference Held in Conjunction with the International Folk Music Festival and Congress in Venice." Retrieved on February 11, 2021, from https://ictmusic.org.
117. Our London Music Critic, "Songs and Dances of Spain," *The Scotsman*, February 23, 1952, AGA, (03)051.023 Caja 60 (Grupo 7, no. 1).
118. "Stole Theatre: Songs and Dances of Spain," *The Times*, February 20, 1952, retrieved on September 5, 2019, from *The Times Digital Archive*: http://tinyurl.gale.com/tinyurl/BdZpx4.
119. G.S., "Spanish Serenade: Songs and Dances of Spain." *Theatre*, March 1, 1952, ES-AGA, (03)051.023 Caja 1460 top. 23/25.406–30.103.
120. G.S., "Spanish Serenade."
121. Ibid.
122. Ibid.
123. Ibid.
124. Carol Hess, *Sacred Passions: The Life and Music of Manuel de Falla* (Oxford and New York: Oxford University Press, 2005), 218.
125. "Spanish Serenade: Songs and Dances of Spain," *Theatre*, March 1, 1952, (03)051.023 Caja 1460 top. 23/25.406–30.103.

126. "84 Top Spanish Showmen Booked," *Talespinner: Lackland Air Force Base*, October 29, 1953.

127. Danielle Fosler-Lussier, *Music in America's Cold War Diplomacy* (Oakland: University of California Press, 2015), 3.

128. Martínez del Fresno, "Women, Land and Nation," 99–126; Grugel, *Franco's Spain*, 139; Moreda Rodriguez, "La mujer que no canta no es . . . ¡ni mujer española!," 630.

129. Linz, "An Authoritarian Regime," 323.

Chapter 2

1. The *sardana* is a traditional circle dance of Catalonia. The *chistu*, sometimes spelled "*txistu*," is a traditional Basque flute.

2. "Levante" refers to the eastern regions of Spain, not the "Levant" of the Eastern Mediterranean.

3. "Nos metimos en la Falange porque España no nos gustaba. Y la Falange cambió todo nuestro ser. De frívolas e insustanciales que éramos antes, nos hizo darnos cuenta de que podíamos servir para algo, de que en España había una música que desconocíamos, de que había montes, de que había ríos, de que había mares que nos unían con el mundo, de que había hombres capaces de morir por España. Que el ser español es una de las pocas cosas serias que se pueden ser en la vida. . . . Cuanto todos los españoles tengan metido dentro de sí las consignas de Falange Española Tradicionalista y de las J.O.N.S., cuando los catalanes sepan cantar las canciones de Castilla; cuando en Castilla se conozcan también las sardanas y se toque el 'chistu'; cuando del cante andaluz se entienda toda la profundidad y toda la filosofía que tiene en vez de conocerlo a través de los tabladillos zarzueleros; cuando las canciones de Galicia se canten en Levante; cuando se unan cincuenta o sesenta mil voces para cantar una misma canción, entonces sí que habremos conseguido la unidad entre los hombres y entre las tierras de España." Pilar Primo de Rivera, "Discurso de Pilar Primo de Rivera en el III Consejo Nacional de la Sección Femenina de F. E. T. y de las J. O. N. S. (Zamora), 1939," in *Pilar Primo de Rivera: Escritos* (Madrid: Sección Femenina de F.E.T. y de las J.O.N.S., 1942), 10.

4. For example, "En el portal de belén," ES-BNE, M.SEC.FEM./25/1; ES-BNE, M.SEC.FEM./25/27; "Hacia balan," ES-BNE, M.SEC.FEM./25/29; "Zapatillas encamadas," ES-BNE, M.SEC.FEM./26/6; "Canción de cuna ¡cuando mi niña llorosa!," ES-BNE, M.SEC.FEM./28/6; "Malagueña," ES-CDMA, R.30.809; "El cebollinero," ES-AHP, Cádiz, Caja no. 13326, no. 3 Tomo 1; "La Torre," "Cuando Herodes," "Era la media noche," "La Pastorcita," "La virgen va caminando," "Hacia Belén," ES-AHP, Cádiz, Caja no. 13327, tomo 5.

5. "Es un baile propiamente del campo ya que es donde se acostumbra a bailarlo, aunque en la actualidad tan sólo lo conocen los ancianos por lo que es difícil se vea bailar, ya que la juventud lo desconoce . . . no se ha sacado de ningún archivo sino de los ancianos de la localidad." "Fandango Agarrao," AHP-Cádiz, Caja 13324, Libro 2, no. 6.

6. "De los ancianos de la localidad ya que no existen documentos alguno sobre este baile, tan solo . . . los ancianos que lo conocieron en su tiempo." "Fandango de callejero," AHP-Cádiz, Caja 13324, Carpeta 4 Libro 1.

7. "This dance, born in the mountains around Grazalma, was danced by old women of today when they were children." "Este baile nacido en la sierra de Grazalma lo bailaban las ancianas de hoy cuando eran niñas enseñados por sus abuelas." " 'La Bata' de Grazalema," ES-AHP, Cádiz, Caja 13324, Carpeta 4, Libro 1.

8. "It is collected to Toribio Campos Muñoz of about 80 years. He only knows that both were danced a lot in his time." "Es recogida a Toribio Campos Muñoz de unos 80 años. Sólo sabe que ambas cosas se bailaban mucho en sus tiempos." ES-BNE, M.SEC. FEM./27/29.

9. Ibid.

10. "Gitana," ES-AHP Cádiz, Caja 13325, num. 3, libro 1.

11. "No existan. Solo lo hay (muy parecidos) en la fábrica de muñecos 'Marín' en dicho pueblo." Ibid.

12. Maja/o: A fashionable working-class citizen of Madrid of the late eighteenth and early nineteenth centuries. "The costume, characteristic of the *maja jerezana*, is reproduced from the famous paintings of Goya. They are very colorful garments"; "El traje es típico de la maja jerezana, está reproducido de los célebres cuadros de Goya. Son de muy vistoso colorido," "Maja jerezana," AHP-Cádiz, Caja No. 13324, Libro. 2 H Danzas Cádiz Tomo I, *fandango*; Carpeta num. 4, Libro 1.

13. "The accompanying information is taken from (indicate documents, archive, etc): The work 'Popular Dances of Small Town of the Sierra' by an anonymous author, written in the year 1797." "Los datos que se acompañan están tomados de (indicar documentos, archivo, etc.): La obra 'Danzas populares de algunos pueblos de la Sierra,' de autor anónimo, escrita en el año 1797." "El gazpacho," ES-AHP Cádiz, Caja 13324 Libro 3, Tomo 1, Carpeta 3.

14. The second letter in the initials of the organist as recorded on the song file by the instructora Angustias Franco is almost certainly a typo due to the use of a type-writer ("F" in place of "R"). Rafael Salguero Rodríguez was a *maestro de capilla* of the Cathedral of Granada during the early twentieth century. Transcriptions made by Salguero are currently held in the Archives of the Cathedral of Granada, although this seems to be entirely liturgical music. I have yet to find the transcription of the fandango to which Miguel del Castillo set his choreography of "La reja." See José López-Calo, *Catálogo del Archivo de Música de la Catedral de Granada, Vol. 1 Catálogo (I)* (Granada: Junta de Andalucía, 1991), 57–59.

15. "The music is an authentic Granada fandango collected by D. F. Salguero, organist of the Cathedral of Granada who did not provide details because he had already died." "La música es auténtica de un fandango granadino recogido por D. F. Salguero organista de la Catedral de granada sin poder tener detalles porque ya ha muerto." "La reja," ES-CDMA, R.30.809.

16. Ibid.

17. The Spanish word "*Gitano*" usually refers to the settled Roma of Spain.

18. "Don Miguel del Castillo was inspired by the gypsy dances of the Sacromonete when he choreographed the steps. There are choreographic influences of the *arbolá*, as can be seen in the starting posture, the turns, shifting steps, isolated and whole figures that clearly show us their origin." "D. Miguel del Castillo se inspire en las danzas gitanas del Sacromonte por elegir sus pasos y se observan influencias corográficas de la arbolá por cuanto en su formación entran, ruedas, desplazamientos, figuras aisladas y de conjunto que nos demuestran claramente su procedencia." "La reja," ES-CDMA, R.30.809.

19. "canción puede tener una gran belleza musical y no ser folklórica." "El gazpacho," ES-AHP Cádiz, Caja 13324.

20. Ibid.

21. "Este villancico es muy popular y antiguo, conocido y cantado por todas las clases sociales desde nuestros abuelos y antepasados." "'Alegría alegría,'" ES-BNE, M.SEC. FEM./13/64.

22. "lo hemos cantado de niños, nosotros, nuestros padres, nuestros abuelos. No hay duda de su antigüedad y autenticidad y no nos explicamos cómo no figura en alguien cancionero." "Picaros gitanos," ES-BNE, 29/56 M.SEC. FEM./29/56.

23. Eva Moreda Rodríguez, *Music Criticism and Music Critics in Early Francoist Spain* (New York: Oxford University Press, 2016), 103.

24. Ibid.

25. Blas Infante, *Ideal Andaluz. Varios estudios acerca del renacimiento de Andalucía* (Sevilla, 1915); Blas Infante, *La Verdad sobre el Complot de Tablada y el Estado libre de Andalucía* (Sevilla, 1931).

26. Adolf Schulten, *Tartessos. Ein Beitrag zur ältesten Geschichte des Westens* (Hamburg: L. Friedrichsen & Co., 1922).

27. "Un canto que ya estaba levantado en Andalucía desde Tartesí, amasado con la sangre del África del Norte y probablemente con vetas profundas de los desgarrados ritmos jidíos, padres hoy de toda la gran música eslava." Federico García-Lorca, "Arquitectura de Cante jondo," *F. García Lorca: Prosa, 1* (Madrid: Ediciones Akal, 1994), 230.

28. Such references do not seem to have posed a huge ideological problem for the Sección Femenina. While the instructoras never directly cite Blas Infante, they frequently refer to García Lorca's essays, poems, and song collections. This inclusion may be because García Lorca's international fame was too pronounced to simply ignore. A surviving script that was read aloud during performances of the Coros y Danzas provides the audience with the origins of *Los muleros*, a dance from the neighborhood in Granada called the Albaicín, harmonized and adapted by García Lorca: "[This is a] popular dance collected by the poet Federico García Lorca of Granada from a Christmas Carol of the Albaicín [neighborhood of Granada]. This cheerful, lively, and funny dance is to the rhythm of 'Bulerias' and is currently sung with the poet's words." "Danza popular recogida por el poeta granadino Federico García Lorca de un Villancico Albaicinero. Su baile es alegre movido y gracioso a ritmo de 'Bulerías' y en la actualidad se canta con la letra de dicho poeta." "Los muleros," ES-CDMA, R.30.809.

29. "¿Eran estas danzas el origen del fandango cortijero? No hay datos escritos que puedan confirmarlos pues el fandango se transmite a través de las generaciones solo de una forma oral pero el estudio comparativo del Folklore español nos lleva a la conclusión de que esta hipótesis está totalmente fundamentada." Ibid.

30. "Fandango de Almuñecar," ES-CDMA, Fondos de la Sección Femenina R.S.93.

31. Peña Tú is a sandstone outcrop in the region of Asturias on which paintings and engravings were made during the megalithic age.

32. Original English from a narration from a North American tour, 1953. ES-AGA, (03)051.023, Caja 12/666 top. (03)14.51.

33. Ibid.

34. Ibid.

35. Stanley Brandes, "The Sardana: Catalan Dance and Catalan National Identity," *Journal of American Folklore* 103, no. 407 (1990): 30.

36. "Viva Pérez de Guzmán, / viva su bendita tierra, / y viva también Graná." ES-CDMA, Fondos de la Sección Femenina R.S.93.

37. See Gil y Zárate, *Guzmán El Bueno. drama en cuatro actos* (London: FB&C Ltd., 2017).

38. "Documentos de actividades de la Sección Femenina," ES-CDMA, Fondos de la Sección Femenina, R.S.93.

39. Ibid.

40. "Sultán: (Se arrodilla ante la Virgen) El hombre mas atroz, mas atrevido tenéis, Señora, a vuestros pies, rendido. Pues hasta ahora . . . ¡Que delicia, que gloria, que contento! Hoy he de hacer de fino esclavo alarde recibiendo el bautismo en esta tarde. Y aunque tenéis a todos mil soldados por fuerza de armas cautivados por esa obligación mas excelente, tus esclavos te aclaman justamente todos piden tu gracia y asimismo sienten se les retarde ya el bautismo." "Fiestas de moros y cristianos," ES-CDMA, PAR D 162.

41. Carmen Ortíz García, "The Uses of Folklore in the Franco Regime," *Journal of American Folklore* 112, no. 446 (1998), 483.

42. The term "moor" is a highly derogatory term that refers to Muslims and Berbers who lived in the Iberian Peninsula during the Middle Ages. Of course, this was ironic, considering that the Nationalists heavily relied on Moroccan troops during the Spanish Civil War. See Michael Richards, *A Time of Silence: Civil War and the Culture of Repression in Franco's Spain, 1936–1945* (Cambridge: Cambridge University Press, 1998), 49.

43. Jean Grugel, *Franco's Spain* (London: Arnold, 1997), 139; Brandes, "The Sardana," 35.

44. Josep Benet, *L'intent franquista de genocidi cultural contra Catalunya* (Barcelona: Abadia de Montserrat, 1995); Francesc Vilanova, "Did Catalonia Endure a (Cultural) Genocide?," *Journal of Catalan Intellectual History* 1, no. 11 (2018): 28.

45. Vilanova, "Did Catalonia Endure a (Cultural) Genocide?," 20.

46. Beatriz Martínez del Fresno, "Women, Land and Nation: The Dances of the Falange's Women's Section in the Political Map of Franco's Spain (1939–1952)," in *Music and Francoism*, ed. Gemma Pérez Zalduondo and Gan Quesada (Turnhout: Brepols, 2013), 109.

47. Ortíz García, "The Uses of Folklore in the Franco Regime," 488.

48. Ibid.

49. "La primera cosa que llama la atención al contemplar este espectáculo es la diversidad del folklore español. Cada provincia tiene sus trajes, sus danzas, su música totalmente diferente de las otras y toda elle refleja mejor que cualquier estudio de erudito podría nacerlo, el alma de cada una y de España también." "Viaje a Marruecos 1955: Actuación de 'Canciones y danzas de España." ES-AGA, (03)051.023, Caja1460 top. 23/25.406-30.103.

50. Original English from a narration from a North American tour, 1953. ES-AGA, (03)051.023, Caja 12/666 top. (03)14.51.

51. Ibid.

52. Ibid.

53. Ibid.

54. Ibid.

55. Grugel, Franco's Spain, 142; Ortiz, "The Uses of Folklore by the Franco Regime," 489.

56. Fernando Martínez López and Miguel Gómez Oliver, "Political Responsibilities in Franco's Spain," in Memory and Culture of the Spanish Civil War: Realms of Oblivion, ed. Arora Morcillo (Leiden and Boston: Brill, 2013), 105.

57. Ibid.

58. Stanley Payne, The Franco Regime: 1936–1975 (Madison: University of Wisconsin Press, 1987), 48.

59. Original English from a narration from a North American tour, 1953. ES-AGA, (03)051.023, Caja 12/666 top. (03)14.51.

60. Lauren Chuse, The Cantaoras: Music, Gender, and Identity in Flamenco Song (New York: Routledge, 2003), 104.

61. "Su gracia resida en la sencillez, tosquedad e ímpetu que todo él respira, es una agitación de saltos rítmicos y vueltas, propios de pozos y mozas fuertes, curtidos por el sol que nada saben de estilización en la figura . . . es antiquísimo y se baila en la actualidad con toda su pureza." "Fondos de la Sección Femenina," ES-CDMA, R.30.809, Caja 1, Carpeta 3.

62. "El traje de coquinera lo usaba la clase pobre y era esencialmente—vestido cotidiano, de trabajo. Derivado del traje de gitana, tiene modificaciones que buscan la sencillez y la comodidad. Más corto, para no entorpecer los movimientos. Adornos simples y sobrio." "Tanguillo de la isla," ES-AHP Cádiz, Caja 13324.

63. Antonio Cazorla Sánchez, Fear and Progress: Ordinary Lives in Franco's Spain, (1939–1975) (Chichester: Willey-Blackwell, 2010), 6.

64. Ibid., 6.

65. Ibid., 12.

66. Payne, The Franco Regime, 390; Cazorla Sánches, Fear and Progress, 9.

67. Cazorla Sánchez, Fear and Progress, 9.

68. Ibid., 10.

69. Ibid., 9; Joan Esteban, "The Economic Policy of Francoism: An Interpretation," in Spain in Crisis: The Evolution and Decline of the Franco Régime, ed. Paul Preston (Hassocks: Harvester Press, 1976), 90.

70. Cazorla Sánches, Fear and Progress, 8.

71. "los hombres y las tierras . . . y las clases de España . . . que no se malogre ningún talento por falta de medios económicos." Pilar Primo de Rivera, *4 discursos de Pilar Primo de Rivera* (Barcelona: Editora Nacional, 1939), 22–23.

72. "los que trabajan, que merecen toda nuestra consideración, y los vagos, a los que no se les concederá jamás ningún privilegio. . . . El estado nacionalsindicalista no tributa la menor consideración a los que no empleen función alguna y aspiren a vivir como convidados a costa del esfuerzo de los demás." Ibid.

73. Martínez del Fresno, "Women, Land and Nation," 99–126; Grugel, *Franco's Spain*, 139; Moreda Rodriguez, "La mujer que no canta no es . . . ¡ni mujer española!," 627–644.

Chapter 3

1. "En la santa ciudad [de Chauen] la bella iluminación de su Alcazaba, junto al rumor del agua de sus fuentes, canta un himno de paz y de alegría, de fraternidad, que la gran familia hispano-marroquí allí presente, jubilosamente exteriorizaba. Frente a la ciudad los altos picachos del Kalaá . . . son también nidos de sosiego, de laboriosidad y de convivencia. . . . Los Coros y Danzas de España, no había más remedio que evocar tiempos pasados como un puente de oro tendido entre aquellos y estos tiempos." "Paz y Alegría en Chauen," Telegrama del Rif, July 10, 1951. ES-AGA, (03)051.023 Caja 1460 top. 23/25.406–30.103.

2. Susan Gilson Miller, *A History of Modern Morocco* (Cambridge: Cambridge University Press, 2013), 42.

3. Ibid., 42

4. Ibid., 46.

5. Hisham Aidi, "The Interference of al-Andalus: Spain, Islam, and the West," *Social Text* 24, no. 2 (2006): 68; Stanley Payne, *The Franco Regime: 1936–1975* (Madison: University of Wisconsin Press, 1987), 418.

6. Aidi, "The Interference of al-Andalus," 68.

7. Jonathan Holt Shannon, *Performing al-Andalus: Music and Nostalgia Across the Mediterranean* (Bloomington: Indiana University Press, 2015), 131.

8. Miller, *A History of Modern Morocco*, 147.

9. Ibid., 150.

10. Jonathan Wyrtzen, "National Resistance, Amazighité, and (Re-)imagining the Nation in Morocco," in *Revisiting the Colonial Past in Morocco*, ed. Driss Maghraoui (London and New York: Routledge, 2013), 185.

11. Ibid.

12. Ali Al Tuma, "Moros y Cristianos: Religious Aspects of the Participation of Moroccan Soldiers in the Spanish Civil War (1936–1939)," in *Muslims in Interwar Europe: A Transcultural Historical Perspective*, ed. Umar Ryad Bekim Agai and Mehdi Sajid (Leiden and Boston: Brill, 2016), 151; Eric Calderwood, *Colonial Al-Andalus: Spain and the Making of Modern Moroccan Culture* (Cambridge, MA, and London: Harvard University Press, 2018), 169.

13. Calderwood, *Colonial Al-Andalus*, 169. In fact, Franco himself spent more than a decade in Morocco prior to the regime and utilized his garrison in Melilla to launch one hundred thousand Muslim mercenaries into Iberia at the beginning of the Spanish Civil War. See Shannon, *Performing al-Andalus*, 131.

14. Calderwood, *Colonial Al-Andalus*, 169.

15. Clare Croft, *Dancers as Diplomats: American Choreography in Cultural Exchange* (Oxford: Oxford University Press, 2015), 5; Cynthia Schneider, "Cultural Diplomacy: Hard to Define, but You'd Know It If You Saw It," *Brown Journal of World Affairs* 13, no. 1 (2006): 192.

16. Jean Grugel, *Franco's Spain* (London: Arnold, 1997), 139.

17. John Haines, "The Arabic Style of Performing Medieval Music," *Early Music* 29, no. 3 (2001): 370.

18. Julián Ribera, *La música de las Cantigas. Estudio sobre su origen y naturaleza* (Madrid: Real Academia Española, 1922); Julián Ribera, *La música andaluza medieval en las canciones de trovadores, troveros y minnesinger* (Madrid: Real Academia Española, 1922), 5.

19. Ismael Fernández de la Cuesta, "Relectura de la Teoría de Julián Ribera sobre la influencia de la música arábigo en las cantigas de santa maría en las canciones de los trovadores, troveros y Minnesingers," *Revista de Musicología* 16, no. 1 (1993): 385.

20. Gerhard Steingress, "El cante flamenco como manifestación artística, instrumento ideológico y elemento de identidad cultural andaluza," in *Flamenco y nacionalismo*, ed. Gerhard Steingress and Enrique Balantás (Seville: Universidad de Sevilla, 1997), 32–53.

21. William Washabaugh, "The Politics of Passion: Flamenco, Power and the Body," *Journal of Musicological Research* 15, no. 1 (1995): 94; Shannon, *Performing al-Andalus*, 128.

22. Eric Calderwood, "In Andalucía, There Are No Foreigners," *Journal of Spanish Cultural Studies* 15, no. 4 (2014): 410.

23. Rodolfo Benumeya, *Andalucismo africano* (Madrid: Instituto de Estudios Africanos, 1953), 412; Rodolfo Benumeya, *Claroscuro andaluz* (Madrid: Editora Nacional, 1966).

24. Calderwood, *Colonial al-Andalus*, 170.

25. Eric Calderwood, "Moroccan Jews and the Spanish Colonial Imaginary (1903–1951)," *Journal of North African Studies* 24, no. 1 (2019): 87.

26. Ali Al Tuma, *Guns, Culture and Moors* (London and New York: Routledge, 2018), 154.

27. Ibid.

28. For more information on *Telegrama del Rif*, see Francisco Sevillano Calero, *Propaganda y medios de comunicación en el franquismo (1936–1951)* (Alicante: Universidad de Alicante, 1998), 85.

29. "La prensa que publican en idioma árabe o en español ha destacado la visita de los coros y dances . . . tiene interés para el mundo de cultura arábiga en el Mar Mediterráneo. . . . En el repertorio melódico español la medida carácter parece ser la parte que pertenece al mismo fondo musical que los turcos y lo que dice es genuino que está en el fondo las composiciones esenciales han tenido su origen en el Sur de la Península, es decir, en Andalucía que fue la base del Sestado hispano-arabo medieval.

Así los Coros y Danzas de España no resultan cosa extraña para el sentimiento estético ni para el recuerdo patriótico de los turco, sirio, libanés y palestino. . . . Ellos esperan que las muchachas de los coros y las danzas de España se lleven a cabo un día con la misma sustancia de arte y sensibilidad común de Marruecos en Egipto y Siria en Jordania . . . un lodo en el Levante mediterráneo donde lo hispano en contra de los familiares." Gil Benumeya, "Coros y Danzas de España en el mundo árabe," *El telegrama del Rif*, January 12, 1950. ES-AGA, 14-51, 12/643.

30. "la asimilación de otras culturas como nutrición para el futuro." "Bachillerato curso cuatro: Interpretación falangista de la Historia de España," ES-AGA, 51.023, 12/421.

31. "como transmisora de lo oriental al mundo cristiano." Ibid.

32. Rafael Benedito, *Historia de la música: La música a través de los tiempos* (Madrid: Sección Femenina de F.E.T de la J.O.N.S, 1946), 39–40; Abraham Zevi Idelsohn, "Parallelen zwischen gregorianischen und hebräischorientalischen Gesangsweisen," *Zeitschrift für Musikwissenschaft* 4 (1921/1922): 515–524.

33. Richard Taruskin, *Oxford History of Western Music: Music from the Earliest Notations to the Sixteenth Century* (Oxford: Oxford University Press, 2010), 7–9.

34. For the history and analysis of the reception of *cante jondo* during the twentieth century, see Timothy Mitchell, *Flamenco Deep Song* (New Haven, CT: Yale University Press, 1994).

35. "aportaremos el de un autor moderno que encuentra un semejanza no solamente en espíritu y en intensidad expresiva, sino también en la forma melódica . . . entre ciertos cantos que aun hoy día se conservan y practican en las sinagogas y ciertas modalidades del 'cante jondo,' como la saeta, la seguidilla y el fandanguillo, llegando, incluso a suponer que la denominación de 'cante jondo' sea una transformación de Jon do, derivación a que puede haber llegado bajo la presión del desgaste vulgar de pronunciación la voz Jom tob, cuya traducción es 'díz de fiesta,' o, aún más literalmente, 'buen día.' Faltos de elementos de juicio, y no habiendo ahondado en la investigación nos limitamos a aportar este dato a guisa de curiosidad." Rafael Benedito, *Historia de la Música* (Madrid: Almena. Rústica, 1960), 39–40.

36. Máximo José Kahn (published under pseudonym Medina Azahara), "Cante jondo y cantares sinagogales," *Revista de Occidente* 88 (1930): 53–84.

37. Mario Martín Gijón, "Una reflexión sobre el judaísmo desde el exilio republicano español: sobre 'Arte y Torá'. Libro inédito de máximo José Kahn," *Hispanic Review* 81, no. 3 (2013): 285–307.

38. "El folklore español es el más rico de los europeos, incomparablemente más variado y emotivo que el de cualquiera Nación. . . . La fogosa inspiración oriental se ha encontrado en nuestras tierras con la dulzura céltica y como matiz fundido de dos luces contrarias. . . . Resucitar, entonar en fondos armónicos estos cuadros maravillosos y ofrecérnoslos para regalo de nuestros ojos y nuestros oídos es alta labor de Patria y de arte." "Ángel Barrios." ES-AGA, (03)051.023, Caja 1086.

39. The reference to *cante jondo* may have been made to emphasize the shared musical characteristics between the traditional repertoires of Andalusia and the Arabic world even though it was inconsistent with the Sección Femenina's own performance

practices. "Narration from North American Tour," 1953. ES-AGA, (03)051.023, 14
51–12/00666.

40. "Historial de la Danza: El centro de dispersión se supone que es en España tarifa.
Su introducción parece remontarse al siglo 9º después de J.C. y la persona que lo
introdujo se supone que fue alguno de los más adisctos [sic] servidores de Omar-ben-
Hafsum que como se sabido fundo un reino en la serranía de Ronda, comprendiendo
como centro la montaña de Balastro." "Ocho y zangano" (1948). ES-AHP Cádiz, Caja
13324, Carpeta núm. 4, Libro 1.

41. "Fandango agarrao" (1950). ES-AHP Cádiz, Caja 13324, Carpeta núm. 4, Libro 1.

42. Manuela Cortés García, "La mujer árabe y la música. Transculturación en el área
mediterránea," *Música oral del sur* 5 (2002): 91–106 at 92 f.n. 5.

43. "The Moors that remained in the country after the Reconquista preserved their
own songs and dances. The *Zambra*, *Leyla*, and *Caña* were adapted to the popular
customs of the victorious [Christians]. This was also the case of the *Polo*, *Tirana*,
Rondeña, *Olé*, *Malagueña*, *Caña*, etc." "Los moros que quedaron en el país después de
la reconquista, conservaron sus cantos y bailes. Su Zambra, Leyla y Caña se adaptaron
a las costumbres populares de los vencedores. Así el Polo, Tirana, Rondeña, Olé,
Malagueña, Caña, etc." Dance File for "La Caña," 1957. ES-AHP Cádiz, Caja 13324.

44. "a unas bellas jóvenes cristianas que habitaban en un Castillo de Tarifa." "Fandango de
Tarifa," 1948. ES-AHP Cádiz, Caja 13324, Carpeta núm. 4, Libro 1.

45. Ibid.

46. "Cuando una chica de Cádiz sale a bailar 'El chacarrá' envuelto en una capa que
cubre su cara, inevitablemente se recuerda a las mujeres del Antiguo Islam. Y cuando
bailan al ritmo de las castañuelas, las cuerdas de la guitarra llevan la mente muy
atrás en el tiempo, hacia los tiempos de los Califas de Córdoba. ¿Quién no olvida
sus preocupaciones mientras mira los pasos intrincados y atemporales de estos
bailarines? El origen musulmán de estos bailes, hoy ya hispánicos, por haber sido
aclimatados en la interesantísima civilización hispano-árabe, salta a la vista lo mismo
por sus movimientos y técnica como por la prenda con que sale bailarse, el 'Cobijar'
prenda moruna del más puro sabor folklórico, que cubre a la mujer ocultando en
gran parte su forma y la casi totalidad del rostro, descubriendo solamente los ojos."
Historial del traje del baile Regional: "El Chacarrá," 1948. ES-AHP Cádiz, Caja 13324,
Carpeta núm. 4, Libro 1.

47. Amelia Mas Gorrochategur and Antonio Muñoz Rodriguez, "El cobijado de vejer y
su leyenda morisca," *MAGAzin. Rivista de Germanística Intercultural* 1 (2009): 74;
Richard Ford, *A Handbook for Travelers in Spain and Readers at Home* (London: J.
Murray, 1845).

48. Ford, *A Handbook for Travelers in Spain and Readers at Home.*

49. Moriscos, the converted decedents of Muslims of Iberia, were also forced into exile in
1609 by a royal decree of King Philip II of Spain, although the process was only partially successful.

50. "paz y alegría, de fraternidad, que la gran mayor familia hispano-marroquí." "Paz y
alegría en Chauen," *Telegrama del Rif*, July 10, 1951. ES-AGA, (03)051.023 Caja 1460
top. 23/25.406–30.103.

51. Ibid.
52. For example, this transcript of speech from a tour of Morocco: "The Sección Femenina is happy to offer their most sincere expression of warmth and friendship to the Muslim women." "La Sección Femenina se siente hoy contenta de ofrecer a las . . . Sras. Musulmanas la expresión más sincera de su afecto y amistad." "Festival organizado por la Junta de Servicios Municipales de Tetuán, con motivo de las fiestas de la ciudad," 1955. ES-AGA, (03)051.023 Caja 1460 top. 23/25.406–30.103.
53. The Coros y Danzas of Tétouan, located in the Spanish Protectorate, were lumped together with those from Andalusia during the regional portion of the competition. The following is a record of a judge's comments on a troupe of Coros y Danzas of Tétouan after their performance during the national competition of 1958: "In second place was the Mixed Choir of the Medina Circle of Tétouan, they sang the set pieces and another for the 'free choice' category—outside of the contest they sang an Arabic [song] and a 'Hallelujah.' They were directed by Father Emilio Soto, and the result was good." "En segundo lugar acto el Coro Mixto del Circulo Medina de Tetuán, igualmente cantaron las obligadas y la de libre elección y fuera de Concurso una canción Árabe y un Aleluya, fueron dirigidos por El Padre Emilio Soto, y resulto bien." "Informe de la prueba de sector del concurso nacional de coros y danzas en África del Norte," ES-AGA, (03)051.023 14-51, 12/546 top. 23/25.406–30.103.
54. Carten Stahn, *The Law and Practice of International Territorial Administration: Versailles to Iraq and Beyond* (Cambridge: Cambridge University Press, 2008), 57.
55. "espléndido conglomerado de razas y nacionalidades que constituye nuestra ciudad . . . trayendo el viento suave de Occidente." "Coros y Danzas de la Sección Femenina en Tánger," review, *Arriba*, July 11, 1951. ES-AGA, (03)051.023 12/644 top. 23/25.406–30.103.
56. Ibid.
57. "I am sure you will achieve great success and it will be a magnificent act of propaganda." "estoy seguro que conseguiréis un gran éxito y sería un magnifico acto de propaganda." Correspondence from Luis García Llera (general director of cultural relations in Tangier) to Pilar Primo de Rivera, Madrid, April 29, 1955. ES-AGA, (03)051.023 Caja 1460 top. 23/25.406–30.103.
58. "por su geografía, y por su historia española. Y español es también el idioma en que se habla y la moneda de más circulación." "Coros y Danzas de la Sección Femenina en Tánger," *Arriba*, July 21, 1951. ES-AGA, ES-AGA, (03)051.023 Caja 1460 top. 23/25.406–30.103.
59. Ibid.
60. "no hubo musulmanes ni judíos que no pasaron por la Feria de Andalucía al menos una vez." Ibid.
61. "Una curiosa españolidad en la que no dejaban de existir notas de pluralidad cultural." José Antonio González Alcantud, "Taurolatrías periféricas: París-Tánger," in *Fiestas de Toros y Sociedad*, ed. Antonio García-Baquero González and Pedro Romero de Solís (Seville: Editorial Universidad de Sevilla-Secretariado de Publicaciones, 2003), 475.

62. "the bullfight that was celebrated in the Plaza de Toros of Tangier, had a very pe-
culiar program, in which Slaomón Hachuel—the victor from the *Feria de Ceuta*—
performed, Eleunterio García, José Andreu and Krimo el Mirabet. That is, to deduce
from their names, a Jewish bullfighter, a Muslim, and two Spaniards." "la novillada
que se celebró en la plaza tangerina, tenía un programa realmente curioso, en él
actuaban Slaomón Hachuel—triunfador de la feria de Ceuta—Eleuterio García, José
Andreu y Krimo el Mirabet, es decir, a deducir por sus nombres, un novillero judío,
otro musulmán, y dos españoles." Ibid.

63. "there, in the old arena where the sands still bore the recent traces of the Spanish game
of death." "Allí, en el viejo circo cuyas arenas aun graban recientes huellas del juego
español con la muerte." "La Semana de Tánger," *Arriba*, July 21, 1951. ES-AGA, ES-
AGA, (03)051.023 Caja 1460 top. 23/25.406–30.103.

64. "más de seis mil personas de diferentes religiones, nacionalidades y razas . . .
heterogéneos en su composición, unánimes en sus reacciones." "La Semana de
Tánger," *Arriba*, July 21, 1951.

65. "Coros y Danzas de la Sección Femenina en Tánger."

66. The *djellaba* is a long, loose-fitting shirt and hood that reaches mid-calf to ankle.
Variations of the *djellaba* are worn by men and women.

67. "musulmanes de blanca y perfumada barba con sus mujeres embutidas en chilabas de
rica tela, y también obreros de Málaga y Algeciras, indios del Zoco Chico y moros de
la vieja Medina se apiñaron en los tendidos para conocer nuestras danzas y nuestras
canciones . . . y el pueblo de Tánger supo de nuevo de las cosas de España." "La Semana
de Tánger," *Arriba*, July 21, 1951.

68. George Joffé, "The Moroccan Nationalist Movement: Istiqlal, the Sultan, and the
Country," *Journal of African History* 26, no. 4 (1985): 301.

69. Ibid., 304.

70. Miller, *A History of Modern Morocco*, 148.

71. Stéphane Bernard, *The Franco-Moroccan Conflict: 1943–1956* (New Haven, CT, and
London: Yale University Press, 1968), 76.

72. Schneider, "Cultural Diplomacy," 192; Croft, *Dancers as Diplomats*, 5.

Chapter 4

1. Letter from Sokol to Pilar, August 29, 1953. Alcalá de Henares, ES-AGA, (03)051.023,
Caja 12/666 top. (03)14.51.

2. Cécile Stephanie Stehrenberger, *Francos Tänzerinnen auf Auslandstournee: Folklore,
Nation und Geschlecht im "Colonial Encounter"* (Bielefeld: transcript Verlag,
2013), 118.

3. Cynthia Schneider, "Cultural Diplomacy: Hard to Define, but You'd Know It If You
Saw It," *Brown Journal of World Affairs* 13, no. 1 (2006): 191–203; Danielle Fosler-
Lussier, *Music in America's Cold War Diplomacy* (Oakland: University of California
Press, 2015), 3.

4. Florentino Portero, *Franco aislado: La cuestión española (1945–1950)* (Madrid: Aguilar, 1989), 28.

5. Carlos Caballero Jurado and Ramiro Bujeiro, *Blue Division Soldier 1941–45: Spanish Volunteer on the Eastern Front* (Oxford: Osprey Publishing, 2009), 34; Paul Preston, "Franco's Foreign Policy," in *Spain in International Context, 1936–1959*, ed. Christian Leitz and David Dunthorn (New York: Berghahn Books, 1999), 1.

6. José Luis Neila Hernández, "The Foreign Policy Administration of Franco's Spain: From Isolation to International Realignment (1945–1957)," in *Spain in International Context, 1936–1959*, ed. Christian Leitz and David Dunthorn (New York: Berghahn Books, 1999), 279; Paul Preston, "Franco's Foreign Policy," 3; Boris Liedtke, "Compromising with the Dictatorship: U.S.-Spanish Relations in the Late 1940s and Early 1950s," in *Spain in International Context, 1936–1959*, ed. Christian Leitz and David Dunthorn (New York: Berghahn Books, 1999), 265.

7. Manuel Espadas Burgos, *Franquismo y Política Exterior* (Madrid: Ediciones RIALP S.A., 1988), 157; Portero, *Franco aislado*, 28; Martin Blinkhorn, *Fascism and the Right in Europe, 1919–1945* (Harlow: Longman, 2000), 81.

8. Preston, "Franco's Foreign Policy," 3.

9. Ibid., 5.

10. Ibid., 14.

11. Paul Preston, "The Anti-Francoist Opposition: The Long March to Unity," in *Spain in Crisis: The Evolution and Decline of the Franco Régime*, ed. Paul Preston (Hassocks: Harvester Press, 1976), 125.

12. Lorenzo Delgado Gómez-Escalonilla, *Imperio de papel: Acción cultural y política exterior durante el primer franquismo* (Madrid: Consejo superior de investigaciones científicas, 1992), 237.

13. Stanley Payne, *The Franco Regime: 1936–1975* (Madison: University of Wisconsin Press, 1987), 345.

14. Liedtke, "Compromising with the Dictatorship," 266; Gómez-Escalonilla, *Imperio de papel*, 48; Helen Graham, "Introduction," in *Interrogating Francoism: History and Dictatorship in Twentieth-Century Spain*, ed. Helen Graham (London: Bloomsbury, 2016), 2.

15. Portero, *Franco aislado*, 33.

16. Peter Carroll, *The Odyssey of the Abraham Lincoln Brigade: Americans in the Spanish Civil War* (Stanford, CA: Stanford University Press, 1994), 210.

17. Ibid., 283.

18. Portero, *Franco aislado*, 79.

19. Ibid.

20. Ibid.

21. Graham, "Introduction," 2.

22. Payne, *The Franco Regime*, 390; Portero, *Franco aislado*, 35; Liedtke, "Compromising with the Dictatorship," 267; Nelia Hernández, "The Foreign Policy Administration of Franco's Spain," 279.

23. Nelia Hernández, "The Foreign Policy Administration of Franco's Spain," 279.

24. Portero, *Franco aislado*, 31.

25. Ibid., 29.
26. Liedtke, "Compromising with the Dictatorship," 269; Preston, "Franco's Foreign Policy," 14.
27. Although HUAC was originally responsible for seeking out American citizens with either fascist or communist connections when it was founded in 1938, its concern with the former evaporated after the Second World War.
28. Public Law 601, 79th Congress (1946), Part 2, Rule XI, "Powers and Duties of Comities."
29. Portero, *Franco aislado*, 35; Espadas Burgos, *Franquismo y política exterior*, 158; Preston, "Franco's Foreign Policy," 13.
30. Preston, "Franco's Foreign Policy," 13.
31. Carroll, *The Odyssey of the Abraham Lincoln Brigade*, 211.
32. Ibid., 287.
33. Liedtke, "Compromising with the Dictatorship," 274.
34. Joan Esteban, "The Economic Policy of Francoism: An Interpretation," in *Spain in Crisis*, ed. Paul Preston (Hassocks: Harvester Press, 1976), 94; Liedtke, "Compromising with the Dictatorship," 267; Stephen Ambrose, *Rise to Globalism: American Foreign Policy since 1938*, 5th rev. ed. (New York: Penguin 1988), 127.
35. Schneider, "Cultural Diplomacy," 196; Fosler-Lussier, *Music in America's Cold War Diplomacy*, 2.
36. "El circulo de simpatizantes de España, y el de nuestros amigos, ha aumentado de modo extraordinario en estos últimos años . . . no nos será difícil constituir aquí un Comité amplio—de cuarenta o cincuenta personas, en mayoría norteamericanos de influyente posición—que contribuyan a la publicidad, contactos y ayudas." Letter from Pérez del Arco to Rivera, January 1, 1950. ES-AGA, (03)051.023, Caja 12/666 top. (03)14.51.
37. "explicar lo que era la S.F. y lo que se hacía actualmente en España." Travelogue of 1947 tour of the United Kingdom. ES-AGA, (03)051.023, Caja 12/666 top. (03)14.51.
38. "todo lo que los periódicos ingleses decían de nosotros era propaganda política contraria. Con su filosofía de hombre sencillo me dijo que un pueblo que tenía una alegría tan sana y una cordialidad tan sincera no podía ser malo. . . . También me dijo que esto lo había hablado con muchas personas de allí a que opinaban como él." Travelogue of 1947 tour of the United Kingdom. ES-AGA, (03)051.023, Caja 12/666 top. (03)14.51.
39. "Dancers from Spain," *Brighton and Hove Herald*, March 22, 1952.
40. Antonio Cazorla Sánchez, *Fear and Progress: Ordinary Lives in Franco's Spain (1939–1975)* (Chichester: Willey-Blackwell, 2010), 6.
41. Carroll, *The Odyssey of the Abraham Lincoln Brigade*, 210.
42. Vicente García-Márquez, *The Ballets Russes: Colonel de Basil's Ballets Russes de Monte Carlo, 1932–1952* (New York: Alfred A. Knopf, 1990), 4.
43. "E. Colonel W. de Basil is white Russian. He left Russia 30 years ago after he actively fought against communism. He was [a] creator of the Ballets Russes. At present, he works with the Coros y Danzas of the Sección Femenina, and has directed the performances in Europe. He has contributed through his work and his great spirit to

their success"; "E. Coronel W. De Basil es ruso blanco, hace 30 años que está fuera de Rusia donde luchó activamente contra el comunismo. Fue creador de los ballets rusos. En la actualidad trabaja con los Coros y Danzas de la Sección Femenina habiendo dirigido la tornes que ésta realizó por Europa y contribuyendo con su trabajo y el gran espíritu que puso en éste al gran éxito que esto obtuvieron." "E. Coronel W. de Basil," ES-AGA, (03)051.023, Caja 1460, top. 23/25.406–30.103.

44. "Es gran defensor de España por la que siente una enorme admiración." "E. Coronel W. de Basil," ES-AGA, (03)051.023, Caja 1460, top. 23/25.406–30.103.

45. "El coronel de Basil al servicio de España," *Arriba*, August 7, 1951. ES-AGA, (03)051.023, Caja 12/666 top. (03)14.51.

46. "This spectacle was a revelation for Basil. . . . After his visit, he had witnessed examples of repertoire created by [our] anonymous authors"; "Este espectáculo fue para de Basil una revelación. . . . Ante su vista pasó una cantidad de obras anónimas, sin autor." "El coronel de Basil al servicio de España," *Arriba*, August 7, 1951. ES-AGA, (03)051.023, Caja 12/666 top. (03)14.51.

47. García-Márquez, *The Ballets Russes*, 4.

48. Ibid., 134.

49. For evidence of Sokol's year of birth, see the following article: "Detectives seized Harry L. Sokol, 57: Arrest of Tour Leader Strands Spanish Group," *El Paso Herald Post*, October 23, 1953.

50. Information taken from a report from the Council of Information and Press, October 8, 1953. "Artistas españoles en Norteamérica," ES-AGA, (03)051.023, Caja 12/666 top. (03)14.51.

51. Letter from Pérez del Arco to Rivera, February 9, 1953. ES-AGA, (03)051.023, Caja 12/666 top. (03)14.51.

52. Letter from Arco to Maruja Sampelayo, March 14, 1953. ES-AGA, (03)051.023, Caja 12/666 top. (03)14.51.

53. "Repito, por tanto: Cuidado! . . . Pero viviendo esta posibilidad, vigilada también el tener las espaldas cubiertas, pues así si la empresa no resultara económicamente tan próspera como Sokol proyecta, el único mal sería el que él personalmente sufriría, muy lamentable teniendo en cuenta su buena fe, pero que no dañaría en nada a los intereses de la Sección Femenina." Letter from Pérez del Arco to Maruja Sampelayo, March 14, 1953. ES-AGA, (03)051.023, Caja 12/666 top. (03)14.51.

54. Correspondence from the Regidora central de Servicio Eterio, April 22, 1952. ES-AGA, (03)051.023, Caja 12/666 top. (03)14.51.

55. Ibid.

56. Letter form Pérez del Arco to Maruja Sampelayo, March 14, 1953. ES-AGA, (03)051.023, Caja 12/666 top. (03)14.51.

57. Correspondence from the Regidora central de Servicio Eterio, April 22, 1952.

58. Contract between Coros y Danzas and Office Artistique Continental, January 16, 1952. ES-AGA, (03)051.023, Caja 12/666 top. (03)14.51.

59. "[The Coros y Danzas'] activities should expand [in the United States] in the future, although it would be desirable that if they were at the hands of a more competent entrepreneur;" "sus actuaciones deben departirse en el futuro, si bien sería de desear

que estuviesen a gago de un empresario más competente." Letter from Rivera to the Consejero de Información y Prensa, October 27, 1953. ES-AGA, (03)051.023, Caja 12/666 top. (03)14.51.

60. "No parece que posea gran competencia, como tal empresario, y a esto se deben sus fallos y equivocaciones; ha elegido mal al época para traer a Norteamérica a nuestros artistas, época de verano, insoportablemente calurosa, y en la que el público se retrae de asistir a espectáculos en locales cerraos; la falta de anuncios y, sobre todo, de publicidad acertada, sin la cual o hay éxito posible en este país." Report from the Council of Information and Press, October 8, 1953. *Artistas españoles en Norteamérica*, ES-AGA, (03)051.023, Caja 12/666 top. (03)14.51.

61. Letter from the Director of Cultural Relations to Rivera, June 20, 1953. ES-AGA, (03)051.023, Caja 12/666 top. (03)14.51.

62. Letter from Sokol to Rivera, June 20, 1953. ES-AGA, (03)051.023, Caja 12/666 top. (03)14.51.

63. Letter from Pérez del Arco to Rivera, June 20, 1953. ES-AGA, (03)051.023, Caja 12/666 top. (03)14.51.

64. Letter from Pérez del Arco to Rivera, August 10, 1953. ES-AGA, (03)051.023 Caja 1460 top. 23/25.406-30.103.

65. Letter from Sokol to Rivera, October 15, 1953. ES-AGA, (03)051.023 Caja 1460 top. 23/25.406–30.103.

66. Ibid.

67. "Dancers from Spain," *Lubbock Morning Avalanche*, October 27, 1953.

68. Ibid.

69. "As a matter of fact, Miss Maria Josefa Sampelayo Ruescas could tell you herself that I've hired agents and paid them $1,000.00 per week and behind my back, they sent a young lady to talk to Sampelayo and tell her that they could take the group and do a better job. Sampelayo was honest and told me about it. As a matter of fact, they wrote her a letter which I am bringing with me when I arrive in Spain to show to you." Letter from Sokol to Rivera, November 9, 1953. ES-AGA, (03)051.023, Caja 12/666 top. (03)14.51.

70. Letter from Sokol to Rivera, August 29, 1953. ES-AGA, (03)051.023, Caja 12/666 top. (03)14.51.

71. Stehrenberger, *Francos Tänzerinnen auf Auslandstournee*, 118.

72. Letter from Sokol to Rivera, May 30, 1953. ES-AGA, (03)051.023, Caja 12/666 top. (03)14.51.

73. "This campaign was organized, as is well known, by an American who is an excellent friend of Spain, Mr. Sokol"; "Fue organizada esta campaña como es sabido, por un americano que es excelente amigo de España, Mr. Sokol." *Diario Madrid*, editorial, November 26, 1953. ES-AGA, (03)051.023, Caja 12/666 top. (03)14.51.

74. "84 Spanish Youngsters Here for Part in Fair," *Dallas Morning News*, October 12, 1953.

75. "Una cosa que emocionaba y entusiasmaba al público americano era que inaugurábamos siempre nuestro programa con los dos himnos: el español y el americano, cantado éste en inglés. No tienes idea del efecto que aquello hacía." "Coros y Danzas," *Diario Madrid*, November 26, 1953. ES-AGA, (03)051.023, Caja 12/666 top. (03)14.51.

76. "Nos dijeron era muy bonito y gallardo." Travelogue from 1947 tour of United Kingdom. ES-AGA, (03)051.023 Caja 1460 top. 23/25.406-30.103.

77. "explicamos será el himno que habían llevado las juventudes españolas a la guerra, que con él se había hecho la revolución española y que era el himno que seguía dándonos valor y alegría ante todo." Travelogue from 1947 tour of United Kingdom. ES-AGA, (03)051.023 Caja 1460 top. 23/25.406-30.103.

78. "To distinguish ourselves when we were walking [about town] we wore a ribbon of the Spanish flag with the yoke and the arrows"; "Como distintivo cuando íbamos de pisado llevábamos un lazo de la bandera española sujeto con el yugo y las flechas." *Informe del emplazamiento de los grupos de Segovia, Córdoba y el Ferrol del caudillo (Coruña) al Eisteddfod que se celebra en Llangollen, País de Gales (Inglaterra).* ES-AGA, (03)051.023. Caja 1460 top. 23/25.406–30.103.

79. "The Union would not let me go on with the show here at Carnegie hall, which caused us a loss of over \$30,000. . . . The American Guild stepped in and they said I have to have the boys and girls join the Union before they would let me go ahead with the show. I didn't agree on that and I fought them for several days. . . . Carnegie hall would not open the doors for the performance, because they didn't want to be in any trouble." Letter from Sokol to Rivera, October 5, 1953. ES-AGA, (03)051.023, Caja 12/666 top. (03)14.51.

80. Letter from Sokol to Rivera, November 9, 1953. ES-AGA, (03)051.023, Caja 12/666 top. (03)14.51.

81. Letter from Sokol to Rivera, August 3, 1953. ES-AGA, 14.51-12/00666.

82. "Su admiración por España también parece ser sincera: en Vancouver arremetió contra un español rojo que osó insultar a nuestro régimen, atacándole con tal violencia que el español repelió la agresión a puñetazos." Report from the Council of Information and Press, October 8, 1953. "Artistas españoles en Norteamérica," ES-AGA, (03)051.023, Caja 12/666 top. (03)14.51.

83. "Lo que indica que la propaganda de los enemigos de España no ha dejado de estar en marcha y este envenenamiento progresivo hace que se sientan tan insolentes. Quiero agradecerle vivamente su actitud y siento la incomodidad que ha sentido que pasar por defender nuestra posición." Letter from Rivera to Sokol, October 2, 1953. ES-AGA, (03)051.023, Caja 12/666 top. (03)14.51.

84. "Es hombre tosco, rudo, de violentos 'prontos' en momentos dados, que se turnan con arrepentimientos sinceros por su conducta, e incluso con afabilidades." Report from the Council of Information and Press, October 8, 1953. "Artistas españoles en Norteamérica," ES-AGA, (03)051.023, Caja 12/666 top. (03)14.51.

85. Letter from Sokol to Rivera, June 20, 1953. ES-AGA, (03)051.023, Caja 12/666 top. (03)14.51.

86. Naima Prevots, *Dance for Export: Cultural Diplomacy and the Cold War* (London: Wesleyan University Press: 1998), 13; Damien Mahiet, Mark Ferraguto, and Rebeckah Ahrendt, "Introduction," in *Music and Diplomacy from the Early Modern Era to the Present*, ed. Damien Mahiet, Mark Ferraguto, Rebeckah Ahrendt (Basingstoke: Palgrave Macmillan, 2014), 10.

87. Mahiet et al., "Introduction," 8.

88. Schneider, "Cultural Diplomacy," 192.
89. "Group Called Falangist: Spanish Dancer's Recitals Protested," *San Francisco Chronicle*, July 10, 1953. ES-AGA, (03)051.023, Caja 12/666 top. (03)14.51.
90. Ibid.
91. Letter from "Tex" Sanderson to Coros y Danzas, September 17, 1953. ES-AGA, (03)051.023, Caja 12/666 top. (03)14.51.
92. Ibid.
93. Ibid.
94. "Spanish Serenade: Songs and Dances of Spain at the Stoll Theatre," *Theatre*, March 1, 1952.
95. Ibid.
96. "According to the news that I have gathered on the hundred and five of arrests made, only 16 or 18 of the students were kept with the possibility of being expelled from France"; "según las noticias que he podido obtener de las ciento y cinco de detenciones efectuadas solo se mantuvieron 16 o 18 de los que se estudian los antecedentes con vista a su expulsión de Francia." Letter from the Consul of Spain, August 29, 1951. ES-AGA, (03)051.023 Caja 1460 top. 23/25.406–30.103.
97. "The World Federation of Democratic Youth (WFDY): Based on Data Available as of October 1956," General CIA Records[US], CIA-RDP78-00915R000600140009-1.
98. Ibid.
99. Joël Kotek, *Students of the Cold War* (Oxford: Basingstoke, 1996), ix.
100. "Un spectacle de danses populaires d'Espagne." *Le soir*, April 15, 1951. ES-AGA, (03)15.23, (03)15.23, 12-00644.
101. "[The Coros y Danzas are] a troupe recruited by the women's section of Franco's Falange (the equivalent of the Nazi Hitler-Youth)"; "Une troupe de chœurs et de ballets féminins espagnols recrutés dans la section féminine de la Phalange franquiste (qui est l'équivalent de l'Hitlerjungend nazie)," "Incidents au Palais de Chaillot," *Libération*, April 7, 1951. ES-AGA, (03)15.23, (03)15.23, 12-00644.
102. "Dénonce la politique d'amitié que mène le gouvernement avec le bandit franquiste, qu'était le meilleur ami des nazis oppresseurs de notre pays . . . la reprise des relations diplomatiques avec Franco, l'acceptation de démonstrations de propagande franquiste à Bruxelles constituent une insulte à la démocratie, une insulte à tous ceux qui ont lutté et luttent contre la guerre et le fascisme dont Franco est un des symboles les plus répugnant." "Vive le 14 avril: Journée de solidarité avec le peuple espagnol," *Le drapeau rouge*, April 13, 1951. ES-AGA, (03)15.23, (03)15.23, 12-00644.
103. "Un spectacle de danses populaires d'Espagne," *Le soir*, April 15, 1951. ES-AGA, (03)15.23, (03)15.23, 12-00644; "A bas Franco !," *Germinal*, April 17, 1951. ES-AGA, (03)15.23, (03)15.23, 12-00644; "Une manifestation antifranquiste à Bruxelles," *La dernière heure*, April 17, 1951. ES-AGA, (03)15.23, (03)15.23, 12-00644.
104. The Miranda de Ebro concentration camp held Spanish political prisoners and refugees from Europe from the beginning of the Spanish Civil War until 1947. See Ángeles Egido, *Los campos de concentración franquistas en el contexto europeo* (Madrid: Marcial Pons Ediciones de Historia, 2005).

105. "Un spectacle de danses populaires d'Espagne." *Le soir*, April 15, 1951. ES-AGA, (03)15.23, (03)15.23, 12-00644.

106. Ibid.

107. "'Franco assassin!': Une centaine de démocrates ont été arrêtés," *Le drapeau rouge*, April 17, 1951. ES-AGA, (03)15.23, (03)15.23, 12-00644.

108. "A bas Franco!," *Germinal*, April 17, 1951. ES-AGA, (03)15.23, (03)15.23, 12-00644.

109. Léon Degrelle (1906–1994) was a Belgian politician and Nazi collaborator.

110. "On sait qu'il y a quelques jours le représentant de Franco, bourreau du peuple espagnol, est rentré dans la capitale. Ce n'est pas par hasard que cette troupe de danseurs phalangistes devait passer par Bruxelles, vendredi. Ce n'est pas par hasard, ni pour le plaisir de la danse, que les amis de Franco et de Degrelle avaient mis au point ce programme. Ces gens-là entendaient faire leur propagande pour le régime sanglant du sinistre Franco. . . . Vers huit heures, la salle de l'A.B.C. est vide, désespérément vide. Il faudra attendre huit heures et demie pour voir arriver un peu de monde. Oh ! pas beaucoup. . . . Peu après 9 heures, enfin, le rideau se lève. Une phalangiste vient d'annoncer le spectacle : —Barcelone, crie un spectateur, tandis qu'un coup de sifflet strident coupe l'inspiration à l'envoyée de Franco qui, surprise, s'arrête un instant et rentre derrière le rideau de velours. Voilà la première danse. Les phalangistes sont à peine sur la scène que les cris montent scandés par des dizaines et des dizaines de voix : « Franco assassin ». Ce cri est répété vingt, trente fois. Il vole sur la scène, couvrant la musique, arrêtant les danseuses. La police se saisit de quelques manifestants. Les cris redoublent, ils montent de la gauche, de la droite, du centre. « Franco assassine » « Franco au poteau ». La danseuse chargée d'annoncer chaque danse n'est pas rassurée. Elle n'annonce plus rien et c'est à peine si on la voit. La brève apparition est d'ailleurs chaque fois saluée de huées, de coups de sifflets, il y a même une trompette qui s'en donne à cœur joie . . . les agents avancent matraque en main. On assiste alors à des scènes d'une sauvagerie. Un agent poursuit une femme qui se sauve et la frappe sauvagement par derrière. Cette femme fait trois pas et s'évanouit tant le coup de matraque à travers la figure. . . . Alors la police fait évacuer des rangées entières. On crie, on se cramponne aux banquettes. Les manifestants se séparèrent aux cris de « Franco assassin » , « vive l'Espagne républicaine ». Une centaine de démocrates ont été arrêtés." "Franco assassin!," *Le Drapeau Rouge*, April 17, 1951. ES-AGA, (03)15.23, 12-00644-0044.

111. ". . . *on imagine qu'il a passé le reste de la nuit à rédiger un pitoyable rapport au Caudillo. . . . Nos pays ne sont pas encore mûrs pour le fascisme renaissant.*" "A bas Franco!," *Germinal*, April 17, 1951. ES-AGA, (03)15.23, 12-00644-0042.

112. "Un spectacle de danses populaires d'Espagne." *Le Soir*. 1951. Review, 15 April. ES-AGA, (03)15.23, 12-00644-0038.

113. "Des anarchistes espagnols troublent pendant un demi-heure le spectacle de l'opéra." *Le Méridional de Marseille*, May 26, 1951. ES-AGA, (03)15.23, 12-00644-0046.

114. "Une stupide 'manifestation,'" *La Libre Belgique*, April 15, 1951. ES-AGA, (03)15.23, 12-00644-0036.

115. In French, "*moscoutaires*," a pun on the words "Muscovite" (a person from Moscow) and "Musketeers" (the heroic protagonists in the novel by Alexandre Dumas).

116. "La scène stupide provoquée par les moscoutaires bruxellois a profondément peiné les spectateurs qu'avait attirés à ce théâtre une manifestation artistique de l'Espagne de tous les temps. Car ce n'est ni l'Espagne de Franco, pas plus que celle du « Frente popular » qui s'exprime dans les ballets espagnols. C'est l'Espagne de Goya, de Velasquez, de Granados ; c'est le peuple espagnol lui-même—et le moins qu'on puisse dire des « manifestants » bruxellois, c'est qu'ils ont manifesté autant de muflerie que d'imbécillité." "Une stupide 'manifestation,'" *La libre belgique*, April 15, 1951. ES-AGA, (03)15.23, 12-00644-0036.

117. "Les communistes manifestent aux ballets espagnols," *La nation belge*, April 15, 1951.

118. Of course, many of the veterans who fought in the Republican army *were* communists or anarchists. After returning to the United States several of these Americans continued to aid the USSR in the "murky world of international espionage." See Carroll, *The Odyssey of the Abraham Lincoln Brigade*, 214.

119. Johnson Cartee and Gary Copeland, *Inside Political Campaigns: Theory and Practice* (Westport, CT, and London: Praeger, 1997), 93.

Chapter 5

1. Elizabeth Manley, *The Paradox of Paternalism: Women and the Politics of Authoritarianism in the Dominican Republic* (Gainesville: University Press of Florida, 2017), 8.

2. Jean-Claude Rabaté, *Miguel de Unamuno: Biografía* (Madrid: Taurus, 2009), 240; Juan Pablo Fusi Aizpúrua, "El franquismo: la etapa totalitaria (1939–1959)," in *España: sociedad, política y civilización (siglos XIX–XX)*, ed. Jover Zamora and José María (Madrid: Areté, 2001), 727.

3. Gemma Pérez Zalduondo, "Racial Discourses in Spanish Musical Literature, 1915–1939," in *Western Music and Race*, ed. Julie Brown (Cambridge: Cambridge University Press, 2007), 216.

4. Lorenzo Delgado Gómez-Escalonilla, *Imperio de papel: Acción cultural y política exterior durante el primer franquismo* (Madrid: Consejo superior de investigaciones científicas, 1992), 242.

5. Pérez Zalduondo, "Racial Discourses in Spanish Musical Literature," 216.

6. Vanessa Tessada Sepúlveda, "El Servicio exterior y la Sección Femenina de F.E.T. y de las J.O.N.S. intentos de acercamiento con América Latina," *Historia*, special issue (2019): 21.

7. "Alcance y Acción de la Sección Femenina," ES-AHP Málaga, Caja 1683, no. 29492.

8. "Porque la música une a los más distantes y porque la música nos recuerda, unas veces con pena y otras con alegría, los mejores momentos de nuestra vida, . . . por eso la Falange, que es ante todo unidad, ha preferido la música, mejor que ningún otro medio, para unir nuestros espíritus, y de la música ha escogido la parte más asequible a todos: la canción. La canción, que americanos y españoles cantamos en

la misma lengua. La canción que se pega al oído, que se repite, que no se olvida; la que no tiene autor, sino que ha nacido en el pueblo. . . . Por eso, americanos y españoles tenemos que saber nuestras canciones y cantarlas juntos; porque cuando se unan cincuenta o sesenta mil voces de españoles y americanos para cantar una misma canción, entonces se unirán nuestros espíritus también y nos entenderemos mejor y nos querremos más. Entonces el mar que nos separa será sólo un accidente de la Geografía, que servirá para traer y llevar de acá para allá y de allá para acá la cultura de vuestras Repúblicas y lá de nuestra Patria." Pilar Primo de Rivera, "La Música como unidad," in *Pilar Primo de Rivera: Discursos, circulares, escritos* (Madrid: Gráficas Afrodisio Aguado, 1943), 79.

9. Letter from María Victoria Eirá to Antonio Cano Santillana, Jefe de Intercambio Cultural del Instituto de Cultura Hispánica, November 16, 1953. ES-AGA, (03)051.023, Caja 1460 top. 23/25.406–30.103.

10. Tessada Sepúlveda, "El Servicio exterior y la Sección Femenina de F.E.T. y de las J.O.N.S. intentos de acercamiento con América Latina," 21.

11. "Alcance y Acción de la Sección Femenina" (Madrid, 1952), 69–70. ES–AHP Málaga, Caja 1683, no. 29492.

12. "la responsabilidad y el honor de dar a conocer al mundo hispano-americano la inmensa riqueza de nuestro folklore por el que se sentirán más unidos a España." Circular titled "America 1948: Para todas las camaradas," 1948. ES-AGA, (03)051.023, Caja 1460 top. 23/25.406–30.103.

13. An article announcing the Coros y Danzas' benefit concert in Madrid for the Peruvian city of Cuzco following the devastating earthquake of 1950 is an example of how the Sección Femenina attempted to promote feelings of an international Hispanic solidarity at home: "Cuzco is a city as linked to Spanish history just as much as Seville or Toledo. Cuzco is a source of pride for all Spanish-speaking people. It will be beautiful [once again] when its old towers are rebuilt on the noble palaces and the streets of Spanish court." "Cuzco es una ciudad tan ligada a la historia española como Sevilla o Toledo. Cuzco constituye un orgullo para todos los hombres de habla española. Será hermoso que sus viejas torres renazcan sobre los palacios nobles y las calles de corte español." "Coros y Danzas de la S.F.: Ayuda a Cuzco," *Arriba*, July 9, 1950. ES-AGA, (03)15.23, 12/643.

14. "Las camaradas de la Sección femenina van a realizar una embajada cultural y artística por las tierras de América. Concretamente por las tierras que fueron español de California. Allí, en las ciudades que aún conservan los castizos nombres de santo españoles, vibrará de nuevo el aire con las canciones y los bailes de nuestras jóvenes camaradas, llenos de belleza pura. . . .

"¿El viaje?

"Toda California, y especialmente las poblaciones tan españolísimas como San Diego, Los Ángeles, Santa Bárbara, San Francisco y otras de singular importancia. . . . Los españoles de California, hijos de españoles, van a revivir en su espíritu el claro ejemplo de la pureza española, cuyo arte lleno de misticismo religioso no tiene ejemplo en el mundo." "Coros y Danzas españoles a California, EE.UU.," *Sur: Málaga*, July 6, 1950. ES-AGA, (03)15.23, 12/643.

15. "Allí, en medio de los rascacielos y de las imponentes máquinas modernas, se conservan aún las iglesias que fundaron nuestros colonizadores y se habla el idioma de Cervantes. Allí es donde ellas van a dar lección de buen sabor de la vieja Patria, y resucitarán el amor y el cariño por la España caballeresca y estupenda que se conserva en las leyendas y tradiciones de California. El viaje es sencillamente una embajada. . . . tantas poblaciones españolas volverán a repetir las canciones que sonaban en torno a las caravanas de emigrantes, y los bailes que se bailaban en los coros de los pueblos españoles y cristianos diseminados por la zona más hermosa del nuevo continente. Y nuestra Sección Femenina será la embajadora de esta misión de la raza." ES-AGA, (03)15.23, 12/643.

16. "Old Spanish Days," *San Marino Tribune*, August 17, 1950.

17. "Spanish Dancers," *Olean Times Herald*, September 21, 1950. The contrast between this colorful excerpt and the current state of the Old Spanish Days festival is striking, especially its engagement and with the Mexican American community of Santa Barbara. When I attended the Old Spanish Days festival of 2019, it seemed to be primarily a celebration of local Mexican American culture, a demographic that makes up 36.5 percent of the city's population. The musical performances were almost entirely filled with traditional mariachi bands and dance troupes from around the city, while freshly baked Mexican foods were sold in booths alongside other traditional products. The musical performances supported by the Old Spanish Days Fiesta still have a powerful role in shaping local ideas of ethnicity and perceptions of the history of Southern California and should continue to be studied by researchers in the fields of anthropology and musicology.

18. Albert Hurtado, *Intimate Frontiers: Sex, Gender, and Culture in Old California* (Albuquerque: University of New Mexico Press, 1999), xxii.

19. Ricardo Castro-Salazar and Carl Bagley, "Navigating Historical Borders: Internal Colonialism and the Politics of Memory," *Counterpoints* 415 (2012): 42.

20. Ibid., 43.

21. Ibid., 46.

22. Ibid., 46.

23. "Fiesta, or Ferias or Fairs, There Is a difference," *Santa Barbara News Press*, June 4, 1950. ES-AGA, (03)15.23, 12-00644.

24. "Viva la Fiesta—in Seville and Santa Barbara," *Santa Barbara News Press*, editorial, May 14, 1950. ES-AGA, (03)15.23, 12-00644.

25. Ibid.

26. "Coros y Danzas españoles a California, EE.UU."

27. "flotaba la salve sobre un mar de banderas y se escuchaban vítores a España y a Franco." "Activo programa para el Grupo Folclórico Ibero," *La prensa*, May 28, 1953. ES-AGA, (03)15.23, 12/643.

28. Ibid.

29. Letter from Sokol to Rivera, October 15, 1953. ES-AGA, (03)051.023, Caja 12/666 top. (03)14.51.

30. "Los Coros y Danzas regresan a España," *Diario Madrid*, editorial, November 26, 1953. ES-AGA, (03)051.023, Caja 12/666 top. (03)14.51.

31. Ibid.
32. Ibid.
33. Cécile Stephanie Stehrenberger, *Francos Tänzerinnen auf Auslandstournee: Folklore, Nation und Geschlecht im "Colonial Encounter"* (Bielefeld: Transkript Verlag, 2013), 112.
34. Frank Argote-Freyre, *Fulgencio Batista: From Revolutionary to Strongman* (New Brunswick, NJ: Rutgers University Press, 2007), 124.
35. Edward Gonzalez and Kevin McCarthy, *Cuba after Castro: Legacies, Challenges, and Impediments* (Santa Monica, CA: Rand, 2004), 52.
36. Louis Pérez, *Cuba: Between Reform and Revolution* (New York and Oxford: Oxford University Press, 2011), 232; Gonzalez and McCarthy, *Cuba after Castro*, 52.
37. Gonzalez and McCarthy, *Cuba after Castro*, 52; Pérez, *Cuba*, 232.
38. Katia Figueredo Cabrea, "Carlos Prío Socarrás, Fulgencio Batista, Francisco Franco: La escalada hacia una consolidación 'fraternal,' 1948–1958," *Illes i imperis* 12 (2009): 51.
39. The term "United Nations" here does not refer to the present-day organization founded in 1945, but is a term coined by Franklin D. Roosevelt in 1941 referring to the Allied countries during the Second World War.
40. "Plain Talk in Spanish," *Time*, December 28, 1942.
41. Katia Figueredo Cabrera, "Francisco Franco y Fulgencio Batista: complicidad de dos dictadores en el poder (1952–1958)," *Tzintzun. Revista de estudios históricos* 64 (2016): 299, 313.
42. Ibid., 305.
43. Ibid.
44. "La gratitud sería enorme e imperecedera de cuantos gallegos, asturianos, vascos, catalanes, isleños, en una palabra, de todos los componentes de la nutrida Colonia Española residente en América y de la que la mayor parte de ella por razones económicas, otros de salud, pocos por ideologías políticas, y los más por obligaciones de tipo laboral, verán tarde o tal vez nunca, su amadísima España." Letter from Javier P. Millan Astray to the Cuban consulate, 1953. ES-AGA, (03)051.023 Caja 1460 top. 23/25.406–30.103.
45. "El gran acontecimiento de esta noche: el debut de Coros y Danzas de España," *Diario de la Marina*, January 15, 1954. ES-AGA, (03)051.023, Caja 12/647 top. (03)14.51.
46. "Llegaron a La Habana Grupos de 'Coros y Danzas' de España," *Mundo Habana*, January 1, 1954. ES-AGA, (03)051.023, Caja 12/647 top. (03)14.51.
47. "Existen entre nosotros relaciones de gran amistad y nada mejor para destruir falsas leyendas que el que 'España cante y baile en el amplio y hermoso escenario cubano.'" "Cartas de Madrid," *Excélsior—Habana*, January 21, 1954. ES-AGA, (03)051.023, Caja 12/647 top. (03)14.51.
48. "se estrecharán más ahora en un fraterno abrazo." "Cartas de Madrid," *Excélsior—Habana*, January 21, 1954. ES-AGA, (03)051.023, Caja 12/647 top. (03)14.51.
49. Antonio de Solapeña, "Coros y Danzas de España magnífica embajada en Cuba," in *De la colonia montañesa* (Havana, c. 1954), 5. ES-AGA, (03)051.023, Caja 12/647 top. (03)14.51.

50. "que por ser verdaderamente cristianos en su formación, son ale-gres, con la alegría sana de la fe en Dios y en la patria." Solapeña, "Coros y Danzas de España magnífica embajada en Cuba," 5.

51. "Actúan 'Coros y Danzas' ante la primera dama de Cuba," *Excélsior—Habana*, January 23, 1954. ES-AGA, (03)051.023, Caja 12/647 top. (03)14.51.

52. Michael Kenny, "Twentieth Century Spanish Expatriate in Cuba: A Sub-Culture?," *Anthropological Quarterly* 34 (1961): 85.

53. One such example would be the Galician immigrant Ángel Castro y Argiz, father of the Cuban revolutionary and politician, Fidel Castro.

54. Kenny, "Twentieth Century Spanish Expatriate in Cuba," 87.

55. Ibid., 88.

56. "que es la Casa de España y la Casa de Cuba, también." Pablo Prenso, "Recepción en Centro Gallego a los Coros y Danzas de España," *Información—Habana*, January 2, 1954. ES-AGA, (03)051.023, Caja 12/647 top. (03)14.51.

57. "No sé soy más cubano que gallego o más gallego que cubano." Pablo Prenso, "Obsequiado el 'Grupo vigues' con banderas gallega y cubana," *Información—Habana*, March 16, 1954. ES-AGA, (03)051.023, Caja 12/647 top. (03)14.51.

58. "estos gallegos que aquí están, os ruegan que vayáis al cementerio en Santiago y beséis las tumbas de sus padres, que un día dejaron, y a Santiago nuestra devoción." Ángel Gumbau, "Sociedades y centros españoles," *Avance—Habana*, March 15, 1954. ES-AGA, (03)051.023, Caja 12/647 top. (03)14.51.

59. "Pero como la bienvenida no está lejos del adiós, bueno será deciros que cuando estéis distantes de Cuba, descansando en vuestros hogares, vuestra acción seductora seguirá viviendo con nosotros, no se evaporará, como no se evaporó la de los conquistadores que nos enseñaron a ser caballeros, ni la de los frailes que nos impulsaron a levantar la frente al cielo, porque conquistadores y religiosos era la faz rigorosa y severa de España." Transcript of a speech given by José López Vilaboy at the Centro Gallego, March 15, 1954. ES-AGA, (03)051.023, Caja 12/647 top. (03)14.51.

60. "una representación genuina del folklore hispano." Solapeña, "Coros y Danzas de España magnífica embajada en Cuba," 5. ES-AGA, (03)051.023, Caja 12/647 top. (03)14.51.

61. "madre fecunda de naciones, pueblos y civilizaciones." Daniel Camiroaga, "Los Coros y Danzas de España: Esquela de arte y de formación espiritual," *Diario de la Marina-Habana*, March 15, 1954. ES-AGA, (03)051.023, Caja 12/647 top. (03)14.51.

62. "Cubanos y españoles, unidos todos por el poder irresistible de una sangre común, generosa y ardiente. . . . Ellos he han hecho experimentar el orgullo de pertenecer a esta raza poderosa, que tan bien sabe expresar en sus bailes y canciones el sentir de un pueblo preñado d virtudes y grandezas." "Emisión de radio," February 2, 1954. ES-AGA, (03)051.023, Caja 1460 top. 23/25.406–30.103.

63. Maria Thomas, "Twentieth-Century Catholicisms: Religion as Prison, as Haven, as 'Clamp'," in *Interrogating Francoism: History and Dictatorship in Twentieth-Century Spain*, ed. Helen Graham (London: Bloomsbury, 2016), 28, 36; Geoffrey Jensen, *Irrational Triumph: Cultural Despair, Military Nationalism, and Ideological Origins of Franco's Spain* (Reno: University of Nevada Press, 2002), 166; Stanley

Payne, *The Franco Regime: 1936–1975* (Madison: University of Wisconsin Press, 1987), 199; Pérez Zalduondo, "Racial Discourses in Spanish Musical Literature," 208, 216, 218.

64. "So old and diverse are the songs and dances of Spain. More than one philologist affirms that the song was born even before the language. The guttural rhythmic inflection, in imitation of the song of the birds, which must have pleased primitive man so much, must have been its first expression. The rich aerial fauna that primitive Iberia possessed, had to diversify from the beginning those original expressions of art, and create a wide emotional enclosure in the soul of those primitive Spaniards, warriors and artists at the same time. . . . Tyre and Sidon, the oldest universal emporiums of the Mediterranean civilization, already acclaimed these singers ten centuries before Christ. Rome considered them essential. History, in its course of centuries, did nothing but assert itself in this predilection"; "Tan antigua y diversa como la danza es la canción española. Más de un filólogo afirma que la canción nació aún antes que el lenguaje. La inflexión rítmica gutural, a imitación del canto de las aves, que tanto debía agradar al hombre primitivo, debió ser su primera expresión. La rica fauna aérea que la Iberia primitiva poseyó, debió di-versificar desde un principio aquellas originarias expresiones de arte, y crear un amplio-recinto emocional en el alma de aquellos primitivos españoles, guerreros y artistas a la vez. . . . Tiro y Sidón, los más antiguos emporios universales de la civilización mediterránea, ya aclamaron a estos cantores diez siglos antes de Cristo. Roma les tuvo por imprescindibles. La Historia, en su devenir de siglos, no hizo sino afirmarse en esta predilección." Francisco Mota, "Así canta y baila España: La canción tradicional," *Mañana—Habana*, January 21, 1954. ES-AGA, (03)051.023, Caja 12/647 top. (03)14.51.

65. "*Neñas*" is the Asturian word for "girls."

66. "Pero el público necesita algunas advertencias y creo que sería conveniente hacérselas para cada número. Porque he oído comentar a asturianos, por ejemplo, que nunca habían visto bailar en Asturias como lo hacían las monísimas 'neñas' del grupo astur de Coros y Danzas. Y es natural que, hasta ahora, no hayan conocido cantos, melodías y danzas del siglo XIII, o del XIV, o del XVI." Joaquín Aristigueta, "¡Aquí España!," *Prensa Libre—Habana*, January 23, 1954. ES-AGA, (03)051.023, Caja 12/647 top. (03)14.51.

67. Stephen Ambrose and Douglas Brinkley, *Rise to Globalism: American Foreign Policy since 1938* (London: Penguin Books, 2011), 174, 409.

68. Manuel de Paz-Sánchez, *Zona de Guerra: España y la revolución cubana (1960–1962)* (Tenrife: Litografía Romero, S. A., 2001), 81–82, 132.

69. It is probably no coincidence that "Crixo" was the name of a rebel gladiator who helped lead the Third Servile War (73–71 BC) against the ancient Roman Republic.

70. "El envió de los 'Coros y Danzas de España' por parte del tiranuelo Franco, como vehículo para captarse las simpatías de este pueblo de hondas raíces democráticas, ha sido un tremendísimo fracaso. Lo que debió ser un espectáculo eminentemente popular, en el que lo más sano de nuestro pueblo sintiera en la raíz de su sensibilidad el eco de las bellezas del buen pueblo español, hermano nuestro en mil hazañas por la libertad, solo fue el centro de reunión del franquismo tocinero que vive en nuestra

isla. Para nadie era un secreto, y menos para los pacos de la Embajada española con Lojendio, . . . que nuestros paisanos hubieran brindado su presencia y su emoción al espectáculo, si éste hubiera venido a este país limpio del asqueroso y repulsivo barniz franquista." Crixo, "El envió de los 'Coros y Danzas de España'," *Tiempo—Habana*, January 27, 1954. ES-AGA, (03)051.023, Caja 12/647 top. (03)14.51.

71. Despite their extreme ideological differences, Castro and Franco would attempt to maintain diplomatic relations between Spain and Cuba for at least the first year of Castro's presidency.

72. "acogido con viva satisfacción y claras muestras de aprobación por todos los españoles que lo han conocido." "Repulsa a los Coros y Danzas de la Falange," *España republicana*, January 23, 1954. ES-AGA, (03)051.023, Caja 12/647 top. (03)14.51.

73. "Todos nuestros compatriotas respaldan esa enérgica denuncia de la vil maniobra del régimen franquista que, tras haber sumido a nuestro pueblo en una terrible situación de hambre, miseria y terror—situación que ciega las fuentes de su tradicional alegría y es la menos propicia para que cante y baile—pretende aprovecharse de muestro rico folklore para atraerse el respaldo de los españoles de Cuba. . . . Una muestra de esa creciente repulsa fue lo sucedido en el Centro Andaluz de la Habana. Sirviendo los torvos propósitos perseguidos por el franquismo con esa llamada 'embajada artística', los directivos del Centro Andaluz organizaron una recepción a los componentes de los Coros y Danzas de Falange. Cuando se estaba desarrollando esa recepción, sonaron estentóreos gritos contra el criminal régimen de Franco . . . del que no ha tenido más remedio que hacerse eco la prensa diaria, aun cuando haya pretendido desvirtuar su significación y quitarle importancia," 5. ES-AGA, (03)051.023, Caja 12/647 top. (03)14.51.

74. Jorge Domingo Cuadriello, *Los Españoles en las letras cubanas durante el siglo XX* (Seville: Editorial Renacimiento, 2002), 236, 244.

75. "El mundo ve en vosotras la aristocracia moral de un pueblo que . . . cuando injustamente se le asedia, cuando injustamente se le calumnia y se le excomulga, pone serenamente a revisar su tesoro popular, lo revive y lo purifica, para salir a mostrárselo, incluso a los enemigos, con el fin de que todos los pueblos de la tierra se convenzan de que España, en un clima de odio o de recelo universal, de acechante ferocidad mongólica, o de sombría y ruinosa precaución occidental, levanta las cándidas banderas de sus tradiciones más genuinas, y en un alarde de generosa serenidad expresiva, sale al mundo para demostrar la pureza de sus principios." "Coros y Danzas de España," *Ecos de Sociedad*, January 1954. ES-AGA, (03)051.023, Caja 12/647 top. (03)14.51.

76. Travelogue of Sampelayo during the 1954 Cuban tour: "La embajada de España en Cuba," ES-AGA, (03)051.023, Caja 1460 top. 23/25.406–30.103.

77. Frank Moya Pons, "The Dominican Republic since 1930," in *The Cambridge History of Latin America*, ed. Leslie Bethell (Cambridge: Cambridge University Press, 1994), 510, 517.

78. Humberto García Muñiz and Jorge Giovannetti, "Garveyismo y racismo en e Caribe: El caso de la población cocola en la República Dominicana," *Caribbean Studies* 31, no. 1 (2003): 183.

79. Ernesto Sagás, *Race and Politics in the Dominican Republic* (Gainesville: University Press of Florida, 2000), 3.

80. Eric Roorda, *The Dominican Republic Reader: History, Culture and Politics* (Durham, NC, and London: Duke University Press, 2014), 281.

81. April Mayes, *The Mulatto Republic: Class, Race, and Dominican National Identity* (Gainesville: University Press of Florida, 2014), 2; Sagás, *Race and Politics in the Dominican Republic*, 46.

82. Sagás, *Race and Politics in the Dominican Republic*, 60.

83. Mayes, *The Mulatto Republic*, 3.

84. Pons, "The Dominican Republic since 1930," 518.

85. Sagás, *Race and Politics in the Dominican Republic*, 66.

86. Trujillo's Hispanicization of Dominican music was part of the dictator's complex relationship with his own Afro-Caribbean heritage. Austerlitz points out that Trujillo claimed to abolish all traditions and religious practices associated with Afro-Caribbean culture while he himself practiced voodoo and consulted local holy men to perceive the future. See Paul Austerlitz, *Merengue: Dominican Music and Dominican Identity* (Philadelphia: Temple University Press, 1997).

87. Mayes, *The Mulatto Republic*, 1.

88. Roorda, *The Dominican Republic Reader*, 281.

89. Austerlitz, *Merengue*, 64.

90. Ibid.

91. Manley, *The Paradox of Paternalism*, 68.

92. Ibid., 64.

93. Pamphlet titled "Perspectiva presente y futura de la escuela dominicana a favor de la renovación pedagógica auspiciada: una conferencia," c. 1954. ES-AGA (03)051.023, Caja 1087 top. 23/25.406–30.103.

94. Letter from Alfonso Marqués de Merry del Val to Pilar Primo de Rivera, November 2, 1954. ES-AGA, (03)051.023, Caja 1460 top. 23/25.406–30.103.

95. Letter from Alfonso Marqués de Merry del Val to Pilar Primo de Rivera, March 25, 1955. ES-AGA, (03)051.023, Caja 1460 top. 23/25.406-30.103.

96. "durante la estancia e las mismas en la República Dominicana se las pagaría $100.0." Letter from Rafael Bonnelly (Ambassador to Spain) to Pilar Primo de Rivera, [March?] 1955. ES-AGA, (03)051.023, Caja 1460 top. 23/25.406–30.103.

97. Letter from Alfonso Marqués de Merry del Val to Pilar Primo de Rivera, November 2, 1954.

98. Lauren Derby, "The Dictator's Seduction: Gender and State Spectacle during the Trujillo Regime," *Dominican Republic Literature and Culture* 23, no. 3 (2000): 1122.

99. Letter from Alfonso Marqués de Merry del Val to Pilar Primo de Rivera, November 2, 1954.

100. "existir escasísimos antecedentes folklóricos de este país." Ibid.

101. "Les interesa enormemente se resucite un traje típico nacional que no he podido constatar si haya existido en realidad." Ibid.

102. Letter from Alfonso Marqués de Merry del Val to Rivera Primo de Rivera, April 29, 1955. ES-AGA, (03)051.023, Caja 1460 top. 23/25.406–30.103.

103. "A French girl is studying this question, who even went to Haiti in search of inspiration"; "Está estudiando esta cuestión una chica francesa que, incluso fue a Haití en busca de inspiración." Ibid.
104. "afro-antillana que no tiene, en realidad base histórica alguna en Santo Domingo, donde durante las postrimerías de nuestra soberanía solo existía unos 15 mil negros esclavos y en cambio la gran mayoría de la población era de origen netamente español" Ibid.
105. "If you could find engravings or drawings from the late eighteenth or early nineteenth century of Santo Domingo in the National Library or in the Archivo de Indias, or some of the descriptions of the island and its inhabitants in travelogues of the epoch or even from 1860 when the country was reincorporated to Spain—this would lead you to a great success"; "Si pudieras encontrar grabados o dibujos de fines del XVIII o principios del XIX de Santo Domingo, en la Biblioteca Nacional o en el Archivo d Indias o alguna descripción de la isla y sus habitantes en relatos de viajeros de la época o incluso de 1860, cuando fue reincorporado el país a España, sería una gran éxito para vosotras." Ibid.
106. "the vast majority of the [Dominican] population was of purely Spanish origin and of probable Canary, Andalusian, and perhaps Asturian and Galician ancestry"; "la gran mayoría de la población era de origen netamente español y de probable ascendencia canaria, andaluza y quizás asturiana y gallega." Ibid.
107. "The Hispanic hotbed is located inland in the Cibao, Mao and Santiago de los Caballeros region, regions with a clear Spanish tradition, and not on the coast"; "El vivero hispano se encuentra situado en el interior en la región de Cibao, Mao y Santiago de los Caballeros, regiones de neta tradición española, y no en la costa." Ibid.
108. "If you do not find anything indigenous on the island, I would advise you to try to adapt something inspired by the typical costumes and songs from Cuba and Puerto Rico, since it is likely that those here [in the Dominican Republic] are very similar to those from the nearby islands"; "Si no encuentras nada autóctono de la isla, te aconsejaría procurases adaptar algo inspirado en los trajes típicos y en las canciones de Cuba y de Puerto Rico, pues es probable que los de aquí, haya sido muy parecido a los de las islas tan cercanas." Ibid.
109. Cynthia Schneider, "Cultural Diplomacy: Hard to Define, but You'd Know It If You Saw It," *Brown Journal of World Affairs* 13, no. 1 (2006): 192.

Reflections

1. Paul Lawrence, *Nationalism: History and Theory* (Harlow: Pearson Education, 2005), 44; Svetlana Boym, *The Future of Nostalgia* (New York: Basic Books, 2001), 25.

Bibliography

Aguado, Ana. "Citizenship and Gender Equality in the Second Spanish Republic: Representations and Practices in Socialist Culture (1931–1936)." *Contemporary European History* 23, no. 1 (2014): 95–113.

Aidi, Hisham. "The Interference of al-Andalus: Spain, Islam, and the West." *Social Text* 24, no. 2 (2006): 67–88.

Alcoba, Antonio. *Auge y ocaso del Frente de juventudes*. Madrid: San Martin, 2002.

Al Tuma, Ali. *Guns, Culture and Moors*. London and New York: Routledge, 2018.

Al Tuma, Ali. "Moros y Cristianos: Religious Aspects of the Participation of Moroccan Soldiers in the Spanish Civil War (1936–1939)." In *Muslims in Interwar Europe: A Transcultural Historical Perspective*, edited by Umar Ryad Bekim Agai and Mehdi Sajid, 151–177. Leiden and Boston: Brill, 2016.

Álvarez-Junco, José. *Mater Dolorosa: La idea de España en el siglo XIX*. Madrid: Taurus, 2001.

Ambrose, Stephen, and Douglas Brinkley. *Rise to Globalism: American Foreign Policy since 1938*. London: Penguin Books, 2011.

Argote-Freyre, Frank. *Fulgencio Batista: From Revolutionary to Strongman*. New Brunswick, NJ: Rutgers University Press, 2007.

Austerlitz, Paul. *Merengue: Dominican Music and Dominican Identity*. Philadelphia: Temple University Press, 1997.

Ben-Ami, Shlomo. *Fascism from Above: The Dictatorship of Primo de Rivera in Spain, 1923–1930*. Oxford: Oxford University Press, 1983.

Benedito, Rafael. *Historia de la música: La música a través de los tiempos*. Madrid: Sección Femenina de F.E.T de la J.O.N.S, 1946.

Benet, Josep. *L'intent franquista de genocidi cultural contra Catalunya*. Barcelona: Abadia de Montserrat, 1995.

Benumeya, Rodolfo. *Andalucismo africano*. Madrid: Instituto de Estudios Africanos, 1953.

Benumeya, Rodolfo. *Claroscuro andaluz*. Madrid: Editora Nacional, 1966.

Bernard, Stéphane. *The Franco-Moroccan Conflict: 1943–1956*. New Haven, CT, and London: Yale University Press, 1968.

Blinkhorn, Martin. *Fascism and the Right in Europe, 1919–1945*. Harlow: Longman, 2000.

Bohlman, Philip. "Music before the Nation, Music after Nationalism." *Musicology Australia* 31, no. 1 (2009): 79–100.

Bowen, Wayne. "Pilar Primo de Rivera and the Axis Temptation," *The Historian* 67, no. 1 (2005): 62–72.

Boym, Svetlana. *The Future of Nostalgia*. New York: Basic Books, 2001.

Brandes, Stanley. "The Sardana: Catalan Dance and Catalan National Identity." *Journal of American Folklore* 103, no. 407 (1990): 24–41.

Butler, Judith. *Gender Trouble: Feminism and the Subversion of Identity*. New York: Routledge, 1999.

Caballero Jurado, Carlos, and Ramiro Bujeiro. *Blue Division Soldier 1941–45: Spanish Volunteer on the Eastern Front*. Oxford: Osprey Publishing, 2009.

Calderwood, Eric. *Colonial Al-Andalus: Spain and the Making of Modern Moroccan Culture*. Cambridge, MA, and London: Harvard University Press, 2018.

Calderwood, Eric. "'In Andalucía, there are no foreigners': Andalucismo from Transperipheral Critique to Colonial Apology." *Journal of Spanish Cultural Studies* 15, no. 4 (2014): 399–417.

Calderwood, Eric. "Moroccan Jews and the Spanish Colonial Imaginary (1903–1951)." *Journal of North African Studies* 24, no. 1 (2019): 86–110.

Capdepón, Ulrike. "Challenging the Symbolic Representation of the Franco Dictatorship: The Street Name Controversy in Madrid." *History and Memory* 32, no. 2 (Spring/Summer 2020): 100–130.

Carbajosa Menéndez, Concepción. *Las profesoras de educación física en España: historia de su formación (1938–1977)*. Oviedo: Universidad de Oviedo, 1999.

Carroll, Peter. *The Odyssey of the Abraham Lincoln Brigade: Americans in the Spanish Civil War*. Stanford, CA: Stanford University Press, 1994.

Cartee, Johnson, and Gary Copeland. *Inside Political Campaigns: Theory and Practice*. Westport, CT, and London: Praeger, 1997.

Casero-García, Estrella. *La España que bailó con Franco: Coros y Danzas de la Sección Femenina*. Madrid: Editorial Nuevas Estructuras, 2000.

Castro-Salazar, Ricardo, and Carl Bagley. "Navigating Historical Borders: Internal Colonialism and the Politics of Memory." *Counterpoints* 415 (2012): 3–36.

Cazorla-Sánchez, Antonio. *Fear and Progress: Ordinary Lives in Franco's Spain, 1939–1975*. Chichester: Wiley-Blackwell, 2010.

Cazorla-Sánchez, Antonio. "The Spanish Civil War as a Crisis of Memory." In *Memory and Cultural History of the Spanish Civil War: Realms of Oblivion*, edited by Aurora Gómez Morcillo, 21–50. Leiden: Brill, 2013.

Chuse, Lauren. *The Cantaoras: Music, Gender, and Identity in Flamenco Song*. New York: Routledge, 2003.

Cortés García, Manuela. "La mujer árabe y la música. Transculturación en el área mediterránea." *Música oral del sur* 5 (2002), 91–106.

Croft, Clare. *Dancers as Diplomats: American Choreography in Cultural Exchange*. New York: Oxford University Press, 2015.

Derby, Lauren. "The Dictator's Seduction: Gender and State Spectacle during the Trujillo Regime." *Dominican Republic Literature and Culture* 23, no. 3 (2000): 1112–1146.

Díaz-Andreu García, Margarita. *Archeological Encounters: Building Networks of Spanish and British Archaeologists in the 20th Century*. Newcastle: Cambridge Scholars, 2012.

Domingo Cuadriello, Jorge. *Los españoles en las letras cubanas durante el siglo XX*. Seville: Editorial Renacimiento, 2002.

Egido, Ángeles. *Los campos de concentración franquistas en el contexto europeo*. Madrid: Marcial Pons Ediciones de Historia, 2005.

Encarnación, Omar. *Democracy without Justice in Spain: The Politics of Forgetting*. Philadelphia: University of Pennsylvania Press, 2014.

Encarnación, Omar. "Reconciliation after Democratization: Coping with the Past in Spain." *Political Science Quarterly* 123, no. 3 (2008): 435–459.

Espadas Burgos, Manuel. *Franquismo y Política Exterior*. Ediciones RIALP S.A.: Madrid, 1988.

Esteban, Joan. "The Economic Policy of Francoism: An Interpretation." In *Spain in Crisis: The Evolution and Decline of the Franco Regime*, edited by Paul Preston, 82–100. Hassocks: Harvester Press, 1976.

Falk, Andrew Justin. *Upstaging the Cold War: American Dissent and Cultural Diplomacy, 1940–1960*. Amherst: University of Massachusetts, 2011.

Fernández de la Cuesta, Ismael. "Relectura de la teoría de Julián Ribera sobre la influencia de la música arábigo en las cantigas de santa maría en las canciones de los trovadores, troveros y Minnesingers." *Revista de Musicología* 16, no. 1 (1993): 385–396.

Figueredo Cabrera, Katia. "Carlos Prío Socarrás, Fulgencio Batista, Francisco Franco: La escalada hacia una consolidación 'fraternal,' 1948–1958." *Illes i imperis* 12 (2009): 49–71.

Figueredo Cabrera, Katia. "Francisco Franco y Fulgencio Batista: Complicidad de dos dictadores en el poder (1952–1958)." *Tzintzun. Revista de estudios históricos* 64 (2016): 296–325.

Flesler, Daniela. *The Return of the Moor*. West Lafayette, IN: Purdue University Press, 2008.

Flynn, Angela. *Falangist and National Catholic Women in the Spanish Civil War (1936–1939)*. New York: Routledge, 2020.

Ford, Richard. *A Handbook for Travelers in Spain and Readers at Home*. London: J. Murray, 1845.

Fosler-Lussier, Danielle. *Music in America's Cold War Diplomacy*. Oakland: University of California Press, 2015

Frolova-Walker, Marina. *Russian Music and Nationalism from Glinka to Stalin*. New Haven, CT, and London: Yale University Press, 2007.

Fusi Aizpúrua, Juan Pablo. "El franquismo: la etapa totalitaria (1939–1959)." In *España: sociedad, política y civilización (siglos XIX–XX)*, edited by Jover Zamora and José María, 714–738. Madrid: Areté, 2001.

García, Benito. *Cancionero español (Cuadro primero)*. Madrid, ca. 1940.

García-Márquez, Vicente. *The Ballets Russes: Colonel de Basil's Ballets Russes de Monte Carlo, 1932–1952*. New York: Alfred A. Knopf, 1990.

García Mateos, Manuel. *Danzas populares de España*. Madrid: Sección Femenina del Movimiento, 1971.

García Muñiz, Humberto, and Jorge Giovanetti. "Garveyismo y racismo en e Caribe: El caso de la población cocola en la República Dominicana." *Caribbean Studies* 31, no. 1 (2003): 139–211.

Gienow-Hecht, Jessica. "What Are We Searching For? Culture, Diplomacy, Agents, and the State." In *Searching for a Cultural Diplomacy*, edited by Jessica Gienow-Hecht and Mark Donfried, 3–12. New York: Berghahn, 2010.

Gienow-Hecht, Jessica, and Mark Donfried. "The Model of Cultural Diplomacy: Power, Distance, and the Promise of Civil Society." In *Searching for a Cultural Diplomacy*, edited by Jessica Gienow-Hecht and Mark Donfried, 13–32. New York: Berghahn, 2010.

Gil y Zárate, Antonio. *Guzmán El Bueno. drama en cuatro actos*. London: FB&C Ltd., 2017.

Gómez-Escalonilla, Lorenzo Delgado. *Diplomacia Franquista y política cultural hacia Iberoamerica, 1939–1953*. Madrid: Consejo superior de investigaciones científicas, 1988.

Gómez-Escalonilla, Lorenzo Delgado. *Imperio de papel: Acción cultural y política exterior durante el primer franquismo*. Madrid: Consejo superior de investigaciones científicas, 1992.

Gonzalez, Edward, and Kevin McCarthy. *Cuba after Castro: Legacies, Challenges, and Impediments*. Santa Monica, CA: Rand, 2004.

González Alcantud, José Antonio. "Taurolatrías periféricas: París-Tánger." In *Fiestas de toros y sociedad*, edited by Antonio García-Baquero González and Pedro Romero de Solís, 461–482. Seville: Editorial Universidad de Sevilla-Secretariado de Publicaciones, 2003.

Gottschall, Marilyn. "The Ethical Implications of the Deconstruction of Gender." *Journal of the American Academy of Religion* 70, no. 2 (2002): 279–299.

Graham, Helen. "Introduction." In *Interrogating Francoism: History and Dictatorship in Twentieth-Century Spain*, edited by Helen Graham, 1–26. London: Bloomsbury, 2016.

Graham, Helen. "Reform as Promise and Threat: Political Progressives and Blueprints for Change in Spain, 1931–6." In *Interrogating Francoism: History and Dictatorship in Twentieth-Century Spain*, edited by Helen Graham, 69–96. London: Bloomsbury, 2016.

Green, Lucy. *Music, Gender, Education*. New York: Cambridge University Press, 1997.

Grugel, Jean. *Franco's Spain*. London: Arnold, 1997.

Haines, John. "The Arabic Style of Performing Medieval Music." *Early Music* 29, no. 3 (2001): 369–378.

Harvey, Elizabeth. "International Networks and Cross-Border Cooperation: National Socialist Women and the Vision of a 'New Order' in Europe." *Politics, Religion & Ideology* 13, no. 2 (2002): 141–158.

Hayes, Michelle Heffner. *Flamenco: Conflicting Histories of the Dance*. Jefferson, NC: McFarland & Co, 2009.

Hess, Carol. *Sacred Passions: The Life and Music of Manuel de Falla*. Oxford and New York: Oxford University Press, 2005.

Hobsbawm, Eric. *The Invention of Tradition*. Cambridge: Cambridge University Press, 2012.

Homs, Joaquim. *Roberto Gerhard and His Music*. Sheffield: Anglo-Catalan Society, 2000.

Huret, Romain. "All in the Family Again?: Political Historians and the Challenge of Social History." *Journal of Policy History* 21, no. 3 (2009): 239–263.

Hurtado, Albert. *Intimate Frontiers: Sex, Gender, and Culture in Old California*. Albuquerque: University of New Mexico Press, 1999.

Idelsohn, Abraham Zevi. "Parallelen zwischen gregorianischen und hebräischorientalischen Gesangsweisen." *Zeitschrift für Musikwissenschaft* 4 (1921/2): 515–524.

Iglesias, Iván. "Swinging Modernity: Jazz and Politics in Franco's Spain (1939–1968)." In *Made in Spain: Studies in Popular Music*, edited by Sílvia Martinez and Héctor Fouce, 101–112. New York: Routledge, 2013.

Infante, Blas. *Ideal Andaluz. Varios estudios acerca del renacimiento de Andalucía*. Sevilla: Fundación Pública Andaluza Centro de Estudios Andaluces, 2015.

Infante, Blas. *La verdad sobre el complot de tablada y el estado libre de Andalucía*. Aljibe: Fundación Pública Andaluza Centro de Estudios Andaluces, 1979.

Jensen, Geoffrey. *Irrational Triumph: Cultural Despair, Military Nationalism, and Ideological Origins of Franco's Spain*. Reno: University of Nevada Press, 2002.

Joffé, George. "The Moroccan Nationalist Movement: Istiqlal, the Sultan, and the Country." *Journal of African History* 26, no. 4 (1985): 289–307.

Johnson-Cartee, Karen, and Gary Copeland. *Inside Political Campaigns: Theory and Practice*. Westport, CT, and London: Praeger, 1997.

Jordan, Daniel. "Sección Femenina: Documenting and Performing Spanish Musical Folklore During the Early Franco Regime (1939–1953)." *Music and Letters* 101, no. 3 (2020): 544–566.

Kahn, Máximo José (published under pseudonym Medina Azahara). "Cante jondo y cantares sinagogales." *Revista de Occidente* 88 (1930): 53–84.

Kater, Michael. *The Twisted Muse: Musicians and Their Music in the Third Reich.* New York: Oxford University Press, 1997.

Kenny, Michael. "Twentieth Century Spanish Expatriate in Cuba: A Sub-Culture?" *Anthropological Quarterly* 34 (1961): 85–93.

Korian, Tola. "The Venice Festival: Some Impressions of a Visitor." *Journal of the International Folk Music Council* 2, no. 20 (1950): 3–5.

Koskoff, Ellen. *A Feminist Ethnomusicology: Writings on Music and Gender.* Urbana: University of Illinois Press, 2014.

Kotek, Joël. *Students of the Cold War.* Oxford: Basingstoke, 1996.

Lawrence, Paul. *Nationalism: History and Theory.* Harlow: Pearson Education, 2005.

Liedtke, Boris. "Compromising with the Dictatorship: U.S.-Spanish Relations in the Late 1940s and Early 1950s." In *Spain in International Context, 1936–1959*, edited by Christian Leitz and David Dunthorn, 265–276. New York: Berghahn Books, 1999.

Linz, Juan. "An Authoritarian Regime: Spain." In *Cleavages, Ideologies, and Party Systems: Contributions to Comparative Political Sociology*, edited by Erik Allardt and Yrjö Littunen, 291–341. Helsinki: Transactions of the Westermaark Society, 1964.

Llano, Samuel. *Whose Spain?: Negotiating Spanish Music in Paris, 1908–1929.* New York: Oxford University Press, 2013.

López-Calo, José. *Catálogo del Archivo de Música de la Catedral de Granada, Vol. 1 Catálogo (I).* Granada: Junta de Andalucía, 1991.

López-Ríos Moreno, Santiago, and Antonio Juan González Cárceles. *La facultad de filosofía y letras de Madrid en la Segunda República: arquitectura y universidad durante los años 30.* Madrid: Sociedad Estatal de Conmemoraciones Culturales, 2008.

Losada Malverez, Juan Carlos. *Ideología del ejército Franquista (1939–1959).* Madrid: Selección Fundamentos, 1990.

Machin-Autenrieth, Matthew. *Flamenco Regionalism and Musical Heritage in Southern Spain.* London and New York: Routledge, 2017.

Mahiet, Damien, Mark Ferraguto, and Rebeckah Ahrendt. "Introduction." In *Music and Diplomacy from the Early Modern Era to the Present*, edited by Damien Mahiet, Mark Ferraguto, and Rebeckah Ahrendt, 1–10. Basingstoke: Palgrave Macmillan, 2014.

Malefyt, Timothy Dewaal. "'Inside' and 'Outside' Spanish Flamenco: Gender Constructions in Andalusian Concepts of Flamenco Tradition." *Anthropological Quarterly* 71, no. 2 (1998): 63–73.

Manley, Elizabeth. *The Paradox of Paternalism: Women and the Politics of Authoritarianism in the Dominican Republic.* Gainesville: University Press of Florida, 2017.

Martí Pérez, Josep. "Folk Music Studies and Ethnomusicology in Spain." *Yearbook for Traditional Music* 29 (1997): 107–140.

Martín Gijón, Mario. "Una reflexión sobre el judaísmo desde el exilio republicano español: sobre 'Arte y Torá.' Libro inédito de máximo José Kahn." *Hispanic Review* 81, no. 3 (2013): 285–307.

Martínez del Fresno, Beatriz. "Women, Land and Nation: The Dances of the Falange's Women's Section in the Political Map of Franco's Spain (1939–1952)." In *Music and Francoism*, edited by Gemma Pérez Zalduondo and Gan Quesada, 99–126. Turnhout: Brepols, 2013.

Martínez López, Fernando, and Miguel Gómez Oliver. "Political Responsibilities in Franco's Spain." In *Memory and Culture of the Spanish Civil War: Realms of Oblivion*, edited by Arora Morcillo, 111–144. Leiden and Boston: Brill, 2013.

Mas Gorrochategur, Amelia, and Antonio Muñoz Rodriguez. "El cobijado de vejer y su leyenda morisca." *MAGAzin. Rivista de Germanística Intercultural* 1 (2009): 73–78.

Mayes, April. *The Mulatto Republic: Class, Race, and Dominican National Identity.* Gainesville: University Press of Florida, 2014.

Mikkonen, Simo, Jari Parkkinen, and Giles Scott-Smith. "Introduction." In *Entangled East and West: Cultural Diplomacy and Artistic Interaction during the Cold War*, edited by Simo Mikkonen, Jari Parkkinen, and Giles Scott-Smith, 1–15. Berlin: De Gruyter, 2019.

Miller, Susan Gilson. *A History of Modern Morocco.* Cambridge: Cambridge University Press, 2013.

Mitchell, Timothy. *Flamenco Deep Song.* New Haven, CT: Yale University Press, 1994.

Morcillo, Aurora. *The Seduction of Modern Spain: The Female Body and the Francoist Body Politic.* Lewisburg, PA: Bucknell University Press, 2010.

Moreda Rodríguez, Eva. "'La mujer que no canta no es . . . ¡ni mujer española!': Folklore and Gender in the Earlier Franco Regime." *Bulletin of Hispanic Studies* 89, no. 6 (2012): 627–644.

Moreda Rodríguez, Eva. *Music and Exile in Francoist Spain.* London: Routledge, 2016.

Moreda Rodríguez, Eva. *Music Criticism and Music Critics in Early Francoist Spain.* New York: Oxford University Press, 2016.

Moreno Fernández, Luis. *The Federalization of Spain.* London: Routledge, 2001.

Moya Pons, Frank. "The Dominican Republic since 1930." In *The Cambridge History of Latin America*, edited by Leslie Bethell, 509–544. Cambridge: Cambridge University Press, 1994.

Neila Hernández, José Louis. "The Foreign Policy Administration of Franco's Spain: From Isolation to International Realignment (1945–1957)." In *Spain in International Context, 1936–1959*, edited by Christian Leitz and David Dunthorne, 227–297. New York: Berghahn Books, 1999.

Núñez Seixas, Xosé-Manoel. "Nations in Arms against the Invader: On Nationalist Discourses During the Spanish Civil War." In *The Splintering of Spain: Cultural History and the Spanish Civil War, 1936–1939*, edited by Chris Elham and Michael Richards, 46–66. Cambridge: Cambridge University Press, 2005.

Nye, Joseph. "Public Diplomacy and Soft Power." *Annals of the American Academy of Political and Social Science* 616, no. 1 (2008): 94–109.

O'Donnell, Guillermo. *Bureaucratic Authoritarianism: Argentina, 1966–1973, in Comparative Perspective.* Los Angeles: University of California Press, 1988.

Ofer, Inbal. "Fragmented Autobiographies: A Style of Writing or Self-Perception? The Case of Pilar Primo de Rivera." *Iberoamericana* 9, no. 3 (2003): 37–51.

Ofer, Inbal. "Historical Models, Contemporary Identities: The Sección Femenina of the Spanish Falange and Its Redefinition of the Term "Femininity." *Journal of Contemporary History* 40, no. 4 (October 2005): 663–674.

Ofer, Inbal. *Señoritas in Blue: The Making of a Female Political Elite in Franco's Spain.* Portland: Sussex Academic Press, 2009.

Ortíz García, Carmen. "The Uses of Folklore in the Franco Regime." *Journal of American Folklore* 112, no. 446 (1998): 479–496.

Painter, Karen. "Musical Aesthetics of National Socialism." In *Music and Dictatorship in Europe and Latin America*, edited by Roberto Illiano and Massimiliano Sala, 121–140. Turnhout: Brepols, 2009.

Payne, Stanley. *The Franco Regime: 1936–1975*. Madison: University of Wisconsin Press, 1987.

Paz-Sánchez, Manuel de. *Zona de Guerra: España y la revolución cubana (1960–1962)*. Tenerife: Litografía Romero, S. A., 2001.

Pérez, Louis. *Cuba: Between Reform and Revolution*. New York and Oxford: Oxford University Press, 2011.

Pérez Zalduondo, Gemma. "De la tradición a la vanguardia: música, discursos e instituciones desde la Guerra Civil hasta 1956." In *Historia de la música en España e Hispanoamérica*, edited by Alberto Gómez Lapuente, 101–173. Ciudad de México: Fondo de Cultura Económica, 2009.

Pérez Zalduondo, Gemma. "Racial Discourses in Spanish Musical Literature, 1915–1939." In *Western Music and Race*, edited by Julie Brown, 201–217. Cambridge: Cambridge University Press, 2007.

Pierce, Samuel. "The Political Mobilization of Catholic Women in Spain's Second Republic: The CEDA, 1931–6." *Journal of Contemporary History* 45, no. 1 (2010): 74–94.

Pistrick, Eckehard. *Performing Nostalgia: Migration, Culture and Creativity in South Albania*. Farnham and Burlington: Ashgate, 2015.

Portero, Florentino. *Franco aislado: La cuestión española (1945–1950)*. Aguilar: Madrid, 1989.

Preston, Paul. "The Anti-Francoist Opposition: The Long March to Unity." In *Spain in Crisis: The Evolution and Decline of the Franco Regime*, edited by Paul Preston, 120–140. Hassocks: Harvester Press, 1976.

Preston, Paul. "Franco's Foreign Policy." In *Spain in International Context, 1936–1959*, edited by Christian Leitz and David Dunthorn, 1–18. New York: Berghahn Books, 1999.

Preston, Paul. *The Spanish Holocaust: Inquisition and Extermination in Twentieth-Century Spain*. London: Harper Press, 2012.

Prevots, Naima. *Dance for Export: Cultural Diplomacy and the Cold War*. London: Wesleyan University Press: 1998.

Rabaté, Jean-Claude. *Miguel de Unamuno: Biografía*. Madrid: Taurus, 2009.

Ribera, Julián. *La música andaluza medieval en las canciones de trovadores, troveros y minnesinger*. Madrid: Real Academia Española, 1922.

Ribera, Julián. *La música de las Cantigas. Estudio sobre su origen y naturaleza*. Madrid: Real Academia Española, 1922.

Richards, Michael. *A Time of Silence: Civil War and the Culture of Repression in Franco's Spain, 1936–1945*. Cambridge: Cambridge University Press, 1998.

Richards, Michael, and Chris Ealham. "History, Memory and the Spanish Civil War: Recent Perspectives." In *The Splintering of Spain: Cultural History and Spanish Civil War, 1936–1939*, edited by Chris Ealham and Michael Richards, 1–20. Cambridge: Cambridge University Press, 2005.

Richmond, Kathleen. *Women and Spanish Fascism: The Women's Section of the Falange, 1934–1959*. London: Routledge, 2003.

Rivera, Pilar Primo de. *4 discursos de Pilar Primo de Rivera*. Barcelona: Editora Nacional, 1939.

Rivera, Pilar Primo de. *Discursos, circulares, escritos*. Madrid: Gráficas Afrodisio Aguado, 1943.

Rivera, Pilar Primo de. *Pilar Primo de Rivera: Escritos*. Madrid: Sección Femenina de F.E.T. y de las J.O.N.S. 1942.

Rohr, Isabelle. "'Productive Hatreds': Radical Segregationist Discourses and the Making of Francoism." In *Interrogating Francoism: History and Dictatorship in Twentieth-Century Spain*, edited by Helen Graham, 99–114. London: Bloomsbury, 2016.

Romero Salvadó, Federico. "Building Alliances against the New? Monarchy and the Military in Industrializing Spain." In *Interrogating Francoism: History and Dictatorship in Twentieth-Century Spain*, edited by Helen Graham, 49–68. London: Bloomsbury, 2016.

Roorda, Eric. *The Dominican Republic Reader: History, Culture and Politics*. Durham, NC, and London: Duke University Press, 2014.

Sagás, Ernesto. *Race and Politics in the Dominican Republic*. Gainesville: University Press of Florida, 2000.

Sárez Fernández, Luis. *Cronica de la Sección Femenina y su tiempo*. Madrid: Asociación Nueva Andadura, 1993.

Schneider, Cynthia. "Cultural Diplomacy: Hard to Define, but You'd Know It If You Saw It." *Brown Journal of World Affairs* 13, no. 1 (2006): 191–203.

Schulten, Adolf. *Tartessos. Ein Beitrag zur ältesten Geschichte des Westens*. Hamburg: L. Friedrichsen & Co., 1922.

Scott, Joan. "Gender: A Useful Category of Historical Analysis." *American Historical Review* 91, no. 5 (1986): 1053–1075.

Sepúlveda, Vanessa Tessada. "El Servicio exterior y la Sección Femenina de F.E.T. y de las J.O.N.S. intentos de acercamiento con América Latina." *Historia*, special issue (2019): 19–40.

Serém, Rúben. "A Coup against Change: Repression in Seville and the Assault on Civilian Society." In *Interrogating Francoism: History and Dictatorship in Twentieth-Century Spain*, edited by Helen Graham, 115–138. London: Bloomsbury 2016.

Sevillano Calero, Francisco. *Propaganda y medios de comunicación en el franquismo (1936-1951)*. Alicante: Universidad de Alicante, 1998.

Shannon, Jonathan Holt. *Performing al-Andalus: Music and Nostalgia across the Mediterranean*. Bloomington: Indiana University Press, 2015.

Stahn, Carten. *The Law and Practice of International Territorial Administration: Versailles to Iraq and Beyond*. Cambridge: Cambridge University Press, 2008.

Stehrenberger, Cécile Stephanie. "Folklore, Nation, and Gender in a Colonial Encounter: Coros y Danzas of the Sección Femenina of the Falange in Equatorial Guinea." *Afro-Hispanic Review* 28, no. 2 (2009): 231–244.

Stehrenberger, Cécile Stephanie. *Francos Tänzerinnen auf Auslandstournee: Folklore, Nation und Geschlecht im "Colonial Encounter."* Bielefeld: transcript Verlag, 2013.

Steingress, Gerhard. "El cante flamenco como manifestación artística, instrumento ideológico y elemento de identidad cultural andaluza." In *Flamenco y nacionalismo*, edited by Gerhard Steingress and Enrique Balantás, 32–53. Seville: Universidad de Sevilla, 1997.

Taruskin, Richard. *Oxford History of Western Music: Music from the Earliest Notations to the Sixteenth Century*. Oxford: Oxford University Press, 2010.

Thomas, Maria. "Twentieth-Century Catholicisms: Religion as Prison, as Haven, as 'Clamp.'" In *Interrogating Francoism: History and Dictatorship in Twentieth-Century Spain*, edited by Helen Graham, 27–48. London: Bloomsbury, 2016.

Topić, Martina, and Siniša Rodin. *Cultural Diplomacy and Cultural Imperialism.* Frankfurt am Main: Lang, 2012.

Vilanova, Francesc. "Did Catalonia Endure a (Cultural) Genocide?" *Journal of Catalan Intellectual History* 1, no. 11 (2018): 15–32.

Viñas Martín, Ángel. "La administración de la política económica exterior en España, 1936–1979." *Cuadernos económicos de I.C.E.* 13 (1980): 157–272.

Washabaugh, William. *Flamenco: Passion, Politics and Popular culture.* Oxford: Berg, 1996.

Washabaugh, William. "The Politics of Passion: Flamenco, Power and the Body." *Journal of Musicological Research* 15, no. 1 (1995): 85–112.

Wyrtzen, Jonathan. "National Resistance, Amazighité, and (Re-)imagining the Nation in Morocco." In *Revisiting the Colonial Past in Morocco*, edited by Driss Maghraoui, 184–199. London and New York: Routledge, 2013.

Index

For the benefit of digital users, indexed terms that span two pages (e.g., 52–53) may, on occasion, appear on only one of those pages.
Figures are indicated by *f* following the page number